DR EAMONN O'SULLIVAN

A Man Before His Time

Dedicated to the memory of my beautiful niece, Karen Fogarty who died in a tragic road accident on the Muckross Road, Killarney on August 4, 1996. She was 21 years old.

DR EAMONN O'SULLIVAN

A Man Before His Time

Weeshie Fogarty

WOLFHOUND PRESS

First published in 2007 by
Wolfhound Press
An Imprint of Merlin Publishing
Newmarket Hall, Cork Street,
Dublin 8, Ireland
Tel: +353 1 4535866
Fax: +353 1 4535930
publishing@merlin.ie
www.merlinwolfhound.com

All pictures courtesy of Monsignor Liam Brosnan and the O'Sullivan Family
Back Cover Picture Captions:
Sam Maguire Cup 1953: Ecstatic Kerry supporters welcome Jackie Lyne home
to Killarney following Kerry's win over Armagh in the All-Ireland Final. This
photo was taken on the platform of Killarney Railway Station.
1959: The legendary Mick O'Connell (Captain) rises high for the ball with
Seamus Murphy as Dr. Eamonn looks on approvingly. Players, from left to
right: Dan McAuliffe, Moss O'Connell, Jerome O'Shea, Kevin Coffey, Mick
O'Donoghue, Jack Dowling, John Dowling, Tim 'Tiger' Lyons and Dave
Geaney.

10-Digit ISBN 0-86327-943-0
13-Digit ISBN 978-0-86327-943-0

A CIP catalogue record for this book is available from the British Library.

10 9 8 7 6 5 4 3 2 1

Typeset by Gough Typesetting
Photo section by Artwerk Design
Cover Design by Graham Thew Design
Printed and bound by J.H. Haynes & Co. Ltd., Britain.

Acknowledgements

Thanks to the O'Sullivan Family, Eamonn's four sons Anthony, James, Edward and Robert for their continuous encouragement, letters and e-mails and great faith in entrusting me with their father's writings and documents. Without their blessing this production would never have come about. Sadly Anthony, a true gentleman, died in 2004. It was as a result of his lengthy interview with me five years ago that the seeds of this publication were born.

Eamon Brown of Tralee County Library and Killarney Library who provided wonderful access to *The Kerryman* newspaper and other historical records. *The Kerryman* itself had covered all of Eamonn's achievements from his early days and its records proved invaluable. I must give thanks to the many sources which gave me much needed background information for this book including; *Dr. Croke's Gaelic Century – Their club History, Killarney Legion GAA Club History – A Legion of Memories,* Raymond Smiths *'Complete Handbook of Gaelic Games',* and *Kerry's Football Story* (1944 Edition) written by Paddy Foley (more popularly referred to as 'P.F.' – a virtual treasure of early Kerry football records.

All those who so willingly gave interviews for inclusion. All my meetings with these great GAA personalities remain etched in the memory.

A very special thank you to Monsignor Liam Brosnan of Killarney and Texas who gave me complete access to his magnificent collection of Kerry football photographs. It was invaluable Liam; the finest collection in the world. And to his brother, Monsignor Noel and sisters Phyllis and Ina, for their courtesy and hospitality at all times.

John Kelly of The Spa GAA Club for his advice and encouragement.

C/R Videos Caherceiveen for access to their historical film records. Donie 'Whitty' O'Sullivan. Proof readers Ann Mulligan, Fiona Brennan and Mike 'Curley' O'Sullivan. MacMonagle Photographers, Killarney. Breeda Sugrue for her typing expertise; she is a star.

To the two sponsors of the book launch for their generosity – Pat

Sheehan, Glenbeigh and Killarney and his wife Eileen. Pat a multi-publican and Kerry businessman is in the unique position of being an All-Ireland Senior Medal winner with Kerry and the owner of the licensed premises and home in Firies village where Dr. Eamonn was born.

Thanks to Quills Ireland. This family-run business was established in 1939 by the late Padraig Quill, Senior. Quills shops can be seen along the Ring of Kerry and Cork and the beautiful Lansdowne Arms Hotel in Kenmare Town is also family owned. Quills are delighted to be associated with this publication about one of Kerry's greatest sons – a wonderful family.

Without Merlin Publishing/Wolfhound Press this book would never have happened. It has been a pleasure working with them. My deepest gratitude to Chenile Keogh, Managing Director, Aoife Barrett, Managing Editor, Julie Dobson and Tony Hayes, sales and marketing and Noelle Moran, my Editor. Thank you Noelle for all your hard work, patience and encouragement dealing with a novice such as I. An exemplary team.

World renowned musician Liam O'Connor and wife, Lisa, their music and friendship are very special.

Bill Cullen, Jackie Lavin and the Muckross Park Hotel.

Our first grandchild Lucy arrived in this world 14 months ago at the height of this work. She has lit up our lives.

Micheál Ó Muircheartaigh; a national treasure and Garry McMahon; a true friend.

My daughters Denise and Carol Ann for their encouragement when spirits were down. My son Kieran for his computer knowledge when problems arose. And my wife Joan who encouraged me to take on this task five years ago and kept me at it winter and summer.

Contents

Foreword

When Weeshie Fogarty asked me to write the foreword to his book on the life and times of Dr. Eamonn O'Sullivan, naturally we drifted into discussion about the remarkable man who had the great honour of being trainer to many Kerry teams between 1924 and 1964. It was then I discovered that the title of the treatise was to be *'Dr. Eamonn O'Sullivan: A Man Before His Time'* and my immediate reaction was that those oft quoted words were more appropriate in his case than anyone else that I could recall at that moment.

I am privileged to be able to say that I knew the good Doctor though not as well as the endless train of wonderful footballers who trained for important games under his guidance. I was a great admirer of him as a trainer, as a visionary on the role of football and sport, in general, in the life of communities and as a pioneer in promoting the therapeutic value of sport.

Fate cast him into the role of a healer from the beginning of his sojourn with Kerry teams, though not of the type dictated by his medical qualifications. On the invitation of the captain of the 1924 side, Phil Sullivan, he took charge of preparing the team for the All-Ireland Final against reigning champions Dublin. It was running six months behind time due to the chaos and trauma brought about by the War of Independence and the Civil War. In the circumstances it was amazing that the GAA succeeded in playing the concluding stages of the championships of 1920, 1921, 1922 and 1923 within a two year span.

The mental scars of war were still deep in many parts of the country, notably in Kerry where the Civil War had been especially bitter. Thankfully and almost miraculously the first step of rapprochement between the parties involved was taken in April 1924 when men who had taken the Free State side, those who engaged in the Republican stand and neutrals all joined together in the common cause of Kerry football. That was the birth-pang of the most significant Gaelic football team that ever left Kerry in search of sporting glory and it was into that environment that Dr. Eamonn was invited before the end of the same year.

He was the ideal man to oversee the healing process through the medium of Kerry's religion and by April of 1925 he had trained his first of eight All-Ireland winning sides with many players destined for legendary status on board. He was there again for the 1926 victory but strangely the quiet-spoken, all-round sportsman took no further part until the Championship of 1937. In between Kerry had accomplished a four-in-a row of All-Ireland wins in the absence of the 'Doctor' who had many other interests. He was Resident Medical Superintendent of St. Finan's Hospital that catered for patients with mental illness and his revolutionary idea of involving them in the development of Fitzgerald Stadium in the 1930s was seen as a huge step forward in therapy. Later on he extended the principle by bringing teams from the hospital on trips without a semblance of publicity to play football against suitable opposition, that novel venture also proved to be both worthy and beneficial.

His return as Kerry trainer in 1937 marked the beginning of another six successful All-Ireland campaigns – 1946, when he was brought back to take charge for the replay of the final with Roscommon, 1953, 1955, 1959 and finally 1962. Curiously he was not involved in any losing final until Galway beat Kerry in the All-Ireland Final of 1964. With that he decided to retire, having trained All-Ireland winning teams in six decades.

He frequently used the words 'Kerry Team' with emphasis on the word team and it was the basis of his training philosophy. I am sure the brace of words helped Eamonn in 1924 to mould a disparate group into a team where each individual had a part to play in reconciliation as much as winning the All-Ireland. Maybe it helped that a future archbishop was a member of the side!

The theory propounded in his book *The Art and Science of Gaelic Football*, that players should be confined to their own areas of the field, is not easily understood in these days of attacking defenders and visa versa as occasions demand. I paraphrase a particular sentence from the book to illustrate the steadfastness of his view and I must say that it would be heresy to many of the fine players of modern times: "There is no justification even for a right midfielder to be found on the left."

Perhaps Dr. Eamonn's vision for Gaelic football was that of a game of repeating contests of skill in running, fielding, kicking, blocking, scoring, etc. To him that was most feasible when it was individual cast against individual in fair play without the presence of others with the intention of nullifying or stifling the arts and sciences of the game as he saw it.

Another tenet of his training creed was the absolute necessity for players to be fresh in mind and body for each game. He did not seek total fitness and believed that teams should always have a little in reserve for the bigger games and even give consideration in preparation for the possibility of replays. He treated all players as individuals and was known to allow characters like Paddy Bawn Brosnan indulge in a limited amount of his favourite drink of porter as part of mental tuning for an important game ahead.

Yes, Dr. Eamonn, the son of J.P., who was known as 'The Champion' and the father figure of Kerry football, is rightly regarded as a major figure in the development of the GAA. He was scholarly, dignified, considerate and capable, and perceived Gaelic football well beyond the bounds of his beloved Dr. Croke's and Kerry.

As preparation for the future it behoves all of us to acquaint ourselves with the past now and then and in this context I welcome '*Dr. Eamonn O'Sullivan, A Man Before His Time*' into the fold of books and congratulate author Weeshie on filling a void in the sporting history of 'The Kingdom'. After all Dr. Eamonn was trainer of the Kerry team on the occasion of the first ever radio broadcast of an All-Ireland Football Final in 1926 and almost incredibly guided the county to yet another when RTE television beamed it's first final to sports followers throughout the country 36 years later.

Mo bheannacht leat a scríbhinn
Go h-inis aoibhinn Faithleann.

Micheál Ó Muircheartaigh

Note of Tribute to Weeshie Fogarty

I can only congratulate you on your perseverance in undertaking this project on Eamonn and the successful way in which it has been brought to a conclusion.

Your tribute is wider than Eamonn himself, of course. It embraces all those who provided support and encouragement to his efforts – the staff at St. Finan's; its culture, history and regimentation, the rich vein of footballing talent that was made available to him, the pride he had in his county, his nation; its culture and language and his joy at the peoples' emerging independence and all that he inherited from the reputation of his own father, whose stature in Kerry if not wider afield must have been unique in that era and might explain the sudden, unexpected way in which he was called upon as a very young man to train his first Kerry team.

Your book will provide encouragement to the youth of Kerry coming along now who may not know the full story of their own inheritance.

You have been fortunate to have been given access to Mr. Brosnan's photo collection. I'm glad, in particular, that you have a photo of Eamonn with the patients of the hospital who did so much in the building of the Stadium.

Dr. Sean Murphy's input is particularly significant. Not only was he himself a great footballer but he was also a medic and therefore would have a deeper appreciation of all that Eamonn brought to the training field. My Aunt Máire Griffin has always spoken of her high regard for Sean Murphy to me in the past. His observations of the difference between then and now, in terms of technique and peoples' backgrounds, is of particular interest. Millie Devane had one comment to pass on readings Sean's words: "Eamonn also insisted that when the team stayed at Park Place Hotel they must march off as a compact unit to Mass at the Cathedral every morning, even if

Eamonn himself was still in bed! Even Tadghie Lyne, who lived next door, was not allowed to go home at night." I believe that group training was prohibited later because of the success that Kerry gained from it. Today, what's happening? My father believed there must always be formal training in Gaelic football.

The address that you have obtained from Minister John O'Donoghue is a great tribute to Eamonn and is very supportive of your own efforts too.

Thank you for giving me the opportunity to go back over so many events of my father's life which has given me great pleasure. When your work has been completed, our family will have a tangible, concrete memoir of their father, grandfather and great grandfather.

Ever in your debt,
Jim O'Sullivan.

Introduction

The idea of writing a book about Dr. Eamonn O'Sullivan has been in my head for many years and as I got older the realization of what he had achieved in his lifetime became more and more evident. I never ceased to be amazed that some well-known writer or sports journalist had not taken up the task of getting down in print some of the achievements of this extraordinary Kerryman.

My earliest recollection of seeing Dr. Eamonn goes right back to 1953, the year he trained Kerry to win their Jubilee All-Ireland. In that dramatic and historic match they defeated Armagh in a final that will forever be remembered for Bill McCorry's second half penalty miss.

I was too young to be in Croke Park that day. I was only twelve years of age. Nevertheless, I had a close and personal look at the Kerry team in the weeks before the final as they had then, like now, trained for all big matches in Fitzgerald Stadium.

I can trace the beginning of my passion for Kerry football right back to what I experienced that year. Back then the gates of the field were always open and we would spend our evenings retrieving the football from behind the goals and around the field as the players practiced their point kicking and general football play. The names of the players were revered in the county – Sean Murphy, Jas Murphy, Mixie Palmer, Jim Brosnan, Jackie Lyne, Ned Roche and our own Killarney hero, Tadghie Lyne. And there we were in the very same field as them. The Doctor would line them up in a straight line, blow the whistle and the players would sprint flat out for about 14 yards. He would whistle again and they would slow to a fast walk and this exercise would be repeated up and down the field.

There were other drills as well – piggy back, rope skipping, hand passing in fours up and down the field. Then big groups would stand around in a circle passing the ball alternatively with the right and left hands. While the hand passing was going on he would talk in his low, quiet, measured tones, passing on his vast knowledge to his players. These are just a few of the drills I recall from those days in the early 50s.

It was a regular and much anticipated visit each evening to the Stadium as my boyhood friends and I looked on in awe as these giants of Kerrymen were put through their paces. And there in the middle of the field was this tall, stately man, dressed in a suit, shirt and tie, wearing either brown or black shoes always shining and brightly polished. He had a stop watch in one hand and a whistle in the other and some evenings he would sit down as he regularly carried with him one of these golf sticks you could open at the top to form a little seat. He was never dressed in a tracksuit, never wore a pair of football boots and on a wet evening he would have a brightly coloured umbrella and a gaberdine raincoat.

And my most abiding memory of all, in stark contrast to today's trainers, was this quiet elegant man never once raised his voice to shout at, encourage or berate one of his players. This I remember most of all. It was my first experience of a county trainer in action and little did I realize that I was in the presence of a man who had trained Kerry to win All-Irelands in 1924, 1926, 1937 and 1946. They would, of course, win that 1953 Final and he would go on and add three more to his record: 1955, 1959 and finally 1962.

Let me say straight away that I would never have taken on the task of documenting his greatest achievements except for the fact that his sons very kindly gave me permission to reprint in full his very lengthy and detailed account which he himself entitled, '*Self-Outline of Biographical Details*'. Eamonn wrote this wonderful and previously unpublished document when he retired from his position in St. Finan's Hospital Killarney as Resident Medical Superintendent in July 1962. It contains detailed and specific accounts of his life from the year he was born right up to his retirement.

If published on its own this biographical account would be sufficient to declare that Eamonn was truly one of the great Kerrymen of the twentieth century. I believe it would be fair to say that his written self-outline is an historic document in its own right and deserves to be published and available for future generations.

So the main basis of this book is the wonderful life account of what Eamonn himself has left us. This I have included in its entirety, without any additions or subtractions. I decided on this, following consultations with writers far more eminent than myself. I then decided to include here people and events that we know from his own account touched his life in one way or another. He reveals that, "my old friend the late 'Phileen' O'Sullivan announced to the Kerry team of 1924 that I would train them for the delayed final against Dublin." This was in fact the very first Eamonn had heard that he was the new Kerry trainer. So who was this man Eamonn called 'Phileen' who can now be credited with the honour of beginning Eamonn's Kerry training career? I include an account of Phil's life. Sadly I discovered that the Tousist man is one of two winning Kerry captains to be buried outside Ireland; the other is Gega O'Connor.

When Eamonn trained the Kerry team to win their seventh All-Ireland title in 1924, following a historic replay, Jack Murphy (a brilliant footballer from Balycarbery, Caherceiveen) died tragically between the draw and replay. His death at such a young age stunned the country. He was only 22. Eamonn of course attended Jack's funeral and I am particularly happy to remember him in this publication. Other legendary Kerry names will surface. However, I have tried as far as possible to write about people and events which have been lost and forgotten to an extent in the mists of time.

I am very grateful to those people who took time out to talk to me of their memories of Eamonn and with their interviews included in full I hope to give an overall view of the man. There are three interviews I am especially grateful for. Those are the interviews with three of Eamonn's four sons. Two years before he died, at the age of 70, I did a lengthy interview with Tony O'Sullivan by phone from his home in Oxfordshire. He gave me an open, honest and detailed account of his memories growing up in Killarney and his father's great love for his wife and children. Two years later James O'Sullivan visited Killarney on holiday from his home in England and we sat down together and he too recalled his father and his great love for all things Kerry. Edward was much nearer home; he lives in Killarney and he too gave of his time. Their interviews are vital as they give a previously unknown insight into Eamonn's private life. Robert is Eamonn's fourth son.

Among the other people I spoke to in my research was 90-year-old Jack O'Keeffe from Killarney. Jack was President of the famed Killarney Dr. Croke's GAA Club of which Eamonn was a staunch member. Jack had also been a member of the committee formed by the Croke's to build the Fitzgerald Stadium. He had vivid memories of Eamonn. Sadly, Jack passed away in 2006 and once again I consider myself very fortunate to have spoken before his death to another colleague of Eamonn's.

Dr. Desmond Hayes was a working colleague at St. Finan's Psychiatric Hospital for many years. I visited him in May 2001 at his home in Aghadoe, Killarney where he lived out his retirement with his daughter Catherine and son-in-law Denis Coffey. He gave a wonderful insight into the man away from football and his contribution to psychiatry. His interview is included here in full. There are numerous others as you will discover.

I have personal insights into Eamonn away from the green fields and white lines of the football field as well. When I applied for a nursing position in St. Finan's Hospital in 1962 Eamonn was one of three people who interviewed me. He sat behind a huge desk in the boardroom of the Hospital and naturally I was slightly overawed by the occasion. It was my first ever face-to-face meeting with him. I needn't have worried. He quickly put me at ease as he threw in a few football questions. I was, at that time, a member of the Kerry Under-21 football team and I had included this information in my application form. The interview was drawing to a close when he asked: "If you took up employment in this Hospital would you transfer to play with the hospital football team?" He waited for my reply. This threw me slightly as my club was Killarney Legion. If I answered "No," would my job prospect be finished? I took no chance and after a few moments pause I replied, "Yes, I will play for the hospital team." I was accepted as a trainee nurse, transferred from my beloved Legion Club and played for St. Finan's for a number of years. My friends and colleagues in The Legion never forgave me for that transfer. But the reason was simple; I had met Dr. Eamonn.

As I began my career in the Hospital early in 1962 Eamonn was beginning his last months as Resident Medical Superintendent (R.M.S.). It was very evident to me in the short time that I worked with him that his influence in the Hospital was huge. He would conduct a round of all the wards once a week. Junior doctors and senior nursing personnel would trail in his wake as he moved from ward to ward. His very presence invoked an urgent response from both staff and patient and it was action stations for one and all when Eamonn was on the move. Following his retirement his very memory continued to cast long shadows throughout the vast building and the older nurses would continue to relate stories of his work and achievements. Even today the name St. Finan's and Dr. Eamonn are synonymous and when one is mentioned the other quickly follows.

Eamonn packed more into his life than most people would in two life times. He was truly a remarkable person and my wish is that this publication will in some small way record for future generations some of his many and varied achievements. While he is generally known for his football training successes little has been written of his work in other fields. His input into the building of Fitzgerald Stadium and the Killarney Golf and Fishing Club, his work as an author, the founding of the Killarney Bridge Club and of course his massive contribution to psychiatry all should be remembered.

Without a doubt, he was a man before his time.

Weeshie Fogarty
2007

The Champion

EAMONN'S FATHER J.P. O'SULLIVAN

James Patrick O'Sullivan (known as 'J.P.') was born in his father's farm in Brookhill, Killorglin, in 1867, the eldest of a family of four. His father, Patrick, was a well-known Gaelic scholar and Court interpreter. He died about 1900. J.P. took part in athletics and played football from an early age. At the age of 17, he caught a chill playing games and contracted rheumatic fever. Unknown at the time, this must have caused damage to his aortic heart valves. (Dr. Eamonn explained some years later that this weakness led inevitably to his untimely death at the age of 42 – date written in margin note by Dr. Eamonn: January 13, 1909). This tragic event occurred in Midleton, between Cork and Youghal, during a coursing meeting at which he ran his own dogs. J.P. was accompanied to the coursing that day by a relative, Tos O'Sullivan of Waterville, father of Thomas ('Toddy') O'Sullivan, Manager and Director of the Gresham Hotel, Dublin. (Anecdotal family recollections record the fact that the doctor attending to J.P. at his deathbed was fellow sportsman and greyhound trainer, Dr. Edward W. Griffin, at that time R.M.S. of the Killarney Mental Hospital – who would be some 21 years later the father-in-law of J.P's younger son, Eamonn).

J.P. was a successful local athlete at the age of 19, at a time when Irish athletics were on the ascendancy. At a meeting in Tralee a year later, he came second to the world record holder, J.S. Mitchell, in the weight competition. He won the open hop-step-and-jump. J.P's fame spread quickly: sprinting, hurdles, weight events and cycling, where he won the Silver Cycling Shield at the Lee Sports, Cork, in 1887, at the age of 20. He defeated recognised experts in the 'Rise and Strike' hurling event popular at that time. It was said that J.P. frequently beat the world record hop-step-and-jump of 47ft 4inches in training with 50ft jumps at Firies, where he lived, after he married Annie Spring.

The Sports Championship of 1888 held at the Market Fields, Limerick, was a landmark in J.P's career. He entered and was placed in a number of events. The world hop-step-and-jump record was broken three times on that day! J.P. came second in those jump-offs. The record set that day by Dan Shanahan of Kilfinane, Limerick, of 50ft ½ inch, stood for 25 years.

J.P. competed in the annual IAAA Championship held in Ballsbridge, Dublin, in 1890 and finished well up in third place. In August of the following year, J.P. won the high jump, the long jump, the hammer and the shot events and was close in the hurdles, the 56lbs and the one-mile flat race against the reigning champion, Dr. T.M. O'Donovan, of Rathduff, Blarney. J.P's score was 31 points, against O'Donovan's 30. J.P's reputation was established, thereafter, for all times. He retired from athletics after that great success, but continued to take a great interest in events.

J.P. really began his football career when he captained the Laune Rangers at the age of 25 in the All-Ireland Final of 1892, in Clonturk Park. They were defeated in that final by the Dublin Young Irelanders. Though on the defeated side, J.P. was described by the victors as being as fast as a deer and as strong as three men. "Them Kerrymen were good men and gave us all we wanted of it. They were maybe unlucky and rushed us hard at the end. They were great men with the ball on the ground; we bate them overhead," were the comments made by Dick Curtis at Croke Park in 1948.

J.P. was in his late 30s by the year of 1904. He became a county councillor and supported the Nationalist cause. He was a hard-working, progressive farmer. He was a member of the Kerry GAA County Board and followed the county teams to home and away games. J.P. was paymaster during the building of the Farranfore-Cahirciveen, narrow-gauge railway. This railway interest prevailed, for Dr. Eamonn remembered being taken by his father to see the mono-rail Lartigue (1882-94) between Listowel and Ballybunion.

He was a fine figure of a man; at least 6ft in height. He was remarkably light-footed for his size and girth. He had a leonine head and sported a heavy drooping moustache popular at that time. He had an open, strong face, with a kindly but determined expression. Kerry people universally called J.P. O'Sullivan – 'The Champion', as he was, in their eyes, the greatest athlete and noblest of souls. He was a man of so many interests: athletics, cycling, Gaelic football and coursing.

A true family man also – a lodge in a row of terraced houses in the approaches to the beach at Rossbeigh, existing still today, was taken for family summer holidays in the early years of the twentieth century. How much of an influence J.P. was in inspiring the success of his son Eamonn's own sporting and training career cannot be underestimated.

Eddie O'Sullivan

EAMONN'S SECOND ELDEST SON
REMEMBERS HIS FATHER

Well over the years, he was a very nice father to have, not too strict. He was strict enough, if you like, but not really too strict at all. People often say to me, he was a great man for discipline, did you find that? No. But he was always the boss. They're the early memories of my dad, Weeshie.

There were four boys in the family. Jim's the eldest, myself the second, and Tony and Bob.

I can remember the building of Fitzgerald Stadium. Dad put a huge amount of his life into that project. We would go down on occasions just to see what was going on. Everybody knows the patients and the staff built the Fitzgerald Stadium. Of course that time there was no great medicine for the mentally ill, nowadays everything has changed. That time it was a question of 'keep them occupied as best you can' and in the building of the Stadium my father saw a great opportunity of occupying the patients of his hospital. I believe he was way ahead of his time in this. Indeed, it helped many patients to a better life.

On the football side, I remember around 1944 Kerry were playing in the All-Ireland against Roscommon. I have one memory of coming home and the paper was opened one day and I said to my mother, "What do you think of the Kerry team? Will they win?" She said they would not. I said "Why?" "Because they didn't pick Dan Kavanagh," she replied. She was correct, Roscommon won and Dan Kavanagh was only a sub, he came on in that game.

Another memory of home I have is that there was always this photograph in the living room. For a long time we took no notice of it until one day I decided to ask my mother, "Who was that?" It was my father's father, J.P., she told me. Then I came across some small magazines, and there were various articles, if I remember right, by

Carbery. He was with *The Cork Examiner*. I saw it mentioning J.P. I hadn't a clue who this 'J.P.' was. It was my mother who told me all about him. And I saw these magazines and I used read to them. And as a result of that I was carried up to the All-Ireland Final in 1946 when I showed interest in football. He was thrilled when Kerry beat Roscommon that day and Dan Kavanagh, who was a great favourite of my father, was playing corner forward.

He never spoke a lot at home in front of us about his football involvements. If you drew it down he would. But generally he wouldn't. But of course we later realised that he was fierce interested. I suppose the fact that his father captained the first Kerry team to play in Croke Park – the Laune Rangers, inspired him. His father died suddenly when Eamonn was 11 years of age. That was an awful blow to him. He was sent to school up the country and then got back to the Seminary in Killarney. He idolised his father, Weeshie. He was a well-known athlete and footballer. I'd say he never got over the shock of it.

My mother was a great pillar for him, she always encouraged him to follow what he loved to do and she would go to matches. She'd go to the All-Irelands when they'd be playing in the Fitzgerald Stadium. She had a fierce interested in it, fair play.

When he got older he would reminisce alright. And he'd always tell us to open a scrapbook and keep the cuttings of the paper, which of course we did for a bit and then we stopped it. He had a fierce interest in Gaelic football. And he always maintained nobody could play Gaelic football except Kerry. They were the best of all. He was fully convinced of that and I suppose results have proved him correct.

Yes his name often comes up today, God it does. A friend of mine came up to me one day, a long time ago. "Your father's dead a bit now," he said. "Yeah," says I. "Well of course hardly anybody in Killarney remembers him," he continued. "Well, I suppose," says I, "a lot of them have him forgotten." But he's not forgotten, fair play. I think yer man was being a bit sarcastic. Yes, his name is often mentioned now but it's mostly if you meet people in town that they draw down about him. Up the country they draw down about him a lot. I suppose, I never go round telling people who I am, if you like, but they'd hear and they'd start asking me questions.

His sons were all different, however. My eldest brother is now retired. He was at sea all his life. He was an officer on board oil tankers. Then he became First Officer. The next was myself. Tony was the next boy. He played football more than any of the rest of us. He was very good and dad was very proud of him as a footballer. The youngest Robbie, he's in England. He's called Bob. Bob was a good footballer; he played for the Croke's once or twice. He preferred to play rugby actually.

Eamonn was a man apart I'd say. People often draw down about him to me. They would question me a lot, especially about my interest in football. "Were you involved in the GAA?" "Were you involved in all these things?" I was not. I wasn't that kind of person at all. I lived my own life but I was, naturally, very proud of my father. I suppose the other brothers then were much attached to him too I'd say.

He was involved in practically everything: Bridge, golf, the whole lot. He was a great believer in life, moderation in everything. Too much of anything in this life is bad for you.

He'd be very proud when Kerry won. He was that type of person. More outgoing than I'd be. He was very proud of the staff of St. Finan's also. They gave him a beautiful presentation when he retired. The Killarney Golf Club, it was called the Killarney Golf and Fishing Club at the time, asked what he would like, when he was retiring and he said he would like somebody to paint him. And so it was done! The artist was a Ryan man, and very good he was. He did a beautiful painting of him with the Ladies' View in the background. Now Tony has that over in England. He got several presentations. He trained the Killarney team to win the County Championship and he got a nice plaque. He got presentations following the finals of 1946, 1953, 1955 and 1959. The one after 1946 was a big plaque and it shows seven or eight footballers and the captain of each team at the end. Tony has that. I have the one in Killarney.

When he retired he had two years of good health. Then he had two years of very bad health, and he died in October, 1966. People didn't realise that he was a very heavy diabetic. There are different degrees of diabetes. If I remember rightly he would have to inject himself four times a day. And one of the times was every morning at 4 O'Clock. But he took it in his stride, he never complained about anything Weeshie. Now when I think back I only realise the massive amount of time he devoted to others – his family, the patients, the Kerry footballers, the Bridge and Golf Clubs, and much more. I remember him at home in the winter evenings sitting by the fire writing his books, a board on his lap as a desk top and his little pencil and rubber for correcting spelling mistakes.

I always regretted that no person has written about his life and all he was involved in. Even though he was my father I must say he was a remarkable person. He achieved so much and was a man way before his time. The family will be thrilled Weeshie that you are going to preserve his memory and his works. Of course you worked with him in the Hospital and you knew him fairly well through that and the football. Well done.

Tony O'Sullivan

DR. EAMONN'S THIRD ELDEST SON

On Sunday October 10 of last year Tony O'Sullivan died following a short illness at his home in Oxfordshire, in England. The 68-year-old Killarney born native was the third eldest son of the legendary Kerry football trainer Dr. Eamonn O'Sullivan. Six years ago, (2001), in an exclusive Radio Kerry *Terrace Talk* interview, Tony spoke to me from his home in England and recalled in vivid detail the private man behind the national high profile which his father held. It would prove to be a fascinating, and beautiful account of a son's memories of the father who could be considered one of the great Kerrymen of the last century. Hereunder is the first of a two-part narrative of Tony's interview which, in my opinion, captures a segment of Kerry's football history previously untold.

A RARE INTERVIEW WITH TONY O'SULLIVAN

The late Tony O'Sullivan remembers his father, legendary Kerry football trainer Dr. Eamonn O'Sullivan.

The first recollections I have of my father's football involvement was 1946. That was the year Kerry beat Roscommon in the famous replay and he was called back to train them in that game because they had done rather badly in the drawn match. Actually I'll tell you a story: listening to the drawn game on the radio in the Mental Hospital, one of the patients, his name was Euge Reidy, said with about two are three minutes to go, "I think it's all over." Roscommon were two goals ahead, and then the late Paddy Kennedy, who actually studied dairy science like I did, scored a goal; Tom 'Gega' O'Connor got another. In their hour of need my father was brought back and they succeeded in winning the replay.

I remember being at the Cork game in Killarney that year, I was ten years of age and was very close to my father. I used to go playing golf with him but it was really when I started playing football myself that I got close to him, from the sports side of things. Also it was then that some of the other brothers and I began to realise the esteem in which he was held and the contribution he made to Kerry football. He was a legend really. I remember 1953 well when he trained the team to beat Armagh, because then I was going to university, and was at home in Killarney that summer and saw the team training. It was the last time of 'collective training', as it was banned the following year by the other counties because Kerry were doing so well. Despite this, Kerry won again in 1955. I would say from 1953 on I got more involved and I was playing myself with UCC. My father knew people there like the late Jim Hurley, a Cork hurler who he was secretary of UCC and Professoor Atkins, the President who also had a GAA background. These people knew him and I suppose that was helpful to me.

In all honesty I think his sweetest victory was the one against Dublin in 1955. The famous Dublin machine, with Kevin Heffernan at full forward, represented the new concept of the roving full forward in Gaelic football. Kerry had problems because Ned Roche was full back. Now Ned was a very solid full back but he was not the roving type, the semi-finals were drawn and they were replayed. I remember it was Mayo versus Dublin and Kerry versus Cavan. Kerry won and Dublin won and I remember the next day Sean Flanagan and other Mayo players saying to my father, "Well what are you going to do with Kevin Heffernan because he is very mobile?" My father kept saying to everybody, "My belief is that the full back should stay in the square and mark the square." In fact he gave an example from the Mayo/ Dublin game where Paddy Prendergast was following Heffernan and there was no one in the square, and one ball actually hopped in the square and went over the bar for a point. It was a very close game and my late father said, "If the full back was there that point would not have been scored because he would have been in his position."

Fortunately in a way for Kerry, Heffernan probably thought that he didn't have to roam very much and that he could beat Ned Roche in the square. This played into Kerry's hands and they won very convincingly. I think the media were very much playing up this great Dublin machine, as a result, my father was very happy with this win.

My father was a very low-key person. He had his own ideas, which come across clearly in the book he wrote: '*The Art and Science of Gaelic Football*'. He felt players should stay in their own areas of play. He had very firm and fixed views and was confident these were right.

He was relaxed and never panicked, often understating things. He had this innate confidence that what he was doing was the right thing and the way he trained the team best prepared them for the game. For example, at that time you would see players preparing for sprinting, they would go down on their hands and knees and they would sprint from that position, now he would argue that in Gaelic football you would of course never do that. He would have the players walking along and he would blow a whistle and they would break into a sprint from a standing position, which I suppose physiologically you would do in the game itself. He had it very well thought out and did it in a relaxed, confident manner. He wasn't bombastic at all. I would say at that time in the 1940s and 1950s he brought a professional approach to Gaelic football in the way the teams were trained and the way the players were treated. For example, he took them out of Barry's Hotel in Dublin and took them to hotels outside Dublin City, where they would be less pestered the night before a game. Everything was very well-planned and prepared.

A lot of people might say that my late father had a very austere appearance and wasn't very approachable. I disagree. As you got to know him he was a very nice man, and I was very close to him through the football and other things; he loved to discuss these things. It is fair to say that he had a very constructive approach to Gaelic football; he always thought it through in his head.

My father loved to reminisce about the past and often would go back to the 1955 Final against Dublin. However he was very disappointed in 1964 when Kerry lost the final to Galway, it was his last year and the only final in nine which he lost. I was not at that game; I was working in Cork University but I rang him up afterwards. There are many reasons why this team may have lost. He had just retired from the Mental Hospital and he wasn't as on top of his game as he might have been previously. Also, the team mightn't have been as good as previous Kerry teams. I think that was a disappointment which he hid well. I'm sure he would have liked to have gone out with an intact record.

When he retired he wrote the (previously unpublished) biographical account of his life. It's great to see it appear in this book. I will read out to you Weeshie what he said about that time in his career: "The late Phileen O'Sullivan, the Captain, had asked me to train the team for the 1924 All-Ireland Final against Dublin. I devised a 24-hour schedule of training which differs little from that published in my book of 1958, *The Art and Science of Gaelic Football*', which had worked out successful on all eight subsequent final occasions; 1924, 1926, 1937, 1946, 1953, 1955, 1959 and 1962. These successes were not due to any personal magical touch, as has often been stated, there were other factors at play. Given a bunch of first class footballers and putting them under a few weeks regimental and satisfactory training schedule, with the material such as Kerry has regularly produced, an understanding coach could not fail. The final factor, which is all important, is that the element of luck in the course of the game is not markedly against your team.

True this success story did not apply to the All-Ireland Football Final of September 1964 in which Galway deservedly defeated Kerry by 15 points to 10 points. It is no reflection on Galway's victory to say that Kerry, on that date never reproduced their magnificent football when subsequently defeating Cavan 2-12 to 0-6 in the semi-final, it was not Kerry's lucky day, beset by injuries of a most dislocating nature and other factors, they had to bow to Galway and did so sportingly. Naturally I had some disappointment as it was a break in previous success, but Kerry will be back – remember that they have won 20 All-Ireland titles in the last 60 years and four in the last 11, on the law of averages they are due another title in the next few years."

So you see Weeshie, he was sad at having lost his great unbeaten record.

My father was interested in a lot of things. He read all the newspapers avidly – the Dublin ones and the *Cork Examiner*. At night he spent a lot of time writing, he wrote a textbook on Occupational Therapy for which he received a M.D. Degree. He put a lot of work into that in his free time. I remember him sitting in an armchair with a board on his lap and writing away with a pencil, rubbing out and correcting mistakes. He also wrote a book of which I have a copy here in my home, *'The Art and Science of Gaelic Football'* (which was also published in Gaelic). Mentally, he was very active and inquiring. He played a bit of golf and he was a left hander, I think he got down to a nine handicap he told me one time. He didn't hit the ball very far but he had a nice swing and he enjoyed playing. He got very friendly with an Irish-American who came to retire in Killarney – a Jerry Coffey. Jerry had a very New York since of humour. They would play together and I would join them when I was at home. The golf would be secondary to the banter and jokes and what have you.

My father was very active in Bridge as well and he was the driving force behind the Bridge Congress coming to Killarney in the 1940s. My mother and he would play with two others in a four person competition and I think they won a competition nearly every year. He was quite keen on Bridge but didn't play chess.

When in charge of teams he was very measured and relaxed and instilled great confidence. Some people would be running up and down the sidelines shouting at the team with the best will in the world but my father was not that kind. He would just say that the opposition was a good team with good players, but "But you're a better team, you play your game and stick to your man."

I'll tell you a story Weeshie. In the area of defence he would say that each of the six backs should stay in their own area and not roam out of it very much. I was playing in a county championship game with Dr. Croke's one day and my father was our trainer; I was marking Billy McCarthy. Bobby Buckley came soloing through, I was not sure whether to stop him. I decided to stay with my man. Bobby scored, and after the match my father nicely berated me for not challenging the man going through, saying there are times when you should be flexible and do something different.

We were all very fond of my mother. She stayed behind the scenes mostly, that time women did. She was happy my father was enjoying the football and training Kerry, and that he was out with younger people, she was relaxed in that. She certainly would have travelled to All-Irelands but to support of my father rather than being avidly interested in the match. She preferred to stay behind the scenes but was always very supportive and loving of my father. It pleased her so that he got great satisfaction from what he did.

He was very proud of the Fitzgerald Stadium and spoke highly of the Hospital patients that helped build it. It was Occupational Therapy for them, even though it was hard physical work. When it was opened in 1936 I remember he kept a scrapbook of the matches played there. It is a lovely stadium, but he was not too happy that it was not used as much as it should, due to the fact that it was far removed from Dublin and other places. He was very proud to be associated with it especially as it was called after Dick Fitzgerald.

He was so devoted to his work in St. Finan's and it was quite a challenge to balance his work with his interest in football, but he was able to do it. As I said, he did a lot of his writing at night and at weekends, so he was always doing something, I never remember him being idle. He drank in great moderation, I never saw him drunk, and I never heard him swear. He was a great example to me and my brothers as a father. I found him very approachable and very interesting, I could talk to him for a long time on many subjects.

I think his favourite song was Killarney's *'Lakes and Dells'*. The year he went to the States in the 1960s was the 75th anniversary of the Kerryman's Benevolent and Patriotic Society. They published a book and there was a lovely statement in the front of it which greatly appealed to me and my father. It said, "There are but two kingdoms in this world, the Kingdom of God and the Kingdom of Kerry" – such a statement would have been something that would have encapsulated my father's own beliefs.

He was also a very religious man. I don't know if you are aware, but at one stage he studied for the priesthood in Rome. However his health broke down and he took it as a sign that he didn't have a true vocation. He was a religious man in the very good sense of the word – very proactive and positive. He was a very proud Kerryman as well, so maybe the "two Kingdoms" of the quote would be a very good encapsulation of his feelings about both religion and his home County.

Towards the end of his years he was in ill health and wasn't quite the same man he used to be. That affected him a little I think. I went to the America and when I came back in 1966, my father was dying. He died later that year. Of course he was a great family man. His children and grandchildren greatly appreciated him. I'm away from Killarney now for a long time and not au fait with things, but I feel sure that they're all very proud of him too.

The recantation he has got in Killarney is well deserved. The stand in Fitzgerald Stadium, for example, is called after him. I was home for that event and all of his family were very proud of him and the recognition he obtained on that occasion.

I had met Tony O'Sullivan just once when he was on a visit to Killarney some years ago and I played against him in an O'Donoghue Cup Final in the late 1950s as The Legion and The Croke's clashed. He stood about 6'3 in height and played some games with Kerry. A lovely, quiet, gentle and unassuming person, I am delighted to have had the privilege of recording for posterity some of his memories regarding his legendary father.

An Interview with Jim O'Sullivan

ELDEST SON OF DR. EAMONN

In his one and only interview on the subject, Jim O'Sullivan, son of Dr. Eamonn, talks to the author and provides a remarkable insight into the family, career and sporting endeavours of his father.

I was born in my father's quarters in the Hospital where he lived with my mother. The quarters itself was a small self-contained house that would appear to have been built as an afterthought by Pugin, the designer – a master English architect. It was there in the top upper bedroom I was born in the year 1931 and I was the eldest of Eamonn's four children.

It was a wonderful experience growing up around St. Finan's and even though the Hospital was a part of Killarney it had an existence of its own. It was slightly remote and was subject to certain strict orders such as arriving back at certain times in the evening when the gates were closed, so an element of isolation occurred. I can clearly remember being impressed by the way the staff survived as a community in this environment. Sons and daughters of staff members married and followed into the Hospital as a career path. All of this led to a very close community sense, which we were all part of as children growing up.

And of course in the background, ever present in our consciences were the patients themselves. Sometimes these were forlorn figures, sad but none the less very human and treated with great dignity and respect by all of us. It was a pleasure to grow up in that environment. There were over 1,000 patients in the Hospital at that time. Now there are less than one hundred.

History moves on and Kerry today is a very different place to what it was in the 1930s and during the war years, when everything was so quiet and isolated. The science of psychiatry has also progressed wonderfully to the benefit of the patient. Now, of course, there isn't the same need to virtually incarcerate people in vast numbers in old Victorian institutions and in many instances back then, that was the case.

My own father was always keen to alleviate the burden the patients were faced with by their isolation. In his particular case he concentrated on Occupation Therapy as a means to soften their burden and in that I am proud to say he was very successful.

Eamonn came to Killarney as a locum doctor and while he was there a vacancy occurred for an assistant at St. Finan's. He had to undergo a canvassing process to win that appointment. It was, he reminded me later, a very complex and detailed process but it turned out that he was to be successful. He took up the post under Dr. Edward Griffin who came from Ballyheigue.

Now Dr. Griffin had a bevy of daughters – the second of which caught Eamonn's eye and within a year or two they were involved in a secret courtship. My mother Marjorie was at school in Drishane at that time and when Eamonn went to visit her, the nuns thought he was her medical adviser. They did not realize it was a more personal relationship. So that is how we came into being, as it were.

On one visit to Kerry I discovered a remarkable coincidence of an earlier event that had taken place. There was another Dr. Griffin who was no relation to the family or had no blood relationship. Now he had come to Killarney at the request of the Earl of Kenmare who had an epileptic son and Dr. Griffin lived in the Priory in Killarney, near the Flesk River. This Dr. Griffin acted as a medical adviser for this boy who wasn't very healthy. Eventually the young boy died and Lord Kenmare was able to use his influence to obtain for that Dr. Griffin the appointment of Medical Superintendent of the Hospital – in those days known as the Killarney District Lunatic Asylum or KDLA. You know, those are letters that are emblazoned in my mind because in my early childhood I remember the brooms that were used in the Hospital all had those letters burned into their handles.

Anyway, Dr. Griffin took up that appointment. He was a married man, in fact it was his second marriage. His second wife, an English lady called Marjorie Stokes, had her own ward. Some time later my grandfather, Dr. Griffin from Ballyheigue, returned to Kerry from work in the medical service in England and obtained the appointment as Medical Assistant at the Mental Hospital. He went on to marry Marjorie Stokes, my maternal grandmother, who was the ward of Dr. Griffin, my grandfather's superior at that time. So twice in the history of our family there was a connection with the Hospital and an inter-marriage between the Assistant Doctor and the daughter of the Superintendent. I really think that this was a remarkable thing.

My grandfather, Dr. Griffin, came from farming stock in the village of Ballyheigue and quite remarkably for the times, he graduated through the National University and became a doctor. He went to England to work for a number of years, eventually specializing in mental health. We know he worked in the Mental Hospital in Wakefield and I have a photograph of him from that era standing with a cricket team. So in his own right he was a great sportsman.

When he came back to Kerry he continued his interest in sport. He began training greyhounds as a hobby during his time as Resident Medical Superintendent and by the end of 1919 he had a remarkable winning dog called 'Guard's Brigade'. He then took him over to England for the Waterloo Purse in 1921. The dog won at this event. Guard's Brigade was trained in the Hospital by Nurse O'Connor. My aunt-in-law, Mai Griffin, has a portrait of him. Tragically there was a foot-and-mouth disease outbreak in England which prevented the dog being brought back to Ireland so Dr. Griffin had to sell him to an English lord, Lord Tweedsmouth.

My mother, I presume, was born and reared in St. Finan's where her father worked and like so many of our family she also grew up in that environment. And of course it was there she met my father. She was a member of a large family; there were three boys and five girls.

When I look back now, my memory of my father is that of a large man. He was a very dignified and imposing figure and had to be treated with respect. He wasn't a strict disciplinarian but nonetheless he wanted us to obey certain rules. Still, I would imagine we were brought up in a very strict way by today's standards. However, he was a tolerant man and my feelings for him even as a young teenager and later as a young man were one of love, and respect came from that love.

Eamonn was a wonderful man with a warm spirit and it came across to you when you were in his presence. He was never boring. A journey in the car with him to the country, maybe to attend a sports meeting, was an adventure. He knew exactly all the stories of the places where we travelled through. He loved talking about the towns we passed and the great footballer or hurler they had produced in their time and all of this was presented to me as a young child growing up. He was always close to his county, to his country, to his sport and that rubbed off on us very much.

He was an official with the Irish team at the 1936 Berlin Olympic Games. Now, I don't know much about it but what I do remember is when he came back he was very impressed by Germany as a country and by the organization of the games. He came back and talked about the cleanliness of the country, the punctuality of the trains, the facilities made available for the athletes and so on. He had in fact very strong respect for the Germans as a result of that experience and it wasn't until later when the world war broke out that we began to learn of the more sinister aspects of National Socialism and then he had to review his outlook and attitude.

He studied for the priesthood in Maynooth for two years and then went to the Irish College in Rome but his tenure there came to a sudden end when his health broke down. Now he never really discussed the details of it but it was sufficient to interrupt his career. He came home, recuperated and it was then that he began his medical career and went to college in Dublin.

He was a native speaker of the Irish language even though we didn't speak Irish in the home but he had a great love for all things Irish and promoted the language every chance he had. He was proud of Ireland, proud of the heritage of place names, mountain names and so on. He was constantly bringing these things to our attention as children so we also had a great love for all these things as well.

I was five years old in 1937 and we took our summer holiday in Ballyheigue to be near the retired Dr. Griffin and his family and we were staying in a lodge in the village. That year of 1937 Kerry had drawn with Laois in the All-Ireland semi-final in Cork, Kerry 2-3 : Laois 1-6. Eamonn was approached by officers of the County Board and asked to train the team for the replay. However, he told them he was on holidays and he really could not upset his family by abandoning the holiday. Then he said to them if they brought the team to Ballyheigue he would train them and they did this without hesitation. I have vivid memories of the team behind the Castle Hotel in the village of Ballyheigue undergoing their training regime under Eamonn's supervision.

The replay took place at Waterford City on August 29 and with five minutes to go the sides were level. Just before the final whistle Mickey Lyne (one of the famous Lyne brothers from Cleeney) sent a high ball between the posts and Eamonn had once again guided the team to another final. They then drew with Cavan in the final and won the replay 4-4 to 1-7. I was not aware then of my father having trained Kerry to win the 1924 and 1926 All-Irelands and I was not fully aware of the significance of what I was seeing but I knew it was important and I had a feeling of respect and a great interest in what was going on.

As regards Eamonn's involvement in the planning of the Killarney Golf Course (which most people are unaware of) – I vividly remember going out with him to O'Mahoney's Point on the shores of the Lakes of Killarney one day to meet Valentine, the 5th Earl of Kenmare. We knew him as 'Lord Castlerosse'. He came out with his chauffeur and a bevy of beautiful miniature collie dogs. Now the purpose of the visit was to examine the gamekeeper's lodge at O'Mahoney's Point which was being considered as a temporary clubhouse for the new Killarney Golf Course. I can also vividly recall fighting our way through vast rhododendron bushes to get to the cottage. That event took place about 1936. Eamonn was present with Castlerosse in those early formative years when the Killarney Golf Club was being planned, as Castlerosse was prepared to donate the land to the club and its members. In fact, my father was the very first Club Captain in 1939 and was Honorary from 1940-42.

Another aspect of Eamonn's life Weeshie, unknown to many, was his great interest in Bridge. He became a renowned International Tournament Director in Killarney in the years during and after the war. My recollection is quite vivid about all of this because I was then a young teenager. Auction Bridge was popular in Killarney and there was a club in existence at that time. I'm referring to the late 1930s here. Bridge is a very skilful game and requires a lot of strategy and interpretation. Now the contract bidding type of Bridge was gaining momentum around the world and Eamonn took a great interest in this and he produced a foolscap type sheet of paper on which he designed a two club bidding system which he later introduced to the town. It became very popular and helped people become familiar with the contract type Bridge and then led to the explosion which took place. My father was very happy with the success of Bridge in Killarney.

I remember how he never tolerated bad language. In fact, he had to end a partnership in golf because of that very problem with more than one player. At home he was a quiet man. I did have my disagreements with him as a child growing up, and young children get headstrong ideas and revolt a little. He disapproved of many things I did but he always did it in a gentle way. He never raised his voice and appealed to your better sense rather than your instincts. I learned over the years to adjust to that and to accept that as a way of making decisions.

He was a homely man and his family meant a lot to him. He spent a lot of time following the news in the press and listening to the radio but he had time for his children. Our meal times were enlivened with conversations about a variety of topics, so we grew up in a very stimulating family circle that I'm sure has benefited all of us through our life.

We attended Mass every Sunday in the Hospital. A priest would come up from town to the Chapel which would be full of patients and staff members and often the priest would stay on to have breakfast with our family. That church was very personal to me. In fact I served my first Mass there as a youngster.

Dr. Griffin, as my father's predecessor, had developed the concept of Occupational Therapy. This is the concept of giving tasks to patients to fill their day and keep them mentally active and alert in order to overcome the terrible burden of institutionalisation and isolation. Now Dr. Griffin in his day started this programme that Eamonn, my father, was very happy to continue and to specialize in. Significantly, it was part of the concept of Occupational Therapy that encouraged him to look out from the second floor of St. Finan's Hospital down towards the town, overlooking huge vast expanse of green fields and to think that here was the location for a stadium or a playing field. It would also provide an opportunity for Occupational Therapy for the patients in the Hospital. We should remember that these patients were mostly of rural background, farming stock and physical labour, and so using a spade and shovel was part of their lives growing up. Being given work of this nature was of great benefit to them both physically and mentally.

There was a great need and an opportunity to build Fitzgerald Stadium. There was a requirement to collect funds and all of this gelled together. There was a remarkable bringing together of many influences that led to this great event. It was a natural development for my father to include the staff and patients in the building, as a form of therapy. I remember in particular one member of the staff, Denso Hurley, who was a male charge nurse at that time, was given the responsibility of taking a group of male patients and getting them to turn the sod in this beautiful green field just below the Hospital.

Around this time the former great Kerry footballer Bill Landers, one of three fine brothers, had returned to Killarney from America where he had been for a few years. I remember Bill well. A tall, dignified man, he had a great presence and possessed a great charm and his first job when he returned to Killarney was to get an appointment to the Hospital as the driver of the hospital lorry that was used in the construction of the Stadium. I remember distinctly riding around with Bill in that lorry when earth was being moved from the high part of the field to the lower tier of the field.

Sometime later, as the park was taking shape, I was present when the late Henry Downing, a Killarney solicitor came up with a chain to measure out the pitch. Eamonn was always adamant that they would make the pitch the largest in the country and that it would be wider and longer than any other football field in Ireland. There were many people who shared this vision which my father had and the Dr. Croke's Club was fully behind him in getting the project up and running.

My father had a great love and respect for Dick Fitzgerald whom the Stadium is called after. This extended back to his student days in St. Brendan's. He related to me a story when they had been training for some match with Brendan's. Dick Fitzgerald came into the field and stood watching them for a while. When they took a break Dick approached them and said, "Let me have the ball for a moment boys and I'll show you something that might interest you." He took the ball to the corner flag placed it on the ground and put it over the bar; he was wearing his Sunday boots. My father was so impressed with his kicking that it remained with him all his life and I am sure when it came to naming the Stadium in honour of Dick it pleased him greatly.

I believe Eamonn was far ahead of his time and he had a vision of Gaelic football not just being a national game but becoming an international game. I'm certain that was an aspiration he had. He saw the Australian rules and its similarity and common origin with our game as a means to achieve this. It has now happened. It is not a perfect merging of the games yet but we are on the road to possibly achieving an international status for the game and that would have pleased Eamonn greatly. He had a great fascination with Australian rules and in our home we had a lot of textbooks on football history in places like America, Australia and England.

I feel it is my responsibility to present these recollections of my father, mother and family to guide your activities, Weeshie. In parallel with this, I hope to finalize our family tree for our grandchildren in England, to keep their Irish roots firmly before them.

As I re-read Eamonn's *Outline of Biographical Details* I feel, although very comprehensive, there is still much omitted in these pages that deserve to also be recorded. I would like therefore to take a look at his illustrious but lesser-known career in certain fields.

For one, my father's involvement in the formative years of Irish athletics should not go unnoticed. The 1930s was an important period in Irish life, as the British yoke was being cast off. There is no reference in his autobiography to the fact that he attended the 1936 Olympics in Berlin as an official with the Irish team.

As an official Dr. Eamonn saw O'Callaghan win Ireland's first gold medal at 1936 Olympic Games, for throwing the hammer. Eamonn was impressed by the image that Germany projected at that time – trains running on time, cleanliness, etc. We had an English language copy of Hitler's book, *Mein Kampf*, at home.

A German company was awarded the contract to re-wire the

Mental Hospital for change to National Grid in the very late 1930s. All of us, including Eamonn, were very impressed by the calibre of the German workers – they looked like the Afrika Corps troops of a few years later. This admiration suffered a setback however when their foreman driving a blue sports car crashed into Eamonn's new and treasured Morris 12HP Saloon one evening in 1939 at the top of High Street. Eamonn does not recount the accident in his autobiography however.

The incident that he suffered circa 1920 in Dublin as a medical student also does not get a mention. Dr. Eamonn was knocked off his motorbike by a British Army armoured car and received £15 compensation, equivalent to €2,600 in today's prices.

No reference is made by my father, in his writing, to his involvement in the Croke Park atrocity. Apparently the authorities machine-gunned the supporters at a football match as a reprisal for the shooting the night before of British Secret Service Agents. Eamonn normally attended the Sunday football matches at Croke Park. On this occasion, a fellow student with whom he shared digs asked him to accompany him on a visit to an aunt of his who lived in Malahide. As they approached their digs in the evening they were warned off and told to disappear for a while.

I wonder how he would react now to the opening up of Croke Park. He touched on the history of football in his book but discounted the notion that Webb-Ellis at Rugby School might have been influenced by seeing the early versions of Gaelic football in Ireland. Yet, we see today that the different codes exercise influence on each other – yellow, red cards, etc. Sport and TV was just starting at the end of his life; he would have delighted in the coverage we have today.

There is a lot to be said about my father's political views. I remember my father saying at the outbreak of war: "John Bull will have his come-uppance now!" He read all Irish and English newspapers and his views on current affairs were knowledgeable and balanced. I have no recollection of his having ever read anything like a novel.

DeValera visited the Hospital and persuaded Eamonn to sit on his platform at a public meeting in the Market Square, which I attended. I don't think he enjoyed the experience. He said there was a lot of heckling from a rough crowd.

Eamonn had an earlier encounter with Dev. As a student at Castleknock College (1909-1911) Eamonn attended specially-arranged evening classes in Mathematics given by a mysterious visiting teacher. It was some years later, while attending a political rally, that he recognized his mathematical teacher as DeValera himself.

Later, as I expressed a wish to pursue a sea-going career, Eamonn expressed his disagreement by telling me "I'll have no son of mine in the British Navy!" My career was as a civilian in the Merchant Navy. Later however, Eamonn softened in his views and even enjoyed the experience of being an ESSO inviting guests on board the 36,000-ton tanker, called the "Esso Dublin", for its ceremonial visit to Whitehaven. I was the 2nd Officer on board and the young Radio Officer was from Cork.

My father encountered some difficulty when first introducing Occupational Therapy to the Hospital. In his time, there was a formal protest at one point by jealous neighbours who resented the assistance that the hospital patients provided to senior male nurses who occasionally took them home with them on their two days off to help. They complained that the patients were being abused. Eamonn went to the official records to find approval from Dr. Griffin's time for this excellent therapeutic approach. Most male patients had farming backgrounds and the chance to accompany a senior male nurse on his two days off to join his family and work on his land was a pleasure that they enjoyed. The same principles applied to using the patients to work in constructing the Fitzgerald Stadium and the boat harbour at Reen Point. He stood his ground.

Cork University conferred a Doctorate for Medicine on my father, as a result of Eamonn's published work. This gave him a great sense of satisfaction for all his hard work and dedication.

Eamonn led by example as we grew up, never forcing religion on us. He was a member of the Third Order of St. Francis. He spoke highly of the Easter Week celebrations in Rome that he attended while he was a student there.

A few days before he died, surrounded by his wife and sons, he paid tribute to his worthwhile life and his happy family and went on to say that his only regret was that he was unable ever to say Mass.

Eamonn received an invitation to become a member of the Knights of St. Columbanus. He was uncertain of the right approach to adopt and he consulted with Dr. Moynihan of Rathmore, then Bishop of Ross. His advice was that membership would do nothing to foster his spiritual well-being and in the end Eamonn declined the invitation.

Eamonn was such a proud Kerryman – it is difficult to put this into words. Everything he did was a tribute to his home county, to the people in it whom he served both as a trainer and a physician. He had a passionate love for all and a tolerance and a great pride in Kerry nature, its geography, in its climate. He actually ran a weather station at St. Finan's where he kept records for the meteorological service of the rainfall throughout the year.

Eamonn was a very good speaker and had a great passion for the things in life that interested him. This applied to his professional work as a psychiatrist and also to his deep knowledge of Gaelic games. To me it was obvious he would want to put down in print his feelings and recollections so it came as no surprise when he wrote two books on separate issues. So it was natural for my father to put into print a record of his achievements and opinions of those two major fields of his life. His book on Gaelic football was a very careful study of the history of the game he so loved. This publication impressed me as it did everyone who read it. Our family is so proud of him. It must be unique anywhere in the world that a father and son have stadiums in the one county called after them! The GAA grounds in Firies are called after my father, Dr. Eamonn and J.P. O'Sullivan, my grandfather, is commemorated in Killorglin in the grounds they have kindly dedicated to his great name. It is very special having both of them honoured in this way.

Your background, Weeshie, brings an independent viewpoint as psychiatric nurse, athlete, referee, journalist and broadcaster to your project on Eamonn. This work will be a rewarding achievement from which we, the family, will receive special and lasting benefit.

Jim O'Sullivan Pays Tribute to his Father

(The following is taken from a letter by Jim O'Sullivan).

Dr. Eamonn N.M. O'Sullivan, B.A. M.D. D.D.M.
1897 – 1966
Native of Firies, Co. Kerry.

The popular image of Dr. Eamonn is based on his greatly admired achievements as the trainer of many successful Kerry Gaelic football teams over three decades. His views on football were encapsulated in the '*Art & Science of Gaelic Football*', published by *The Kerryman* in 1958. This long association with the game of football was a matter of great importance and a source of pride to my father. His own father had also had a very illustrious career himself in the same sport. But Dr. Eamonn was a multi-faceted individual and it is important to recognise and pay tribute to experiences and achievements in other fields.

Community Activities
Eamonn played an important part in the creation of the 18-hole Killarney Golf and Fishing Club. I was with him on an occasion in probably 1937-38, when he met with Lord Castlerosse and together they clambered through the dense bushes at O'Mahoney's Point to locate the gamekeeper's lodge that was to become the initial temporary clubhouse. Eamonn himself was an enthusiastic but middle-order golfer. Mental Hospital patients excavated the original mooring at O'Mahoney's Point.

He played an important part in establishing 'Contract Bridge' as a leisure pursuit in Killarney. Though never a great card player, he had a great enthusiasm for the game as a means of bringing people together and putting Killarney on the Bridge Tournament map. For many years he was Director of Tournaments which had become an international event. Bidding in Contract Bridge was a difficult skill to acquire. He had a two-page typed script prepared explaining the intricacies of bidding and used this at beginners' classes he organised. It was a 'two club' system he devised; a convention frowned upon by the experts for many years after that time. In the late 1940s Culbertson, the American Bridge Guru, relented and accepted this convention as legitimate. Eamonn drew great pleasure from this about face.

Behind these activities there was an earnest wish to promote Killarney and Kerry's reputation further afield and assist the tourist industry in its early years.

Professional Work In Medicine
This is an area, which is perhaps less well-known; yet his achievements were a source of great satisfaction to him. A large institution like the Mental Hospital in Killarney required skill and dedication in its administration. Eamonn passed a stiff selection process and joined the staff under Dr. E.W. Griffin (Ballyheigue) soon after qualifying as a doctor. In an era before the availability of drugs to treat mental illness, he set himself to work with enthusiasm to improve the lot of the patients under his care. A family atmosphere prevailed at the Hospital. Eamonn instilled in us, a respect and affection for these patients. "Remember," he said to me, when I was about ten years old, "there is not a family in this country – including our own – that has not had a member here in this Hospital at one time or another." I never forgot that lesson.

Following in the footsteps of Dr. Griffin – by now his father-in-law, for Eamonn married Marjorie Griffin – without means for curing mental illness, he set about ways to improve the lot of the patients. He undertook pioneering in Occupational Therapy – 'O.T.' – as it was called. He established mini-industrial activities throughout the Hospital. The female patients were encouraged to participate in carpet-making, using Celtic designs created by Mr. Maurice Reidy of Killarney Technical School – a skilled artist and architect. Others worked at basket-making. The male patients continued their traditional work on the hospital farm. They were then commissioned to assist in the early building of the Fitzgerald Stadium – this was a form of recreation and a means for building morale. And it was successful. A range of office printing products were created and sold under the banner: 'Ross Products'. There was a tacky hair oil containing glycerine that the Killarney barbers purchased throughout the war years. There were Sugán chairs manufactured.

All this work culminated in Eamonn's second published work: *'Textbook of Occupational Therapy'* published by H.K. Lewis & Co., London, in 1955 (with chief reference to psychological medicine).

Finally – The Family Man

Eamonn led a busy, challenging and rewarding life, yet had time to play the part of 'Pater Familias' with a quiet strength of purpose. I'm sure that he treated his four sons in much the same way as he treated successive generations of Kerry athletes that attended his training sessions. He was a knowledgeable man in the affairs of the world and was deeply steeped in the folklore and history of Kerry and Munster. He was proud of his Firies origins and his closeness to the rugged and wild terrain of his native country.

Were he alive today, he would view his achievements, prosperities and the well-being of The Kingdom with pride, knowing that he had been a guiding influence in some of it. He would be thrilled with the ready availability of all sports in the T.V. media in particular.

May he rest in peace!

J.P. O'Sullivan
April 28, 2000.

Background to Dr. Eamonn's Testimony (Written by his Son Jim P. O'Sullivan)

A project was initiated in 1966 by the late Mrs. Suzie Casey, Tralee, through the auspices of the Irish Countrywomen's Association for people with memories of the Volunteers in Kerry of the period from 1912 up to the Civil War (but not that sad event itself) to compile recollections while witnesses were still alive. Lots of people submitted written testimonies – Eamonn amongst them – and these have been deposited in the Tralee Library. The text that follows was transcribed on May 1, 2000 from the original handwritten text signed and dated as indicated above.

DR. EAMONN'S TESTIMONY

1914 – 1917 and Afterwards in Firies

As a student in St. Patrick's College, Maynooth, from September 1914, I was introduced to summers previously to a vivid appreciation of supporting the national spirit, which was at a low ebb throughout the country generally. I was, from 1912, deeply involved in the GAA, playing football with the Firies team, St. Brendan's College, Killarney and St. Patrick's College, Maynooth. The 1914 Annual Congress of the Gaelic League was held over a fortnight in Killarney towards the end of July. I remember seeing Dr. Douglas Hyde and Lord Ashbourne (who donated the Ashbourne Cup for the Intervarsity Camogie Championship). Lord Ashbourne was a striking figure, because he was dressed in Irish kilts, in the typical green and brown shades. It was towards the end of the Congress that the 1914-1918 War broke out between Germany and England.

The Irish Volunteers were organised that year under the

leadership of Eoin McNeill and John E. Redmond, MP, head of the Irish Parliamentary Party. As I said above, the country at that time was riddled with 'seoneenism' and the usual hotbed of imperialism was centred in the Dublin Pale, but in 1914, at the outbreak of the war, Dublin was outrivaled by many centres through the country generally, mainly in cities and towns. This was clearly evidenced when John Redmond got over 60,000 of his volunteers to fight in France in the British Army, on the understanding that they were fighting for invaded Belgium and "Small Nationalities" (to use the then much-publicised words of the daily papers). This recruiting campaign of Redmond was reinforced by all the members of the Irish Parliamentary Party, who, each individually, spoke at meetings from recruiting platforms throughout the country, with the Union Jack flag prominent throughout. The late Judge Tom O'Donnell, then MP for West Kerry, came in for some severe criticism in the national weekly papers for this anti-national attitude in addressing one of these recruiting meetings at Keel, Castlemaine.

This new change of policy by Redmond (his son, the late Capt. Willie Redmond, subsequently C. Na nGaedheal T.D. for Waterford, fought in Flanders for the British) tended to rouse the national spirit throughout the country and the bulk of the Irish Volunteers under Eoin MacNeill remained true to the cause. There was a company of Irish Volunteers, at least 100 strong, organised in Firies, under the local Capt. Jim Fitzgerald of Goulane.

The country as a whole was now definitely divided into nationalist and imperialists and this was the outstanding reason why Pearse, Clarke and Connolly, etc. decided that it required a revolution, involving the supreme sacrifice, to convert the country to a proper sense of nationalistic pride. This is exactly what occurred immediately after the 1916 executions. The country developed strong anti-British feelings, which instantly made them realise the value and claims of our national culture. Language classes were established all over the provinces and there was no attempt made, as before 1916, to object to Irish Ireland activities, as is so much evident now by the cliques of the affluent societies, which have become so vocal in recent years.

The real turning point came in early 1917, when Count Plunkett (father of the executed 1916 leader, Joe) decisively defeated the John Redmond Party candidate in a by-election in Roscommon. Plunkett was the first elected Sinn Féin MP at a time when all the leading Sinn Féiners were in prisons. Apparently, Plunkett's success went to his head and on his own he decided to call a convention of representatives of all the Irish Public Bodies (Co. Councils, Boards of Guardians and Rural Councils which then existed) as well as two representatives of each Sinn Féin club in the country. I should have mentioned that (between) winter 1916 and early 1917 these clubs were inaugurated in almost every parish in the nation. I happened to be home from Maynooth College during the 1916-1917 winter and established the first Sinn Féin club in Co. Kerry. I also succeeded in selling over 90 copies of Arthur Griffith's weekly paper – *Nationality*.

The Firies delegates to the Plunkett Convention consisted of Rev. Fr. W. Ferris, Acting P.P. of Firies and Ballyhar Parishes (now Parish Priest of Ballylongford), the late Henry Spring and myself. The Convention (which incidentally has [not] been given any mention in recent representations of the 1916 period) was very historical, because, were it not for the intelligent intervention of Fr. Ferris, who was sitting beside me, after two hours of futile discussion, when nearly half the delegates left the meeting in disgust, this convention could have disbanded in failure. This could have meant such a setback to the national movement of the time that it could easily have prevented the subsequent conversion of the entire country to its deep and widespread sense of nationality. The cause of dissension at the meeting arose immediately following Count Plunkett's announcement that the title "Sinn Féin" of the very many clubs should be changed to "Liberty Clubs". On the platform with Plunkett were the late Arthur Griffiths and Rev. Fr. Michael Flannagan, who was Count Plunkett's right-hand man in the Roscommon election. One could see the marked disappointment of Arthur Griffiths when he heard Plunkett's proposal. He made an impassioned plea for the retention of the name "Sinn Féin". He asked was all the work, which he had put into Sinn Féin for so many years to be now set aside because one man wished otherwise.

Fr. Ferris – a straight and dignified figure – foreseeing a possible national calamity that could affect the whole future of our beloved country, strode up to the platform. A hushed silence spread over the Round Room of the Mansion House, followed by a violent bout of hand clapping when he proposed that, "This question be decided by Arthur Griffiths and Fr. O'Flannagan." There followed a short adjournment of about 15 minutes. It was obvious to Fr. Ferris and to all of us that Plunkett's vanity had warped his judgement and this was confirmed by the relatively unimportant role played by Count Plunkett (thereafter) in the Nation's affairs. Fr. O'Flannagan wisely decided with Arthur Griffiths that the words "Sinn Féin" should prevail. An interesting fact arising from the Convention was that Tralee was the only place to use the words "Liberty Club" and continued to do so until they saw that "Sinn Féin" was accepted universally and when De Valera, Austin Stack and the other leaders were released from prison some months later, in the summer of 1917, (they supported the Convention). The rest has been confirmed by history.

I was in Maynooth College during Easter Week of 1916 and I can remember the local company of Volunteers under the command of Domhnal O'Buachalla marching into the college to receive the blessing of the then President, Monsignor Hogan, before joining the insurgents in Dublin. Danny Brinchley had a shop in the college mart and was well-known and liked by all the students. He will be remembered, particularly in later years, when De Valera made him Governor General of the Free State, just to comply with the existing law of the time, until the position was changed to "the Presidency" in the 1937 Constitution.

In Maynooth during the latter part of Easter Week 1916, the red glow in the sky of the burning Dublin (12 miles away) was clearly visible in the dark and there was a general feeling of sadness in the College when news of the capitulation reached us. I came home some time later at the end of term and it was then that I was informed of the fatal shooting of the R.I.C. policeman in broad daylight in the middle of the village and the wounding of another Peeler who was with the man shot.

There was no Cumann na mBan group in Firies, as far as I can recall. The Volunteers remained active and continued their regular drill in the various parts of the parish. Some of the latter formed part of the East Kerry Flying Column headed by the late General Humphrey Murphy of Carrow (who subsequently won All-Ireland football medals with later Kerry teams), Tommy McEllistrum and the late John Cronin, etc. The late Charles Daly of Ballyfinnane, Firies, who was executed later by the Free State Government, operated as Commandant in Donegal and the North during the Black and Tan war.

The East Kerry Flying Column was one of the most active in the country. They carried out many successful ambushes – Headford Station, where Danny Allman, of Rockfield, Firies, was killed. They joined up with the North Cork column under the late Sean Moylan in the famous Clounbannion Ambush (five or six miles from Rathmore on the Mallow Road) where a British General (I forget his name) was shot through the rifle hole of his armoured car. The column had regular rendezvous throughout the area and were regular visitors to our home in Firies, often staying overnight. Spies must have informed on my late brother, Patrick, because the Black and Tans paid a visit to the house and held up Patrick at the end of a rifle, threatening to shoot him. They rifled the shop and burnt out the full haystack.

E.N.M. O'Súilleabháin,
B.A., M.D., D.P.M.
Beataine 12, 1966.

Dr. Jack O'Connor Writes in Appreciation of Dr. Eamonn

Dr. O'Sullivan's death came as a great shock to me. I had known Eamonn for close on 40 years. I met him first when I was in my early teens. At this time I was competing in schoolboy athletics in the country and he was then, I think, Honorary Secretary of the Kerry County Board N.A.C.A.I., and we travelled together to sports meetings all over the country.

He was even then an outstanding personality, and I remember that I regarded him with a certain amount of awe and at the same time I was extremely grateful for, and rather mystified by, his interest in me. I was to appreciate later that he was at all times only too willing to help any newcomer to any form of sport in which he was interested. It is correct to say that many great Kerry footballers reigned supreme during Dr. Eamonn's time as trainer, but it would be equally correct to say that he took many mediocre and ordinary players and inspired them to greatness. Because Dr. Eamonn's way was not merely that of achieving physical perfection – it was more of the mind, more of instilling into his players those finer qualities of manliness, of sportsmanship and of that legitimate pride which the artist is entitled to have in the art in which he excels.

Dr. Eamonn was an eminent doctor and psychiatrist who contributed much to his profession and it was our privilege in the GAA that he brought his personal qualities and his professional qualifications to bear on the promotion of Gaelic football.

He was a whole man, a man of culture, a man of dignity and one who had a true sense of values. He was a man of uncompromising principles and high ideals – there was no place for the second rate in the scheme of things for Dr. Eamonn. He was a great Irishman who recognised the potential of the language, the national games and athletics as vital factors in working towards a full life of national endeavour.

We were also associated as members of the Killarney Dr. Croke's

GAA Club. It was, however, in 1943, when I was appointed to the staff of St. Finan's Hospital, where he was then R.M.S. that I really got to know him intimately. At that time, and for some years previously, he had an excellent Occupational Therapy Department in the Hospital. This department produced a wide variety of articles, which were marketed as Ross Products and found a ready sale. He was, therefore, the pioneer of the Industrial Therapy activities in psychiatric hospitals, which we hear so much about today. He wrote an excellent textbook on Occupational Therapy, and this has been translated into many languages, and is widely regarded as the standard work on this subject. He was awarded a Medical Doctorate by the National University of Ireland for this. The building of the Fitzgerald Stadium, to which he and the patients in the Department contributed so much, is a fitting memorial to his activities in this field.

When he was appointed Medical Superintendent he instituted an organised system of nurse training, and from this has resulted the efficiency of the present nursing services of St. Finan's Hospital – this as one of his finest achievements. During his later years in the Hospital he was quick to avail of all the modern aids for to the treatment of mental illness. He was at all times most solicitous for the welfare of his patients, and they in turn admired and respected him for this. He was also at all times deeply concerned with the welfare of the staff, and his advice and encouragement were always freely available. I shall always be deeply grateful for the training I received during the 16 years that I served under him.

Shortly, before his retirement in 1962 he established an outpatient treatment centre in St. Catherine's Hospital, Tralee. He was captain of the Killarney Golf Club on two occasions and was a director of the Club up to his death.

He was completely devoted to his wife and family, and his indeed was a devout Catholic home. It is all the more regrettable, therefore, that his enjoyment of his well-earned retirement was so short lived.

On my own behalf and on behalf of the staff of the Hospital, I wish to convey our deepest sympathy to his widow and family.

Dr. Jack O'Connor
Resident Medical Supt.,
St. Finan's Hospital,
Killarney

Dr. Eamonn's Eight All-Ireland Winning Teams

1924 All-Ireland Winning Team
Kerry 0-4 : Dublin 0-3.

The Troubles of the 1916-1922 period probably put a shadow over any All-Ireland aspirations Kerry may have had during that time and although they reached the 1915 and 1923 finals, they had to wait until 1924 for title number six. A relatively trouble free Munster campaign which commenced on May 11 was followed by a semi-final win over Mayo on December 7. A long gap ensued before the Final on April 26 and Kerry, under renowned trainer Dr. Eamonn O'Sullivan for the very first time, arranged two good challenge matches with Wexford in the weeks preceding the Final. The Dublin game was a close, tense affair with little separating the sides. Indeed Kerry had to rely on a 21-yard free from Con Brosnan to win the day.

Kerry: Jack Sheehy (goal), Phil O'Sullivan (Captain) (Tuosist, Kenmare), Joe Barrett (Tralee), Jerry Moriarty (Tralee), Johnny Murphy (Caherceiveen), Paul Russell (Killarney), Jack Walsh (Asdee), Con Brosnan (Newtownsandes) (0-2), Bob Stack (Ballybunion), Jackie Ryan (Tralee) John Joe Sheehy (Tralee), Mundy Prendeville (Castleisland), John Baily (0-1), Jimmy Baily (both Ballymacelligott), Bill Landers (Tralee) (0-1).
Subs: Mossie Galvin (Tralee), Eugene Moriarty (Killarney), John 'Gal' Slattery (Tralee), and Eamonn Fitzgerald (Caherdaniel).

Eamonn Fitzgerald represented Ireland in the hop, step and jump in the 1924 Olympics Games in Los Angeles. He finished fourth.

Referee: Tom Shelvin (Roscommon).

1926 All-Ireland Winning Team
Kerry 1-4 : Kildare 0-4.

A Kerry team full of famous names – Brosnan, Sheehy, Russell, Stack, Barrett and Walsh, among others – had a reasonably smooth passage to the 1926 All-Ireland Senior Football Final. However matters did not proceed as anticipated in the final against Kildare on September 5. Kerry's physical catch and kick methods were pitted against the slick hand-passing methods of their opponents. Kerry, trained by J. M. Collins of Dublin, were lucky to escape with a draw, 1-3 to 0-6 with Rock Street's Bill Gorman scoring the all-important goal.

Between that and the replay however tragedy struck in the Kerry camp with the death after a sudden illness of 22-year-old corner back Jack Murphy of Caherceiveen. His death evoked strong emotions and sympathy was extended from many quarters including his Kildare opponents of a few weeks previously.

For the replay, Dr. Eamonn O'Sullivan took control of Kerry's training, with eleven selectors also in the backroom team. With three personal changes and after a titanic struggle, Kerry won the day, with Moyvane's Tom O'Mahoney's getting the vital goal on this occasion. A record 37,000 spectators watched the game.

Kerry: Johnny Riordan (Boherbee), Pat Clifford (Ballymac), Joe Barrett (Rock Street), Jack Walsh (Craughdarrig), Paul Russell (Killarney) (0-1), Jerry Moriarty (Rock St.), John Slattery (Rock St.), Con Brosnan (Moyvane), Bob Stack (Doon), Jackie Ryan (Boherbee) (0-1), John Joe Sheehy (Captain) (Boherbee), Denis O'Connell (Rock Street), Tom O'Mahoney (Moyvane) (1-1), Bill Gorman (Rock Street) (0-1), Jim Baily (Ballymac).
Subs: Dan Joe Conway, Mike Coffey, Paul O'Sullivan, John Baily, Paddy Whitty.

Referee: Tom Shevlin (Roscommon).

1937 All-Ireland Winning Team
Kerry 4-4 : Cavan 1-7.

After they had drawn 1-8 to 2-5 the sides met again on October 17. The tackling was over-robust from the start. Kerry, despite losing Tim O'Donell, took an early lead when Tim O'Leary scored a goal. Magee had two Cavan points before Johnny Walsh hit the Cavan crossbar and Devlin levelled with a point for the sides to go in equal at the interval (1-0 to 0-3). Cavan, through Magee and Devlin took a two point wind assisted advantage before Kerry hit back with crucial scores which set them on their way to victory. Team captain Miko Doyle finished a fine movement to the net before J.J. Landers set up Tim O'Leary for his second of the day. Tim Landers added points for Kerry to lead comfortably 3-3 to 0-6. However, after Danno Keeffe had saved well and was bundled over the line, the referee allowed the goal to reduce the margin to three but the Kerrymen promptly killed off any hope of a Cavan victory when John Joe Landers sent a low hurtling shot to the net for Kerry to win another title.

Kerry: Danno Keeffe, Bill Kinnerk, Joe Keohane, Bill Myers, Tim O'Donnell, Bill Dillon, Tim Healy, Johnny Walsh, Sean Brosnan, John Flavin, Charlie O'Sullivan, Tim Landers (0-4), J.J. Landers (1-0), Miko Doyle (Captain) (1-0), Tim O'Leary (2-0).
Subs: *Tom (Gega) O'Connor, Johnny McCarthy, Eddie Walsh, Gearoid Fitzgerald, Paddy O'Brien, Mick Raymond, Brendan Reidy. *Denotes subs that played.

Referee: Mick Hennessy (Dublin).

1946 All-Ireland Winning Team
Kerry 2-8 : Roscommon 0-10.

Kerry met Roscommon in a final that was delayed because of the poor harvest. In the first of two dramatic games between the sides, Kerry scored only once in the first half – J.J. Fallon's goal giving Roscommon a deserved 1-5 to 0-1 lead at the interval. Despite Paddy Kennedy's move to mid-field, Kerry still trailed by six points with time running out. Two dramatic goals by Paddy Burke and 'Gega' O'Connor gave Kerry a fortuitous draw. Kerry made wholesale changes for the replay, Captain Gus Cremins being one of the unlucky players to lose out. Kerry had the better of the first half and led by 6 points to 4 at the interval. A great goal by Paddy Burke gave Kerry a slender lead but the sides were level when Gus Cremins regained the lead with a late goal. This ensured that Danno Keeffe became the holder of a then record seven All-Ireland medals. Paddy Kennedy of Aunascaul captained the side for the replay instead of Gus Cremins.

Kerry: Danno O'Keeffe, Denny Lyne, Joe Keohane, Paddy Bawn Brosnan, Jackie Lyne, Bill Casey, Eddie Walsh, Teddy O'Connor, Paddy Kennedy (Captain) (0-1), Jackie Falvey, Gega O'Connor (1-4), Batt Garvey (0-2), Frank O'Keeffe, Paddy Burke (1-0), Dan Kavanagh.

Note: Gus Cremins (Captain) and Bill O'Donnell played in the drawn game. Frank O'Keeffe and Jackie Falvey came on for the replay. Gus Cremins replaced Jackie as a sub during the replay. In the drawn game Eddie Dowling replaced Paddy Kennedy and Brendan Kelleher replaced Jackie Lyne.
Subs: *Tom Long, *Gerald Teahan.
*Denotes subs that played.

Referee: Paddy Mythen (Wexford), Bill Delaney (Laois) refereed the drawn game.

1953 All-Ireland Winning Team
Kerry 0-13 : Armagh 1-6.

"A novel pairing, between Kerry and Armagh, the first of the segregated counties to contest an All-Ireland Final", was how the official programme previewed the 1953 Final which was played before a record attendance. Armagh had the better start, with a goal by Mal McEvoy giving them a 1-1 to 0-2 lead. Two pointed frees by Tadghie Lyne had the sides level and Armagh held a slender lead of one point, 1-3 to 0-5 at the break.

The sides were still level at the end of the third quarter before Tadghie Lyne and John Joe Sheehan gave Kerry a two point lead. The defining moment of the game came when Bill McCorry shot wide from an Armagh penalty. Taking advantage of the let-off, Kerry finished with points by John Joe Sheehan and Jackie Lyne to bridge a gap of seven years without a title – their longest since the Sam Maguire was first presented in 1928.

Kerry: Johnny Foley, Jas Murphy (Captain), Ned Roche, Donie Murphy, Colm Kennelly, John Cronin, Micksie Palmer, Sean Murphy, Diarmuid Hannifin, Jim Brosnan (0-4), John Joe Sheehan (0-3), Tadghie Lyne (0-4), Tom Ashe (0-1), Sean Kelly, Jackie Lyne.
Subs: *Gerald O'Sullivan, Jerome O'Shea, Paudie Sheehy, Brendan O'Shea, Mick Brosnan. Mick Murphy, Bobby Buckley.
*Denotes sub that played.

Referee: Peter McDermott (Meath).

1955 All-Ireland Winning Team
Kerry 0-12 : Dublin 1-6.

The 1955 All-Ireland Final remains one of the most talked about finals to this day. Kerry's brand of football has been called into question and the "Dublin Machine" was expected to sweep all before it.

The first half was even, with Kevin Heffernan and Ollie Freeney giving Dublin an early lead, but four points by the masterful Tadghie Lyne gave Kerry a two point lead, 0-5 to 0-3, at the interval. Jim Brosnan threw down the gauntlet to Dublin on the restart with two wonderful points, but at the three quarter stage, their lead was back to two points. Kerry rose to the challenge however, scoring four unanswered points, and despite a late goal by Freeney, John Dowling's men went on to record one of the most memorable victories in the country's history. Kerry's traditional catch-and-kick game was alive and well! *The Kerryman* newspaper summed it up beautifully: "Up Kerry, Up Dr. Eamonn. Up catch-and-kick."

Kerry: Garry O'Mahoney, Jerome O'Shea, Ned Roche, Micksie Palmer, Sean Murphy, John Cronin, Tom Moriarty, John Dowling (Capt. 0-1), Denny O'Shea, Paudie Sheehy (0-1), Tom Costello, Tadghie Lyne (0-6), Johnny Culloty, Mick Murphy (0-1), Jim Brosnan (0-2).
Subs: *John Joe Sheehan (0-1), Bobby Buckley, Gerald O'Sullivan, Colm Kennelly, Dan McAuliffe, Donal 'Marcus' O'Neill, Ned Fitzgerald, Dermot Dillon.
*Denotes subs that played.

Referee: Bill Goodison (Wexford).

1959 All-Ireland Winning Team
Kerry 3-7 : Galway 1-4.

A spectacular display by Mick O'Connell saw Kerry qualify for the 1959 Final at the expense of Dublin before a record semi-final crowd of 70,148 people. In an even first half of the Final, Galway's Frank Evers got an early goal in response to John Dowling's opening two points. Evers was doing well against an injured Mick O'Connell, but the Kerry defence stood firm, especially the half back trio of Murphy, Coffey and O'Dwyer. The sides were level at the break, 0-5 to 1-2.

Mick O'Connell retired injured, and the sides were still deadlocked at the three-quarter stage. Tom Long's move to midfield brought parity in that area and the game took a dramatic turn when Dan McAuliffe struck for two goals, Garry McMahon added a third and Kerry ran out easy winners to record a League/Championship double in a game that many people still refer to as "Sean Murphy's Final".

Kerry: Johnny Culloty, Jerome O'Shea, Niall Sheehy, Tim Lyons,

Sean Murphy, Kevin Coffey, Mick O'Dwyer (0-1), Mick O'Connell, Seamus Murphy, Dan McAuliffe (2-2), Tom Long, Paudie Sheehy, Dave Geaney, John Dowling (0-2), Tadghie Lyne (0-2).
Subs: *Jack Dowling, *Moss O'Connell, *Garry McMahon (1-0), Tom Collins, Paddy Hussey.
*Denotes subs that played.

Referee: John Dowling (Offaly).

1962 All-Ireland Winning Team
Kerry 1-12 : Roscommon 1-6.

Kerry's twentieth title was never in doubt after Garry McMahon and Timmy O'Sullivan scored a goal and a point in the opening minutes. McMahon's goal was one of the fastest ever scored in a final. Kerry led 1-8 to 1-1 at half time – the Roscommon goal scored from a penalty by Do Feeley. Mick O'Connell scored 8 points.

The Kerry back line dominated all through as Kerry recorded an easy victory. It was a proud occasion for Sean Óg Sheehy who followed nobly in his father John Joe's footsteps as a winning Kerry captain. Sean Óg's brother Paudie and Niall were also on the team and both also captained Kerry in their careers.

Kerry: Johnny Culloty, Seamus Murphy, Niall Sheehy, Tim Lyons, Sean Óg Sheehy (Captain), Noel Lucey, Mick O'Dwyer, Mick O'Connell (0-8), Jimmy Lucey, Dan McAuliffe, Timmy O'Sullivan (0-2), Jerry Riordan, Garry McMahon (1-0), Tom Long, Paudie Sheehy (0-2).
Subs: *J.J. Barrett, *Kevin Coffey, Dave Geaney, Donie O'Sullivan, Seamus Roche, Pat Aherne
*Denotes subs that played.

Referee: Eamon Moules (Wicklow).

1964 All-Ireland Losing Team
Kerry 0-10 : Galway 0-15.

Eamonn's only loss in his nine All-Ireland Finals occurred in this year and Galway were clear winners. He spoke afterwards: "Galway deservedly defeated Kerry and it is no reflection on Galway's victory to say, that Kerry, on that date, never reproduced the magnificent football when substantially defeating Cavan in the semi-final. It was not Kerry's lucky day; beset by injuries of a most dislocating nature and other factors, they had to bow to Galway and did so sportingly.

Naturally I had some disappointment as it was a break in previous successes but I have no hesitating in stating that the current Kerry team is young enough and capable enough of winning another All-Ireland Championship."

Kerry: Johnny Culloty, Mick Morris, Niall Sheehy (Captain), Paud O'Donoghue, Denis O'Sullivan, Seamus Murphy, Gerdie O'Connor, Mick Fleming, Donie O'Sullivan, Pat Griffin, Mick O'Dwyer, Mick O'Connell, Frank O'Leary, Tom Long, Joe Joe Barrett.
Subs: *John McCarthy, *Bernie O'Callaghan, *Kevin Coffey.
*Denotes subs that played.

Referee: J. Hatton (Wicklow).

Con Brosnan of Moyvane

A KERRY LEGEND TRAINED BY DR. EAMONN

Dr. Eamonn's legacy to Kerry football spanned more decades than any other Kerry trainer before or after. It must be unique and rare in any sport world-wide when a person trains father and son to achieve the highest honours in their chosen sport. This was the achievement of Dr. Eamonn O'Sullivan. Con Brosnan, one of Kerry's greatest football sons, was trained by Eamonn in 1924 and 1926 to win two of his six Celtic Crosses (he won his other four in 1929, 1930, 1931 and 1932). Nearly 30 years later, in 1953, Con's son Jim won the first of his two medals, he was also under the tutorage of Eamonn, and Dr. Jim won his second in 1955.

Another fascinating fact not generally known is that Eamonn won A Tailteann Games Championship Medal in 1924 playing at left half-back with Munster. The team consisted of 14 Kerry players and one from Clare. A team-mate of Eamonn's that memorable day was Con Brosnan. It is very evident from his writings that Eamonn was very proud of this achievement on the playing field.

He recalled that victory: "I well remember that I had some compensation in 1924 in the Tailteann Games Inter-Provincial Football Final between Leinster and Munster. We were much depleted due to the loss of five or six famous Kerry Republican players, chief of who were Joe Barrett, John Joe Sheehy and Jackie Ryan.

We were behind coming to the end of the match when our famous right half-back Paul Russell sent a long high ball well beyond the centre line. Two of our inside forwards, the Graham brothers from Dingle dashed away inside their full backs, secured possession and scored a great goal which converted a one point defeat at that stage to a two point lead with only some minutes to go. This was ultimately the final result, creating a first class sensation at the time, and we received the Tailteann Games Championship medals of 1924.

Among those on the Munster team were Kerry's famous midfielders Con Brosnan and Bob Stack, who dominated this section of the game as they did in the subsequent six or seven years for Kerry, each winning six All-Ireland medals. Also including Paul Russell mentioned above, we had another Killarney player goalie 'Denso' Hurley. As well on our team was clerical student Mundy Prendiville of Castleisland who, after his ordination won an All-Ireland medal with Kerry. He was subsequently consecrated Archbishop of Perth, Australia, and was the youngest Archbishop in the church. I was playing at left half-back, being a last minute selection to fill in for one of the Kerrymen who, as stated, refused to play. I feel that my play fell short of that of my colleagues. My sole contribution for my side was scoring two points from fifty yard frees in the second half, which reduced our deficit to that of a single point."

The great sportswriter Paddy Foley (known as 'P.F.') once wrote in *The Kerryman* that almost every parish in Kerry had its "All-Ireland man". At the time of P.F.'s writing this, however, very few parishes, not to mention a relatively small rural parish like Moyvane, could boast an All-Ireland medal-holder six times over. In the intervening years since, this parish has been singularly honoured that so many of its sons have contributed to the Kerry cause by representing their county with distinction at every level of the game.

Names could trip off the tongue for every decade since the selection of Con Brosnan in 1923 to play mid-field for Kerry initiated the trend. However, few will cavil with the assertion that Con Brosnan was the greatest of all and inevitably heads the list of the illustrious of the parish who have achieved this distinction.

Coming events cast their shadows before, and as early as 1919, Con Brosnan, playing at midfield for Moyvane in the North Kerry league, came under the notice of Bob Stack. Bob immediately formed the opinion that Con would become a great county player. He was not to know then or fully realize immediately at least, that he and Con would form a celebrated partnership at midfield for Kerry, which would last for all of nine years and would make them both legendary figures in the annals of Kerry football history.

In the same year, the name of Con Brosnan was becoming widely known for actions beyond the football field. He was a familiar name to the British Auxiliaries (or Black and Tans) who, embittered by the ignominy of their failure to curtail his daring exploits as a freedom-fighter (by apprehension or otherwise), descended on Moyvane one spring morning and burned the Brosnan home to the ground.

After Independence, the emergence of Kerry as a footballing force was probably stifled and delayed by the sad outbreak of Civil War. However, when peace was restored a great young Kerry team – some would still maintain the greatest – began to take shape. Moreover, it is further asserted, and not without conviction, that the readiness and willingness of players who were diametrically opposed politically during 'The Troubles', to combine, merge and pool their talents in the cause of Kerry football contributed in no small way to the healing of old wounds and the assuaging of any lingering bitterness left by those unhappy and unfortunate events.

Sited at midfield on this emerging team was the young Moyvane man facing, in his first All-Ireland Final (1923), two of Gaelic footballs all-time greats; Paddy McDonnell and Larry Stanley of Dublin. Defeat was to be their portion on their maiden voyage. However, the exploits of Con Brosnan did not go unnoticed during the game. His immaculate fielding, precision kicking and unflinching endurance helped his team to almost carry the day.

Dublin, now going for their fourth All-Ireland in a row, provided the opposition to Kerry in the All-Ireland of 1924. A thrilling game ensued. The two great teams were locked in battle with the scores level with just minutes remaining, until a marvellous point from the boot of the Moyvane midfielder broke the deadlock and carried the day for Kerry.

This was Dr. Eamonn O'Sullivan's first victory as Kerry trainer. There are two quotes from a poem commemorating the great victory: "At midfield where the fight was raging shone Brosnan, bright as the morning star, He drove the leather right up to Landers, Who fisted neatly across the bar." The other describes his winning score: "With steady nerve and unerring aim, He scored a point and again we lead them, 'Twas the final score in a hard-fought game."

Kerry now entered a phase of keen and sporting rivalry with Kildare which was to last some seven or eight years and which was to raise Gaelic football to new heights and create new levels of awareness and interest among the public.

The 1926 Final went to a replay. In the drawn game Larry Stanley was Kildare's outstanding performer, bringing down balls at midfield from prodigious heights. However, Kerry held out to draw 1-3 to Kildare's 0-6. Kerry got their goal with only a minute remaining with W. O'Gorman crashing to the net. A new legend was created that day, namely, that Kerry are never beaten until the final whistle! Kerry reasserted themselves in the replay, with Stack and Brosnan dominant at midfield and another Moyvane man, Tom Mahony, fisting the ball to the net. Final score was Kerry 1-4 : Kildare 0-4.

The Leinster Leader (Kildare) in its report of the 1926 Final stated: "Two great teams have met twice in the struggle for the 1926 Championship and both have by their displays done much to raise the status of the grand old Gaelic pastimes." Another paper, *The Voice of Labour* (Dublin) stated four factors contributed to the Munster victory: first and foremost of all; superior grit and the will to victory, secondly; better fielding; thirdly; a stronger midfield and fourthly; the ineffectiveness of Stanley.

However, Kildare came back in 1927 to claim their revenge in the All-Ireland Final on the score of Kildare 0-5 : Kerry 0-3. Commenting on the match, *The Leinster Leader* wrote (among other things): "It was a great game, worthy of two great football counties. In the keen football and sporting rivalry between the counties lies the best guarantee for the future of Gaelic pastimes."

Kerry did not figure in the Final of 1928 but Kildare did, retaining their title, with W. Gannon as Captain was the first to accept the Sam Maguire Cup, which had been newly presented.

The next great contest between Kerry and Kildare was in the 1929 All-Ireland Final when Kerry won the first of four-in-a-row All-Irelands before a record attendance of 43,839 people. The score was: Kerry 1-8: Kildare 1-5. A writer of *The Times* wrote: "It was very fast, very clean and very exciting. Kerry's winning margin does not flatter them. Kerry defeated Monaghan in a one-sided final in 1930. The dominance enjoyed by the Kerry midfield pairing is reflected in the score line: Kerry 3-11: Monaghan 0-2. Comment from *The Anglo Celt* (Cavan): "Those who saw for themselves the prowess of the Kerrymen – Supermen would perhaps be a more accurate description – came away satisfied that at the moment there is no combination in the country fit to cope with them. A selection from the rest of Ireland would scarcely be fit enough to stand up to them for an hour." Clear evidence, indeed, that this team was now being regarded as well nigh invincible by friend and foe alike.

In May of 1931 Con Brosnan and his teammates left on a tour of the United States. In the opening game in New York, the real big test, Kerry beat the locals by 9 points to 1-3. The attendance was over 60,000, a then record for a Gaelic game. Liam O'Shea, Sports Editor of the *New York Advocate* was lavish in their praise: "Man for man they are a credit to the Irish race. It would be unfair to single out any member of the team as having anything on the others. It simply cannot be done. I found them high-class, intelligent young athletes who can feel right at home in any company".

Kerry and Kildare clashed once again for the blue riband of Gaelic football in 1931. Kerry emerged victors by 1-11 to 0-8, the biggest margin that ever separated the teams (attendance 42,350). This win was very significant in Con Brosnan's career due to a wonderfully magnanimous gesture by Joe Barrett. Austin Stacks, allowed Con Brosnan to captain Kerry and accept the Sam Maguire Cup. That Joe

Barrett should have deferred to Con in this way is clear evidence of the esteem of his colleagues and their appreciation of his profoundly important contribution to their successes.

Con Brosnan won every honour the game had to offer. As well as his six All-Ireland medals he won Munster Senior championships, three National League medals and two Railway Cups. Following his playing career he was involved at administration level of the North Kerry Board and County Board and represented Kerry at Munster Council level for a long number of years. He was a Kerry selector and trained the victorious Kerry team in 1939. His record of service at North Kerry Board level was no less impressive, Chairman: 1932-1933, 1936-1942. President: 1955-1975.

Con was called from this life in 1975, the very year that saw the emergence of a young, vibrant team that won the Senior All-Ireland in that year (part of the big treble – Senior, Under-21, and Minor) and were to go on to emulate the achievements of 1929-1932 by winning four-in-a-row in 1978-1981.

A poem praising the great footballer and Gael of former years concludes as follows: "I can't name all in one short verse, I could go on and on, But the greatest man of all the clan, Was the one and only Con."

To the Memory of Con Brosnan (on the opening of Con Brosnan Par, Moyvane 1984).
By: Dan Keane.

> When but a child I heard his name,
> Poured out from lips that spoke with pride.
> I relished every loud acclaim,
> My heart like theirs, felt overjoyed.
> I placed him in the Fianna mould,
> Through childish dreams the vision ran.
> I longed to see the green and gold,
> I longed and hoped to meet this man.
>
> This man in later years I met,
> His manner harboured no disguise.
> His honest heart in goodness set,
> His modesty his greatest prize.
> And, yet, sufficient spirit reigned,
> To stand for right – to raise to flame.
> The bursting cheers that off acclaimed,
> His jewelled movement in this game.

This game he loved and sporting played,
From antiquity's ancient store.
The living spark official made,
And trained the Gael to love it more.
The names with pride we still recall,
Their souls its source, their hearts its shield.
Through time and space we bless them all,
And make their monument this field.

This field through which he calls in trust,
The Gaels to love and play the game.
God keeps his soul, the grave his dust,
We proudly give this field his name.
And here while summer breezes kiss,
The bending grass and steal away.
We play the game in hours like this,
We bless this man, this, field, this Day.

Dan Kavanagh

KERRY'S ELDER STATESMAN OF FOOTBALL

One of the elder statesmen of Kerry football, Dan Kavanagh, gives a wonderful insight into his friendship with Eamonn. Dan makes it very clear that he attributes his All-Ireland medal win in 1946 to the recall of Eamonn as trainer for the replay of that year's final against Roscommon. The West Kerry native holds the unenviable distinction of playing in six All-Ireland finals, but was on the winning side on only one occasion. That winning year was 1946 when Eamonn trained the team. The coveted medal came when he lined out at left corner forward in a much remembered and talked about replay against Roscommon.

Born near Dun Chaoin in the West Kerry Gaeltacht in 1921, much of his free time as a youngster was spend kicking a ball. They played on a type of commonage and there was great inter-parish rivalry in the air in those days. "Every Sunday you'd have two matches in Ballyferriter. I started in the game by standing behind the goals in Dun Chaoin when the big fellows played. Whenever the ball went behind the goals a whole gang of us would fight to kick it back to them again," he recalled.

In 1935 Dan went to secondary school at Coláiste Chaoimhin, Glasnevin in Dublin, where he was to spend four happy years. He played both football and hurling for the college, often on the green sward of Croke Park. He also played on the Leinster Colleges' football team and was on the Kerry Minor team in 1938 and 1939. The Minors were beaten by Cavan in the 1938 All-Ireland Final and by Cork in the Munster Final the following year. He went on to University College Galway, to study engineering in 1939 and played on their Sigerson Cup sides. He was chosen to play for Galway in 1941 and ironically was a member of the Galway team defeated by Kerry in that years' All-Ireland Final.

Dan was also a member of the Galway team beaten by Dublin

in the 1942 Final – a game which has often provided a question for quiz-masters. *'Who were the three Kerrymen to play in an All-Ireland Final in which Kerry were not involved? The answer: Dan Kavanagh, Joe Fitzgerald, a Dingle born Garda, and Jim Falvey a civil servant also from Dingle, played with Dublin.'*

While with Galway Dan won two Connaght Championships and also played in the Railway Cup for the western province. He was working as an engineer in the area at the time. By 1944 he had returned to Kerry, taking up a temporary appointment with Kerry County Council, and he helped Dingle to a County Championship victory in the same year. He donned the green and gold in 1944 being a member of the Kerry team defeated by Roscommon that same year.

In the spring of 1945, he was transferred by the County Council to Killarney. He joined the famed Dr. Croke's Club mainly because of his friendship with Kerry star Billy Myers. Dan was later to marry Billy's sister, Nellie, herself a superb camogie player in her day. It was around this time that he was introduced to Dr. Eamonn and they became firm friends through their work and football.

He played much of his football at midfield but he was also a tenacious speedy attacker. Indeed he was switched from midfield to the corner forward position for the 1946 All-Ireland Final replay, regarded as one of the all-time great finals played in Croke Park. In 1947 he was on the Kerry team sensationally beaten by Cavan in the historic All-Ireland Final played in the Polo grounds in New York. "Things just did not go right for us that day. We had two goals disallowed and we were very unlucky to lose Eddie Dowling when he suffered a bad fall going high for a ball. Eddie was having a great game at midfield and we seemed to collapse when he went off. Also the heat was desperate and the fact that Dr. Eamonn was not taken to America as trainer was also a deciding factor."

He continued to play with Kerry until 1951 and won two more County Championship medals with Killarney and Dick Fitzgerald's in 1949 and 1951 respectively. This feat gave him a hat trick of Kerry Championships, all with different teams; surely a unique achievement. Naturally Dan has great memories of his native place and recalls: "I remember in the 1940s when football was at it's zenith in West Kerry, the Dingle team that won a County Championship one year had 14 men who were on Kerry teams. It was much the same Weeshie with the great East Kerry side of 1960s that won four county titles; you were a member of that great side yourself."

Dan and his wife Nellie, live in retirement at Muckross Road, Killarney. He retired from his post as Kerry County Engineer in 1986 and had previously served as County Engineer in Wexford and Cork.

Their sons Dr. Donal and Sean were very talented footballers; both winning honours with Dr. Croke's, East Kerry and University College Cork. Donal also played with Kerry in 1972-73.

A modest quietly spoken gentleman, Dan Kavanagh has had a fantastic football career and when I visited him during my research he and his wife Nellie greeted me with great warmth. Dan's memory of his own career and his association with Dr. Eamonn O'Sullivan were crystal clear. Listening to him was a fascinating and memorable experience. His parting words were of football as he added: "Kerry should have won the All-Ireland Finals of 1944 and 1947. Typical of every Kerry footballer, it's the ones that got away we remember most of all."

Dan Kavanagh's Memories of Dr. Eamonn O'Sullivan

Weeshie when I came to Killarney in 1945, I met Eamonn. That's about the very first time that I got to know him. Both of us were involved with the Dr. Croke's Club. I also had involvement with him in my work as an engineer with the County Council. There was no such thing as a health authority for the hospital at that time. And the County Council did all the engineering work related to hospitals. I would visit and attend meetings at St. Finan's Hospital from an engineering point of view. I knew him in that situation. I knew him particularly well later on through my involvement in the Fitzgerald Park.

I remember being very much involved with him in the construction of the old terraces in the Stadium way back, I'd say, in the late 1950s. At the time the terracing was all sod and grass. Dr. Eamonn and I, and a couple of others, including Gerdie Moynihan who was Secretary and you could say Secretary Manager in the whole set up of the Fitzgerald Park at the time. There was a decision made that we should put some form of steps on the terrace. What we decided after one consultation or another was that we'd put down a concrete facing and a green sod in order to retain the green and serve the purpose that people could stand and have a good view of a match in progress. That was done for the entire terrace. And looking back over it, I think it served very well.

I'm recalling these kinds of things because Eamonn, from the first day I met him, was a man of ideas. He was a thinker, he was always planning. He didn't take off his coat to do the job. He suggested what could be done. He organised a group or a committee and then looked for professional assistance and all types of assistance. And at the time he was able to avail of the patients in the Mental Hospital, those who were capable of doing the work on the stadium. It was considered at the time as Occupational Therapy for the patients. You're aware Weeshie of what Occupational Therapy meant to patients at the time. I remember in training, on several occasions, we would tog out in the Mental Hospital and afterwards take our showers there. All these things were available to us whenever we were training in Killarney and Eamonn never objected. He made the arrangements all the time. The facilities he provided for Kerry teams down the decades should never be forgotten.

Then years on, I would call into his home in Killarney and chat to him and we became very good friends. Indeed it was many a time we held meetings in his house. I was involved in preparing a residence for him where he lived. The residence at the time, as you know, was supplied by the Mental Hospital.

Of course there was his training of the Kerry teams; I trained under him a numerous occasions. The one year in particular that I remember most of all holds great memories for me because we won the All-Ireland. We played Roscommon in the final of 1946. It was a draw. We had trained in Tralee for the first game and there was a decision made by the County Board that the team should come over and train under Dr. Eamonn's control for the replay. The team was brought to Killarney especially for Eamonn. That was a measure of his importance to Kerry at the time. We were accommodated in Scott's Hotel in College St. Killarney for the two weeks training session, maybe ten or eleven days. At the time it was known as 'collective training'. There was no such thing as ongoing continuous yearly training at the time such as we know today.

The training for that replay under Eamonn was completely different from the drawn game. Remember he had not trained us for the first game and once again the County Board sent for him when they found themselves in trouble. Eamonn handled everything in a very professional manner and was very much aided and assisted by the late Mrs. Scott – owner of the hotel. She treated us like a mother. We had the best of everything. Needless to say we won that replay and Eamonn maintained his 100% record in finals.

The next involvement I had with him was years later. I can't recall the year, but it must have been the late 1950s. He decided he'd go for the Chairmanship of the Kerry County Board, and naturally, our club Dr. Croke's, had proposed him. We canvassed for him very enthusiastically. I remember being at that convention in Tralee. He didn't attend the convention himself. He was in Tralee that particular day, but I think he was very, very disappointed that he didn't succeed and become Chairman. Admittedly there was a very good Chairman, I think it was Frank Sheehy, who was very effective in his period in

Kerry, but I could see that he was very disappointed.

But one thing that can be said about Eamonn – anything that he got interested in, he put his heart into it. He guided his group, his committee, and the people who were aiding him. He kind of felt, that you could, in the end, stand back and say, "Well, I did this." He applied that to everything that he was involved in. You are probably aware Weeshie of what he did as the Resident Medical Superintendent in the Hospital. He applied the same focus to Munster Colleges as he applied to athletics. I know he was involved in camogie in Killarney way back in the early 1940s as well.

Nowadays you hear a lot about strategic management and all the rest of it – seems to be the 'in' thing. But this is something that came naturally to Dr. Eamonn way before strategic management became a study. He had a mission, as I say and he was able to stand back and could convince people. He had that power and that charm of convincing people that they were better than what they thought they were. He probably gave the same feeling of hope in the hospital, in the manner that patients worked and mixed in the community. He was seen as a man that was achieving all the time. And of course he had full control as the R.M.S. in the Mental Hospital. They were the chief people in Mental Hospitals until the administrative people came in, then the County Manager, followed by the 1932 Act. They took control then and the professionals became answerable to the administrative.

I remember the Killarney team at the time in the late 1940s, there were two clubs: your crowd – The Legion and my crowd – The Croke's. There was a decision made that the two should amalgamate. A committee formed once again under Dr. Eamonn. Many people got involved with a view that we should get together and form a single team. We did that and Eamonn became trainer. He became leader and co-coordinator and a man again who was able to fuse people together for a period. It lasted for two or three years, I think you know the number of years, but at least he was capable of bringing people together. If I may say so, he was capable of looking for the right people who would put their shoulder to the wheel to see that the job was done. And again he proved his greatness as a trainer when he led Killarney to a memorable Kerry County Championship victory in 1949.

I'd say as a trainer you could call him pre-professional. He applied the skills he had and the method he had of training people. In addition to that, I often noticed on a wet day we'd be inside in the Mental Hospital after dressing out and he'd kill a bit of time till the shower passed over by lecturing you on medical matters and fitness – fitness from the medical point of view, vitamins, what was good for you; all this kind of thing. It was above the heads of the majority of us but he could convince you and you could see here was a man and I must follow his gospel, what he was saying. He spoke with a degree of knowledge in all aspects of his work. He had a good understanding. He was probably used to authority in his early days.

In his day Dr. Eamonn's name was everything, whether it was in a game of Bridge or other things he was involved in in the County social life. So everybody knew him. He had the advantage as well that he was a local, a native of Kerry and the background of influence from his father, J.P. O'Sullivan of Killorglin, the former great athlete and footballer, also helped. Everybody knew him and he was well respected all over the country.

He was a man well before his time – a doctor, an author, a trainer, a leader, a man of tremendous vision. Without him I doubt very much if Kerry would have won the number of All-Ireland titles they hold today. He should never be forgotten, Weeshie.

An Interview with
Donie Sheehan

Donie's Biography

Donie Sheehan is a native of Listowel and came to Killarney in 1946 when he joined the Dr. Croke's Club. He won a Senior County Championship medal with The Dick Fitzgeralds in 1951 and served as Chairman of his club for 14 years in the mid-50s. He has had the great distinction of being a Kerry selector in all grades. Donie trained the highly successful East Kerry side of the 1960s and 1970s to Kerry, Munster and All-Ireland honours. He owns a family chemist shop on Main Street, Killarney.

I first met Dr. Eamonn around 1951. I started playing cards with the Killarney Bridge Club. He was President and Chairman of that Club and he ran the whole show there. Naturally, we both had an interest in the GAA. Actually, I played cards in his house for a long period, but I used to go up to watch him train the teams and we'd always discuss the GAA. I thought his methods were completely different from any other trainer I had seen. He gave me a formula for a rub, which I still have, which he made especially for the Kerry team. It eased aching limbs and helped cure sports injuries. I still use that rub all the time and I used it successfully during all the years I trained teams myself. It's Dr. Eamonn's secret formula and I will take the secret of it to my grave, Weeshie.

Now Dr. Eamonn was a wonderful man, I'll tell you more about what he did. Eamonn knew the minds of the players and he took each player individually. He knew what way to speak to them. He knew what got them going. He knew what they wanted. Now he would put some of the players off the drink completely. Some of them he'd allow have a few pints as he believed it helped certain individuals relax before the big championship games. But he was a strict man on training. They all respected him. It's rumoured (now I never saw this) he would take the players into a hall, in the Mental Hospital, produce the blackboard and he would divide up the board into a pitch with all separate squares. He would show the full backs and the half backs their squares. And they were never to come beyond that square. The same applied for the rest of the positions. That theory probably wouldn't do now, but that was the feeling of the time and Eamonn was the man who was first to use the blackboard to instruct teams. The corner back marked the corner forward. The full back marked the full forward and so along the line. He did short sprints with the players most of the time and then he played a bit of football.

Mick O'Dwyer applied many of Dr. Eamonn's techniques and fine-tuned them in a modern football setting. He knew modern techniques but he learned a lot from Dr. Eamonn. Dr. Eamonn's real strong point came from the fact that he knew each player individually. He came and he spoke to them and he inspired confidence in them thus making Kerry one of the greatest teams of all time. Dr. Eamonn's record for training winning teams, I suppose, will never again be challenged.

You probably knew him fairly well Weeshie, as you worked under him in the Mental Hospital. He was a strict disciplinarian. The lads respected him and that was half the battle. I played myself in one of the final trials before the 1953 All-Ireland Final against Armagh.

For years there was always a final trial above in the park, the Sunday before the All-Ireland. In latter years we used to charge a few bob; we'd ask people to throw in whatever they liked. And we used to collect a good few pound for the training fund. That was a great occasion I'll tell you. All the young lads and the people of Kerry came in and they could see all their favourite players that day, all playing in the trial. Eamonn was a great believer in a final trial before the final itself. Later I became a Kerry selector and the players were generally picked on that final trial.

I remember myself in 1975 we had the best trial ever the Sunday before the All-Ireland. We had no team picked. We didn't know them as they were all new young lads. Dr. Eamonn started that tradition of the final trials. I think it was a great success. Now they're all behind closed doors. They don't want anyone to know anything. I don't know why. People are not even told now that there is a final trial or that there's any type of trial going on. Dr. Eamonn never played behind closed doors; he loved to see the Kerry supporters present at the training.

He had a huge influence in my own club – Dr. Croke's. He trained some of the Croke teams and he gave us every assistance possible. He would tell you what to do. He'd point out any mistake that you were making.

On a personal level Dr. Eamonn was a reserved type of man. He was a gentleman. He had a lot of loves. He loved playing cards. He loved the GAA but sometimes he didn't agree with the hierarchy of the Association. He had his own ideas. As you know he started the All-Ireland Colleges football. He was a very far-seeing man; he could see into the future. He had a massive influence over Kerry football. Kerry wouldn't have won as many All-Ireland finals if it wasn't for Dr. Eamonn. They can thank Dr. Eamonn for most of the All-Ireland wins that he was associated with.

He was the first fellow to bring the teams in for 'collective training', bringing them in for the fortnight beforehand. As you know they stayed in the Park Place Hotel in Killarney. In 1954 Kerry was winning to such a degree that the Association brought in a motion at Congress that 'collective training' would be banned. Dr. Eamonn would not be put off and got over this hurdle in his own imaginative way. He just brought them in every evening for training but wouldn't keep them in the Park Hotel!

He was way ahead of his time. He was a very nice man to speak to. He respected everybody and he himself was highly respected. I saw Dr. Eamonn doing a lot of things and I thought they were very good. As you know, Weeshie, we won four Kerry Senior County Championships with East Kerry and you were on that great team and I was the trainer. You know the training was brutal at times. We won four and we won the very first club All-Ireland in 1971. That was some feat! We also won a couple of Munster Championships. This is another tribute to Dr. Eamonn.

If I am honest, I must admit I copied and I 'cogged' all his methods. 'Cogged' is the word you'd use long ago going to school when you used some other fella's ideas but I cogged everything that I ever knew about training teams from Dr. Eamonn. And you must know that too Weeshie, because you were a part of those very successful East Kerry teams.

He'll be remembered as one of the people who had great foresight, who looked forward, who saw things, who, way back in those days, would have thought of building the Fitzgerald Stadium. And it was a big stadium. Who'd ever think that there'd be crowds like that going to the GAA games? Who'd ever think that there'd be matches that everybody wanted to see? And look at the crowds today.

Dr. Eamonn should be remembered for all this wonderful work he did for the GAA. He was a marvellous man. I think he has been forgotten in the GAA world of today. In all honesty Weeshie, I believe if he was around today, he would be just as successful. There will never be another Dr. Eamonn O'Sullivan.

'Dr. Eamonn – A Great Leader of Men' by Hugh O'Flaherty

Dr. Eamonn was a remarkable man. As well as the actual training of teams he wrote this terrific book, 'The Art and Science of Gaelic Football' which encapsulated what he believed. There was an art and science in football and I suppose with some of the matches you see nowadays you see so much pulling and dragging; it would not have been what he would have liked. He believed in the basic game of catch and kick and each player should stay in his own zone or square. 'Collective training' was there in his time. He never brought the players together for Munster finals but once they went into the All-Ireland series, no matter who they were playing, then he took it very seriously. 'Collective training' was banned in 1954 which was a shame but what we see today is more or less collective training.

The teams today might not have the same coming together like in Eamonn's time when they would reside in St. Brendan's College or the Park Place Hotel in Killarney. Eamonn had this great belief in Gaelic football. I know Gaelic football seems to be overshadowed by hurling and I think that Brendan Kennelly and myself both think that in a way Gaelic football played properly demands every bit as much art and science as hurling. Football is man to man, you don't have a hurley stick, you have to fend for yourself one hundred per cent that is what Brendan believes and I am inclined to agree with him.

The building of Fitzgerald Stadium was an extraordinarily important step and the fact that he involved the patients in the work meant that they got out of the hospital and the locked wards therein. He fully recognized their contribution. He had a special area in the Stadium for them and a special gate leading from the hospital grounds for the patients to enter the Stadium. That was very thoughtful of him. Of course there was an All-Ireland Hurling final staged in the Stadium in 1937, however a football final is yet to be seen.

Dr. Eamonn has had a huge influence on the whole concept of

football. His idea was that the game should be taken very seriously and in the training, fitness and diet he put huge emphasis. He did not believe that Kerry teams had a divine or God-given right to win All-Irelands and all his winning games had been won by sheer hard work. I believe he has inspired other trainers such as the likes of Michael O'Dwyer, Paudie O'Shea and more. I believe he is someone that they look back on and revere. He played a huge part in putting the whole concept of training and management on the high plain it now occupies.

I would say that my first realization of Eamonn and his name was for the 1946 All-Ireland Final against Roscommon. I remember listening to the drawn game in my grandmother's house in Mangerton View, Killarney and Kerry were being beaten very badly. They trailed 1-7 to 0-4 with ten minutes left to play. Jimmy Murray the great Roscommon Captain, who sadly died recently, lay on the side line, blood streaming from a facial injury which would force him to retire. Legend has it that one of the first aid men came over to him and remarked: "We better wipe the blood from your face so that you will look presentable when you receive the Cup."

Now I left the house in despair and walked down the town and in those days, you will recall, they had the radio loudspeakers on to the street because very few people had radio sets. Outside Pat O'Mara's Pub in College Street, now Lenihan's, a huge shout went up. Paddy Burke, Kerry's outstanding full forward, had scored a goal. I just walked on and said to myself – it is too late now we won't do. I had just got to the Imperial Hotel a few doors down when another shout went up and it was another goal for Kerry. This time 'Gega' O'Connor had found the net. Two lightening goals and the game finished in a draw. I met Michael O'Heir one time and remarked to him, can I trespass on your good nature to tell me did the goals come that quick or is it something in one's imagination. "Oh," he replied, "They did, they came as quick as that. The ball was in the net, it was then kicked out and was straight back in the net for the second goal." Kerry won the replay and Eamonn had them in superb shape because they were up against that great Roscommon side who were probably one of the all-time great football teams.

I met Eamonn on a few occasions but I would have a due difference of a young man towards an elder statesman at that stage. He was a man of fine demeanour and had a fine presence. He handled his player's very adroitly; he didn't force anything on them. If some were smokers, which were common enough in those days, they weren't ordered to give up cigarettes totally; they would have been advised to cut back as much as they could. He could see that to give them up completely would have made them too edgy. They were also to cut back on the pint or two or to confine themselves to a pint or two but he would not have been as dictatorial as to order that they couldn't have a recreational drink. He was a wonderful manager.

With the passing of time and memories dimming people can be forgotten in certain instances. What better way to remember Eamonn than to play more Munster hurling matches in Fitzgerald Stadium which would also help greatly in the revival of hurling in Kerry. Eamonn should be remembered as a great human being, a doctor who was certainly in advance of his time in the treatment of mental illness and the care of his patients and above all, a great leader of men – a man for all seasons.

The Story of Jack Murphy

The winning of Kerry's 7th All-Ireland title in 1926 will forever be associated with one of the saddest events in our footballing story – the death of the brilliant Jack Murphy, hero of the drawn game just eleven days following the replay. Jack had joined Dr. Eamonn and the rest of the Kerry squad for 'collective training' in Tralee, staying in bed and breakfast, which was the norm at the time. He developed pneumonia and lay on his death-bed as his teammates overcame Kildare.

The South Kerry man had given a superb display in the drawn match, and the fact that Kerry were not swamped was due almost solely to his display. Time after time Jack saved Kerry when all seemed lost. He was unbeatable under the dropping ball, fielding safely over the heads of friends and foe alike, driving long-raking clearances to midfield and beyond. His speed and anticipation enabled him to intercept and break up most of Kildare's hand-passing movements. He most certainly kept Kerry in the game. The writers of the time agreed that never before had such a display been seen in an All-Ireland final. Invincible Jack Murphy was the hero of the Kerry supporters.

The Kerryman summoned up the mood of the county when news of his death was announced:

"Jack Murphy is dead! Kerry's wonderful back, the pride of Iveragh is no more. Never was a sadder or more poignant message broadcast to the gales of Kerry. With the cheers of our county men still ringing in our ears, proclaiming victory over Kildare; with the heather still black on the hillsides of Kerry whereon bonfires blazed to celebrate the victory came the doleful tidings. And all Kerry reels underneath the shock. While the waves beat a dirge against our coast and the wind croons a caoine over the hills of Iveragh, let us breathe a prayer for the soul of Jack Murphy, one of Kerry's greatest."

Jack Murphy was born on the June 6, 1904 the youngest of 13 children and was raised in Ballycarbery, Caherceiveen. He played with his brothers in the local leagues and on the South Kerry team. He attended the Christian Brothers School in Caherceiveen and afterwards he went on the study medicine in U.C.C.

He later joined the newly formed Civic Guards and was stationed in Dublin, and had been promoted to Sergeant shortly before his death. Playing outstanding football in Dublin club leagues, he was invited and coaxed to join up and play with that county, but the lure of Kerry was too great and he remained with his beloved native county. Jack was a wonder of his generation, a class above all others, his fielding was superb and we are told no man in Ireland could better him. He first made his mark when he helped Kerry in a number of trial games and he then played with the Munster champions of 1924, 1925 and 1926. He also played in a McGrath Cup final. For that 1924 Final in which Eamonn began his career as trainer Jack, together with Phil O'Sullivan and Joe Barrett, gave great displays in that win over Dublin.

Jack Murphy's death at such a young age stunned the country and *The Kerryman* brought the accounts of his funeral and burial to Kerry followers at home and across the seas:

"Very genuine feelings of the deepest regret were manifested in Tralee yesterday when it became known that Johnny Murphy, the star Kerry left full back who for some weeks past had been in the grip of a very serious illness had succumbed. The fact that he was ill was well-known and anxious enquiries about his condition were relayed from near and far. Few realized that the man who a few short weeks ago, in the flower of a splendid manhood, repelled with such wonderful agility and skills the onslaughts of the Kildare forwards as to mark him an outstanding figure in the Gaelic arena, was making his last appearance on a football field.

Critics and friends were loud in praise of his magnificent display on that occasion and it was felt that if it were possible he would add further lustre to his name on the replay. Such was not to be. When Johnny Murphy reported for training to Dr. Eamonn O'Sullivan it was noticed that he was not looking well and the good Doctor ordered him to lie up immediately. Skilled attention and careful nursing were generously bestowed on him but sadly to no avail. He was unable to turn out for the final and death claimed him for its own yesterday at the early age of 22 years."

Few deaths in recent years have occasioned such widespread manifestations of regret as that of our own Sergeant Jack Murphy. He still retained his boyish characteristics; quiet and unassuming to a degree. Jack was a universal favourite with his colleagues at the Depot, the Gaels of the county with whom he came in contact and with the general public.

A large concourse of people followed the remains to their last resting place. The many messages of sympathy received from all over the country and the large number of floral tributes placed on the grave, all bore testimony to the popularity and respect in which our great Jack Murphy was held. The remains were removed to St. John's Mortuary Chapel on Tuesday followed by an immense number of people. The coffin was borne on the shoulders of his comrades of the Kerry football team, and a large body of Gaels and Civic Guards under Chief Supt. Clinton were also present.

There was Solemn Requiem High Mass for the repose of the soul of the deceased presided over by the Right Rev. Mons. O'Leary, P.P.U.S. Dean of Kerry at 10 p.m. The Church was thronged with people and a most touching spectacle was the placing of Jack's football togs, jersey and boots on the coffin by one of his colleagues.

On Wednesday 27, the remains arrived in Caherceiveen from Tralee and were met by a huge crowd of people and borne to the O'Connell Memorial Church where they remained overnight. High Mass was celebrated on Thursday morning with Very Rev. Canon Browne as celebrant, Rev. T. Carroyne C.C., Deacon and Rev. J. Prendeville, C.C., Sub-Deacon. In the afternoon the funeral took place to the burial ground at Kilavarnogue. Despite the inclemency of the early morning there was a massive attendance. High-placed officials of the GAA including Kerry's trainer, Dr. Eamonn O'Sullivan, were in attendance while Chief Supt. R. J. Clinton, Tralee and Supt. R. J. Heydon were in charge of the Kerry Gardaí of whom there was a large party.

The Kerry County Board and all the Kerry divisional boards were represented. Others in attendance were Paddy O'Keeffe (Secretary of Cork County Board), GAA Chief Superintendent Stack represented by General O'Duffy, Gardaí Paul Russell, P.J. Cryan, John Clifford and J. O'Connor represented Kerrymen at the Depot. The members of the Kerry football team with the Gardaí marched after the remains, as did the members of the Kerry Selection Committee. The cortege was preceded by the Killarney Pipers Band, which played appropriate selections of sacred music.

The Kerry and Gardaí colours were laid on the coffin, along with the deceased footballer's jersey, socks, togs and boots. When the grave had been covered in the Killarney Pipers Band struck up 'Nearer my God to Thee', as many at the graveside wept openly. Very Rev. Canon Browne P.P., assisted by the local clergy officiated at the graveside while Donal O'Donoghue of Cork delivered an oration, referring in eulogistic terms to Jack's worth as a comrade and a Gael. The chief mourners were, Jack's parents; Pat and Kate, brothers; Thade, Pat and Denis, sisters; Bernadette, Minnie Lynch, aunts; Mrs. J. Murphy and Mrs. O'Donoghue, uncles; James and Michael Griffin, brother-in-law;

Michael Lynch and cousins; Mick and Jack Donoghue.

Tributes poured in from all parts of the country and overseas, Jack Murphy's death at such a young age stunned the nation.

General O'Duffy on behalf of the Gardaí wrote as follows:

"Your wire intimating the death of Sergeant Murphy comes as a great shock, as I understand from Dick Fitzgerald on Sunday that he was on the way to recovery. I take this opportunity to ask you to kindly convey to his relatives and to all the County Board and the Gael of Kerry my deepest sympathy. I regret that the rejoicing over The Kingdoms great victory should be so soon marred by the death of one who played his part in that noble achievement. Since the Sergeant joined the Garda Síochana he proved, in his own modest and unpretentious way, a faithful and efficient member. And from my personal knowledge of his character and worth, I believe he would have had a very successful career; but God willed otherwise. Jack Murphy was a credit to the GAA and the Kerry County team and the Gardaí Senior Football team mourn the loss of a stalwart champion in whom both shared pride."

The Cork County Board wired as follows: "Gaels of Cork shocked at sad news, Jack is not alone a loss to Kerry but to Ireland." The great Larry Stanley of Kildare said, "He was greatly shocked to hear of the death of Ireland's best, Jack Murphy." Wreaths were piled high on the grave, one said: "From your comrades of the Kerry team in loving memory of Jack without whom we would not be champions." The Dr. Croke's Club wrote, "In loving memory of Jack Murphy who won the All-Ireland for Kerry, September 6, 1929."

The Kerry players had been determined to overcome adversity and as Dr. Eamonn revealed years later, had vowed before they left the dressing room to win that All-Ireland for Jack Murphy. It was on such adversities and tragedies like this of 1926 that the spirit and tradition of Kerry was formed. Paddy Whitty, one of the stars of this memorable win presented his All-Ireland medal to the Murphy family. His sister Nell brought the medal to America but unfortunately it was stolen when her apartment was raided some years later in New York.

In 1969 the Murphy family donated a cup in memory of Jack. It was handed over to the St. Mary's Club, Caherceiveen for an Inter-County tournament on Whit Sunday. In 1974, the Cup was given to the South Kerry Board and ever since the Jack Murphy Memorial Cup is presented to the winners of the Senior South Kerry Championship – a fitting tribute to one of the greatest footballers ever to come out of the Barony of Iveragh.

In April 1975, Renard were the first club to receive the Cup when they beat Valentia in the final played in Waterville. Joe Joe O'Sullivan was the winning Captain and Michael Lyne, Captain of Valentia and Chairman of the South Kerry Board handed over the Cup.

Jack's brothers were prominent footballers with Caherceiveen O'Connell's and Pat helped O'Connell's reach the County semi-final of 1912, only to be defeated by Tralee Parnell's. Jack's nephew Paddy Murphy, New Market Street, was a prominent member of the St. Mary's Club in the 1950s and in more recent times his grandnephews; John Joe, Gearóid, Tim and Padraig Murphy and Mike and Murty O'Connell have given Sterling service to the Club.

Seventy-five years later, on February 2001, on Valentia Island, my own life was touched in a special way by the tragic death of a young Valentia footballer. Gearóid Lyne was just 11 years old when he died, on February 4, 1996. A brilliant young footballer he had played with Valentia the previous year. Sadly he was diagnosed with cancer on December 8 and was buried on February 8. Gearóid was a great grandson of Jack Murphy. Jack's sister Minnie had married Michael Lynch and their daughter Catherine later married Valentia islander, Con Lyne and his sons went on to star with Valentia Young Islanders in many memorable victories. One of the boys Michael Lyne is one of the island's greatest sons, married to Una Keating of Portmagee. They donated a cup to Gearóid's memory to Bord na nÓg Cíarraí Theas for the Under-12 Competition. Valentia Under-12s won the Cup for the first time in 2000.

In early January of 2001 I was honoured to be asked to present the winning team with their South Kerry Under-12 medals. Kerry led by the brilliant Seamus Moynihan and guided by the magnificent Caherceiveen man, Maurice Fitzgerald who had won the Sam Maguire Cup the previous September. It was my duty to collect the Cup in Killarney and make sure it was at the presentation ceremony in Valentia. My journey to South Kerry that January evening remained etched in the memory. It had snowed all that day leaving the road from Killarney to Valentia like an ice rink. Three hours later with the gleaming new Sam Maguire Cup nestling in the back seat, I arrived at my destination following a hazardous journey driving in first and second gear.

The night was memorable; it was one of those Kerry football occasions which touches the heart. The exemplary young footballers of Valentia stepped forward one by one to accept their medals and there on the table before them stood three trophies, which symbolized all that's great in Kerry football. The previous year I had seen Valentia Seniors bring the Jack Murphy Cup back across the bridge to the Island as they regained the South Kerry Championship and now it stood before us side-by-side with the All-Ireland trophy and the Gearóid Lyne Cup.

Jack Murphy, hero of 1926, and his great grandson are united in death but are now remembered through their exploits on the playing fields. For me an emotional, unexplainable coming together of two Kerry footballers whose memories are perpetuated by the Cups standing side-by-side that night on Valentia Island.

It would be 11 years before Dr. Eamonn would lead his next Kerry team to All-Ireland glory. 1937 seemed a long way off following the triumph and tragedy of 1926. However, in those intervening years he would launch himself body and soul into a massive project, which would commemorate forever one of Kerry's greatest sons. As Kerry began to win the first of their four-in-a-row All-Ireland's in 1929, Eamonn was appointed by his club, Dr. Croke's, to select a site which would be suitable to accommodate a new football pitch. Thus began the first step in the building of what is now the internationally known 'Fitzgerald Stadium'. Historians tell us that it was the foresight, leadership, and organizational skills of Eamonn that brought this magnificent stadium to fruition.

An Interview with
Jack O'Keeffe

Jack O'Keeffe is the Patron of the Dr. Croke's GAA Club, Killarney and follows in the footsteps of the very first Patron of that Club, the illustrious Dr. Croke. Jack was himself an outstanding footballer in his youth and he won an All-Ireland Minor medal with Kerry way back in 1931. He has served the famed Killarney club in many capacities, including Chairman. He also served as Chairman of the East Kerry Board and the local Dick Fitzgerald team.

I interviewed Jack at his home in Killarney in February 2001, approaching his 90th year. He was blessed with a most remarkable memory, crystal clear and his recollections of Eamonn were as if they happened only recently. Jack O'Keeffe is the only surviving member of the original committee set up in November 14, 1930, which arrived at the momentous decision to build a Memorial stadium to commemorate the then recently deceased legendary Kerry footballer Dick Fitzgerald. He had died in September 1930 and he had been Chairman and Captain of his club Dr. Croke's.

Dr. Eamonn Pioneers The Building Of Fitzgerald Stadium, Killarney
It is very likely that Eamonn himself decided on the particular field which would be purchased to develop the Stadium, being Resident Medical Superintendent of the Killarney Mental Hospital which overlooked the field. I think he would often look out the Hospital windows and visualise what could be developed on the land which lay before him. I firmly believe that Eamonn could see a little further than most and looking out from those windows all those years ago he saw well past the 1930s and 1940s and must have seen the future potential in that bare field.

When the select committee was set up by the Dr. Croke's Club following Dick Fitzgerald's death he spearheaded the purchase of that field at the then colossal amount of £750. The field was owned by a Dan Courtney and Eamonn, with Eugene O'Sullivan and John Clifford, carried out prolonged negotiations to secure ownership of the land. He was involved in the setting up of committees at home, in Dublin and in America, to help advance the cause of the project and of course to raise funds also. He was also a member of the Munster Council and led a deputation from the Croke's. On his proposition seconded by a Mr. Considine of Clare it was decided to give £400 to the project.

Eamonn's position as R.M.S. in the Mental Hospital played a huge part in the development of the Stadium. Occupational Therapy in those hospitals had been unheard of up until then. He sought and gained permission at a meeting of the Killarney Mental Hospital Committee in Marsh 1933 allowing the patients to work on developing a field, not the property of the committee. There was some condemnation in the local press of Eamonn's project, nevertheless he was in no doubt that the work was of great therapeutic value to the patients. And he added, "It was the very first undertaking of the subsequently developed Occupational Therapy Department of the Hospital and could be described as its Opus Magnum." In a letter to the Hospital, the Minister of Local Government said he was pleased to learn the work had the beneficial effects on the health of the patients and a number of cures had resulted there from.

It was only fitting that the Pavilion and Stand erected in the 1970s should have been named in honour of Dr. Eamonn. This development was officially opened by Eamonn's son Anthony in 1977. I can tell you Weeshie that everyone involved in the development of the Stadium were all in agreement that his contribution was massive. He always told us of the great help that came from the staff of the Mental Hospital, in particular – Denso Hurley, Myo Murphy, and Tim O'Donoghue and of course the patients, without whom nothing could have been achieved. Remember it was nearly all manual work at that period of our history.

Many thought at the time that he was too ambitious, but as we look back from today we now appreciate that he could see way further into the future than any of us. We can see all club colours in action in the Stadium; the black and amber, the green and white and of course the Kerry colours – the green and gold, all in full view, with adequate accommodation for spectators.

Eamonn had a fine stature, and was well endowed with ability. He fully controlled the fracas that would happen at times. He didn't demand respect but he got it by reason of ability and foresight. He did not force his way, people might have thought that he did, believing that he was a kind of a dictator in his own way, but actually it was always done quietly. You might have disagreed with him, but you always felt that he was always more right than you were.

I would say that it would have been impossible without Dr. Eamonn to have accomplished the building of that magnificent Stadium we have today. I remember in 1937, when the Stadium was only open a year, an All-Ireland Senior Hurling final was played there with an attendance of over 43,000 people. I was privileged to have known him and worked with him in that major project. Dr. Eamonn O'Sullivan was truly a remarkable person to achieve this – a man before his time.

An Interview with Jerome O'Shea

Jerome O'Shea became a close friend and great admirer of Dr. Eamonn O'Sullivan. Jerome from the South Kerry town of Caherceiveen is fondly recalled in the history of Kerry football for his magnificent display in the 1955 All-Ireland win over Dublin, in particular his never-to-be forgotten brilliant height catch in the Kerry Square in the closing minutes of that match. This victory is generally accepted as Eamonn's finest hour as Kerry trainer. Among the vast array of honours won by Jerome his two Senior All-Ireland medals in 1955 and 1959, when trained by Eamonn, he cherished most of all.

In Jerome's own words

Yes indeed Weeshie, I have great memories of Dr. Eamonn, especially throughout the 1950s, because my time with Kerry came in the 1950s and into the early 1960s. Dr. Eamonn was a permanent appointment in the Kerry GAA scene at that time. I suppose over all I think of him as a quiet spoken, friendly, very intelligent gentleman who inspired great belief and the utmost confidence in oneself. I had heard of his great contribution to all aspects of the game in Kerry since the early 1920s and it was generally accepted that it was immense.

Then of course, specifically where would you go from there? Some things spring to mind when you talk about the man. For me it would be going into the training sessions and seeing a few things. For instance, he had this little blackboard and easel and he had five simple rules that he would write on that. Now some people might say that's very simple, we all knew this before, etc. but it wasn't so simple really. To me they tell an awful lot about the man himself. In particular, I always remember the number one, indeed so do the other players, that one was, "Backs – don't foul"; three words, very simple, but words that would stand the test of time.

He would go on to explain this and why it was so important

and he would have statistical arguments to go with it. Now this was amazing stuff, he must have been one of the very first sportsmen to keep statistics. He would research for us back to the time he started training Kerry in 1924 and he would have statistics for all matches he was involved in during that period. If it was an All-Ireland semi-final he would relate them to semi-finals and the same if it was a final we were preparing for. He would say, "Now we take this and we take that and apply it here." He would assume that every team would have a good free kicker on the field and assume that he would get the maximum amount of scores on the day, so if the back doesn't foul the difference between the teams at the end would be minimum. Then he would say, "Now if we had not given away those two extra frees back in the 1920s or 1930s in that semi-final or this final we would have won so many more All-Irelands," he would say. Amazing really when you think of it now.

He made a huge impression on lots of people, in particular the team under his training at that time. He wasn't totally focused on the game in itself all the time but focused on pre-game preparation and this helped us, I believe in a big way. Here his own medical career would have helped as he was also interested in research about sport and the dangers of over-training and minding oneself before games. Now if I could give one example from a practical point of view it would be in relation to training in the summer of 1955. It was a beautiful summer and he totally banned swimming for all of the players and the one thing you always felt like doing when you are born near the sea is to take a dip in the ocean. Eamonn maintained that swimming would have an adverse effect on your speed, so that back then when smoking or alcohol were banned before a match, swimming was also banned. He was always thinking ahead, always breaking new ground, always coming up with new ideas in relation to player's fitness. It was an amazing time in Kerry football!

His influence in 1955 was fantastic, as it was in 1959; he blended the players that year together and made them a great team. His view would be, and he always repeated this: "Now lads, you're as good as footballers now, as when you run out on to Croke Park in two weeks time. What I can do for you is improve your fitness levels and maybe in some way improve your skills and get the team working together." That was a fantastic approach and it was an approach that was particularly true of 1955 and his impact that year. In a way he deserved a great deal more credit than even the players did on that occasion. We had some great players on that team; John Dowling, Tadghie Lyne, Johnny Culloty, Jim Brosnan, Ned Roche etc., but Eamonn would stand out over and above the players because he successfully blended these quality players together.

The Dublin team we beat that day had been playing together as a club team at St. Vincent's and had been winning all before them. They were introducing a new aspect into the game at the time which was the talk of the country, it was known as 'the roving full-forward', (Kevin Heffernan). Dr. Eamonn did not agree with this, in his view it would be breaking with tradition and one of his strongest rules which was: "Players keep in their own sector" and the field will divide up. Now according to Dr. Eamonn you had your sector to play in and stay in; if you were a corner back that is where you would stay; if you were a corner forward you would stay in that corner and you didn't stray out of that sector. Completely different as to what you have today. I think Eamonn saw the Dublin change of tactics as a challenge, both to Kerry and to himself. The traditional game that he had grown up with was something that we had to defend to the last. He came up with a tactic in that 1955 Final to respond to this new challenge and discussed it with us. We would come to call it the 'diamond-type defence'.

Now if you look at this tactic against the individual sectors and players in their own individual sectors, this was a slight variation of that diamond defence. Now if you have a roving full forward playing on a good strong full back which was typical of the Kerry full back lines at that particular time like; Ned Roche, Niall Sheehy etc., strong men who didn't sail into the air and indeed didn't need to do so, then the gambit of playing against a roving full forward was a worry. Kevin Heffernan had played exceptionally well for Dublin that year, both semi-finals were drawn that year of 1955. I must add that Heffernan had been marked in games by two of the great full backs of the time, Paddy O'Brien of Meath and Paddy Prendergast of Mayo. So there was this kind of fear going around unfounded or otherwise that Heffernan had to be well-marked if Kerry were to win.

So tactically Eamonn came up with this new idea. "Right so we must close him down and how do you close down a roving full forward?" he explained to us at a meeting. He was a great believer in using the blackboard to explain his thinking. It was then that he came up with the 'diamond effect', never before seen in Gaelic football. He utilized four defenders, but four defenders to mark one man but move them in field from their sectors (he always described their positions as sectors). Our centre back John Cronin was to move back from the traditional centre back position, five to ten yards, nearer his own goal, left full back Mixi Palmer was to move in and stay 10 to 15 yards from the sideline and the same movement for me, I was right full back. Our full back Ned Roche was to stay within the 21 yard line, so within that small area the ball could be contested by any of the four defenders who could at any time replace the full back once we fully understood what we were all doing. And of course it worked like a dream and Kerry won an historic victory thanks to the genius of Eamonn. It's history now.

Of course his medical background had a lot to do with his great successes. He had us absolutely convinced before that 1955 Final that we were going to win. We were written off all around the country and indeed even here at home in Kerry if the truth was known. Most of the so-called experts said that Dublin were the better team and hinted that we were going to Croke Park to simply make up the numbers. So I believe Eamonn literally threw down the gauntlet to our team. He would say to us on a regular basis: "Now lads this has been the tradition of Kerry down the years and ye will be out there trying to uphold that tradition." He always put in the positive, "A win today will maintain that, this is what tradition means lads and it means so much to Kerry. Winning this All-Ireland would be absolutely fantastic." His impact was immense.

Of course we must remember that he was not a selector for the team, he was the trainer, but at times he would discuss with some of the senior players what his opinion of the first 15 should be. He did sit in on the selector's discussions but only on an advisory basis.

He was very much part of the traditions and myths of Kerry football. Of course he came from a great tradition himself, his father J.P. – 'The Champion' and the early Laune Rangers teams. He was steeped in tradition and always preached this to us. It certainly rubbed off on me and I hope inspired me when I donned the green and gold.

He was a great believer at training in short sprints of say 25 yards or so, and he would say, "Get out there in front, first to the ball, be quick off the mark be first off. You'll never be asked for a sprint of more than that." He literally had the game analyzed down to that and this was before the words 'match analysis' was even invented. He would have us standing around in large circles just punching the ball from one to another. The benefit of this was that a player who was weak punching with one fist, right or left, would eventually become quite competent and strong with that weak punching action. You don't see that perfected today.

I was fortunate to be with him on a few occasions following big matches. He was quite happy following those games to simply go away from the whole scene, the after match celebrations were not for him. He would go off for a nice, quiet meal with his wife and family, maybe to a different hotel from where the team was eating. One or two of us might drop in and we would have a nice quiet chat with him, he much preferred that. He would not be one to get involved in the euphoria of the situation but secretly, of course, he had the very same pride and same delight as all others only he expressed it in a different way.

Dr. Eamonn's contribution to the game and to his county was absolutely immense – more than anyone I have ever known. He was a highly intelligent person who had this unique gift of inspiring others in his own special, quiet way. I never ceased to be amazed that he had not received the acclaim that he so richly deserved. Of all his victories he is most closely linked to that 1955 win over Dublin. He had a major impact on my football career and I consider myself very fortunate to have trained under him and befriended him. We will never see his like again Weeshie and I am thrilled that you are bringing together the various strands of his life. It is long, long overdue.

Johnny Culloty

A Lifetime Of Service To His County

In Dr. Eamonn's time things were very different than they are now. Today a manager is appointed at the start of the year and fulfils his duties for that year. Not so with Eamonn. I remember in 1955 the first All-Ireland I was involved in, there was no training for the Munster Final, we trained for about a week for the semi-final against Cavan; that was a draw and we trained about the same for the replay. However we trained full time for the final, twice a day. Now contrast that with the present time where they train the whole year around and you see the huge difference in the different generations.

Dr. Eamonn O'Sullivan was a man before his time. He wrote books about football and Occupational Therapy and we must remember he was Resident Medical Superintendent of St. Finan's Hospital when there were 1,100 patients there. He must have been a genius not alone in the field of football but also in the psychiatric field as well. He was able to activate all those patients every day of the year; it was a massive undertaking for the man. Where he got the time for everything I just didn't know.

As regards the training of teams, he was completely different to the trainers of today. Now they are all pacing and running up and down the sidelines but not him, he was cool calm and collected at all times. As a matter of fact he had nothing to do with the picking of the Kerry teams he trained. In 1955 Kevin Heffernan was the big name on the Dublin side and he was the talk of the place but I never heard Eamonn mentioning Heffernan's name or how we would mark him or plan for him. He trained his own team to the best of his ability, told us what he expected us to do and put us out on the field to do the job for Kerry. Now in that line he brought his psychiatric expertise into the training of all his teams. In my book he was an expert trainer and I firmly believe he would still be the best if he was here today.

It's great Weeshie to see you getting his many achievements down in print for posterity.

My grandfather worked in the Hospital from 1905 to 1950 and one thing he always spoke about was the great work the patients put into the building of the Fitzgerald Stadium. I remember talking to some patients who had worked on the project in the old days back in the hungry 1930s, for very little reward, and they told me that they found it a great break from the tedium of being confined in the wards of the Hospital. It was free and easy and there was great camaraderie between the workers and it helped to bond a great relationship with the staff members. The field itself was laid with grass sods cut by hand by the hospital patients, can you imagine the amount of work alone that that entailed? This should never be forgotten. We are told that up to 50 patients from St. Finan's helped in the project and it is sad that we do not have a record of their names. However those were the times, when little was recorded.

I began working in the Hospital in 1956 and there was practically no medication of any sort. All the emphasis was on recreation and rehabilitation and trying to get the patients out working on the hospital gardens and farm. Now the one thing that always struck me when I took up my nursing career in the Hospital was the number of great workers that were amongst the patients. Fine, strong, athletic, fit fellows that were from all over County Kerry; they could turn their hand to anything. Now if they were completely confined to the hospital wards it would have been a very long soul-destroying day for them and it was in this area that Dr. Eamonn was so far ahead of his time. Occupational Therapy was a big thing for him, and rightly so. And of course if they had back then what they have now, like the vast availability of medication, those patients would not have been in hospital at all.

Among the people I admired greatly was Dr. Eamonn O'Sullivan, he was years before his time and I certainly learned much from him.

Biography of Johnny Culloty

Johnny Culloty came under the expert guidance of Dr. Eamonn at just 18 years of age. One of the most versatile Kerry sports men ever, Johnny had just come out of minor ranks in 1954 when he was immediately added to the Kerry Senior Panel in 1955. That of course was the year that Eamonn guided his county to their most famous victory of all and the young Culloty was one of the stars when he lined out at left corner forward. It was the beginning of a remarkable career. The Killarney man injured his knee the following year while playing in a Railway Cup match against Ulster. He then began a long innings in goal for The Kingdom and guided by Eamonn, won two more medals in 1959 and 1962. He was also a member of the team of 1964 beaten by Galway in the final – Eamonn's only loss as Kerry trainer.

Killarney is famous the world over for its great natural beauty. Its lakes and mountains have been the subject of many poems and songs – even the great Bing Crosby crooned about them. The town still boasts an enormous tourist trade but, in a more parochial context, it is also famous for producing top class footballers.

Johnny Culloty was arguably one the town's greatest achievers in the county jersey. He won five All-Ireland Senior Football medals and was the winning Captain in 1969. And he won no fewer than 12 Munster SFC medals including a magnificent eight-in-a-row from 1958 to 1965. Although he will always be remembered as one of the game's top goalies, it was not as a net minder that he first came to the attention of supporters, nor was it ever his favourite position, nor was football his favourite game!

In fact, Johnny was an above average hurler whose major regret is that Kerry were unable to make an impact in the Munster Championship during his years on the team. He won an All-Ireland Junior hurling medal with The Kingdom in 1961 when they beat London in the final having beaten Meath in the home decider. Johnny scored two goals against Meath from the right corner-forward position. He played in goal for the county minor hurlers at the age of 14 and was a county minor for four years and played at adult club level from 1951 until the 1980s. Apart from the All-Ireland Junior success in 1961, the victory that gave him most satisfaction was Killarney's lone Senior Hurling Championship title in 1969. That glorious day for Killarney, Culloty almost dragged 'Beauties Home' to victory on his own. Many would agree that he was good enough to grace any Inter-County hurling side in Ireland when he was in his prime.

His first encounter with big-time football was in 1954 when he was centre-half forward on the Kerry Minor team that was beaten by Dublin in the All-Ireland Minor Final. Among his colleagues on the team were; Tom Long, the poet Brendan Kennelly, Teddy Dowd, Frank O'Leary, Brian Sheehy, Freddie Lynch and George White. It was one of the most heart-breaking of all minor defeats for The Kingdom. Five points ahead with just five minutes remaining, Dublin stunned Kerry with two late injury time goals to snatch the title. It was a totally forgettable day for Kerry supporters who also saw their Senior team go under to Meath. There was some consolation for Culloty when he lined out at right-half forward on the team that beat London in the All-Ireland Junior Final some weeks later. Teammates of the rising young star that day included; Tom Spillane, Eddie Dowling, Tom Costello, Dermot Dillon, Pop Fitzgerald and Sean Lovett.

Johnny had impressed sufficiently to warrant a call-up to the Senior Panel for the 1955 Championship and was corner forward on the team that faced Dublin in the All-Ireland Final having required a replay to get the better of Cavan in the semi-final. That memorable year he first appeared as a Kerry senior as a substitute in Killarney in the Munster Final. The showdown between Kerry and Dublin was the first to attract the degree of hype which is so much a part of the modern game. Dublin, with their highly-vaunted half-forward line of Des Ferguson, Ollie Freeney and Cathal O'Leary, and with Kevin Heffernan at full forward, were installed as favourites. Kerry's rating as 'outsiders' had much to do with their hugely disappointing performance against an old Meath team in the previous year's final.

The official attendance was 87,102 people but two gates were broken down and hundreds poured through. It wasn't the greatest of finals but the last four minutes helped to make it memorable. Kerry had dominated throughout but a late Dublin goal left only three points between the teams and there was tremendous drama and excitement in the closing stages. Kerry held out to win the title for the 18th time. All six Kerry forwards, including Johnny, got on the score sheet while only three Dublin attackers managed to register. One report of the match said that young Culloty was the star of the full forward line. Despite a distinct disadvantage in height against his marker Mick Moylan, he fared better in the fielding stakes.

A cartilage injury sustained in a Railway Cup game in 1956 was a serious setback but his somewhat gradual transformation from corner forward to goalkeeper occurred in 1957. As with most of such dramatic switches, it happened purely by chance.

Kerry were due to play Galway in a Gaelic Weekly semi-final and the selected goalie, Donal Marcus O'Neill, couldn't make it on the day. Johnny was placed between the posts and although he subsequently played in a number of league games in outfield positions, the switch became permanent in late 1958 when, once again, the selected goalkeeper did not show. From that point onwards, Culloty became the first name to be pencilled in on The Kingdom team.

In his first Championship year as goalie, 1959, Johnny won his second All-Ireland SFC medal but expectations of continued success were punctured by the arrival of Down's great team of that era. In 1962 Down faltered in Ulster and Kerry took full advantage by beating Roscommon in the All-Ireland Final. It was Johnny's third medal but just as Down had proven to be something of a bogey team for Kerry at the turn of the decade, a new and powerful force emerged from the west in the mid-1960s. Galway won three successive All-Irelands beating Kerry en route to all three titles. It was one of these defeats that saw Dr. Eamonn relinquish his position as Kerry trainer in 1964. It was his only All-Ireland final defeat out of nine appearances.

Cork emerged from Munster in 1966 and 1967 and Johnny's next All-Ireland experience was against old rivals Down, in the 1968 decider. The game will always be remembered for Sean O'Neill's goal when he beat the Kerry custodian from close range, after the ball rebounded from the upright. The goal emphasized the genius of O'Neill. There was little that Culloty could have done, especially as his defenders were not as alert as the Down man.

Having won his second of four county SFC medals in 1968 with East Kerry, Johnny was made Captain of the Kerry team for the 1969 campaign and The Kingdom footballers went all the way, with victory over Offaly in the All-Ireland Final providing the Killarney man with the opportunity of being presented with the Sam Maguire Cup. His brilliant full-length diving save from Sean Evans just after half-time sent Kerry on their winning way to their 21st Senior All-Ireland.

In March 1970 he led Kerry on an unbeaten tour as his side played a series of games on a memorable world trip which took them to; Australia, New Zealand, America, Fiji Islands and Hawaii.

His fifth All-Ireland medal came in 1970 when Kerry defeated Meath in the final. The former psychiatric nursing officer played in nine senior All-Ireland finals.

It appears to be forgotten these days but when Johnny retired from the Inter-County playing scene he became manager or 'trainer', as it was then called, of the Kerry team. He held this position for three years. As expected, it was a major disappointment in his first year in charge of Kerry when they lost to Offaly in the replayed All-Ireland Final of 1972. Mick O'Dwyer had punched a point to give Kerry a deserved draw and in the replay it took one of the most remarkable goals ever seen in a final to bury Kerry's hopes. Early in the second half after going two points up, came the score that deflated Kerry's hopes and buried Johnny's dreams of training The Kingdom to victory. It was as bizarre as anything that has ever been seen in Croke Park. The Offaly corner forward Paddy Fenning, lobbed a high centre in the general direction of the canal end goal and as Paud O'Donoghue and Eamon Fitzgerald were caught frozen in a state of indecision, the ball hopped in the square between them and ricocheted into the roof of the net. This was in all probability the one single score that decided Johnny's fate as Kerry trainer. Such is the paper thin line between victory and defeat. Although Kerry lost the Munster Finals of 1973 and 1974 he guided them to successive league titles in 1972, 1973 and 1974, bringing much needed cash to the coffers of the Kerry County Board.

Team trainers back in the early 1970s received little or no recognition. How times have changed! Johnny retired as trainer following a defeat by Cork in the Munster Final played in Killarney in 1974. This game also signalled the final appearance in a Kerry jersey of the magnificent Mick O'Connell.

Shortly after this Mick O'Dwyer became Kerry trainer and the golden era of Kerry football was about to begin. However what has been completely forgotten and completely ignored by writers and GAA historians alike is that under the guidance of Johnny Culloty the seeds of that greatest side ever had already been sown. Culloty, one of the shrewdest brains ever on the Kerry football scene, had seen the light and began to introduce young blood to the side. On that 1974 team beaten by Cork he included; Paudie O'Mahoney, Paudie O'Shea, John O'Keeffe, (Captain), Ger O'Keeffe, Paudie Lynch, Mickey O'Sullivan, Ger Power, John Egan, Jackie Walsh and Mickey Sheehy. It must also be pointed out that all of these up-and-coming young stars helped Kerry win the 1973/74 league title under Culloty and one Pat Spillane won his first league medal as a substitute the same day. The winds of change for Kerry football were well and truly blowing. The Killarney Legion man had laid the most firm of foundations. Johnny's team won three successive National Leagues in 1972, 1973 and 1974 but they couldn't get their hands on the Sam Maguire Cup.

Following a successful stint with trainer Paudie O'Shea as an Under-21 selector, Johnny again answered The Kingdom's call when Jack O'Connor became Senior Team Manager and with his many years of experience he directed the thinking of the management team of Pat Flanagan, Ger O'Keeffe and Jack O'Connor and thus Kerry entered another glorious era of victories. They won the All-Irelands of 2004 and 2006 together with two League titles. Any true blood Kerry supporter will tell you that the Killarney man's vast experience was vital as he directed operations from the sideline. Now his direct involvement with Kerry had stretched from his minor days in 1951 to 2006 – an amazing 55 years. And during all this time he continued to train and coach his clubs under-age and adult teams and still continues to do so to this day.

He has won practically every honour the game can bring. How many players can boast five senior All-Ireland medals, 12 Munster Championship medals, an All-Ireland junior hurling and football medal, five National Football League medals and four Division Two National Hurling League medals. And of course at home in his beloved Kerry he has won top honours in all competitions during his illustrious career. Amazingly when he collected his five Kerry Senior County Championship medals, four football medals with East Kerry and one hurling medal with Killarney, he was playing outfield while being the regular net-minder for Kerry. Such was his versatility. It is extremely doubtful if any other player in history could match a record such as this.

His playing career coincided with that of many Kerry greats including; Mick O'Connell, Donie O'Sullivan, Pat Griffin, John Dowling, Paudie, Niall and Sean Óg Sheehy, Jerome O'Shea, Liam Higgins, Seamus and Sean Murphy, Tadghie Lyne and Mick O'Dwyer. Many of the forwards he faced went on to become legends of the game. Johnny Culloty was also a legend and will be remembered as a great servant of Kerry football and of the Legion Club in Killarney. And all of this despite the fact that he was a most reluctant goalie; preferring to play in outfield positions and a slightly reluctant footballer, preferring hurling as a game!

It must also be recorded that he can be rated as one of the greatest all-round sportsmen that Kerry has ever produced. As well as his expertise at football and hurling he was prolific at basketball, golf, rowing, snooker and billiards. Johnny Culloty's life has been consumed by Kerry football. Unassuming, quite-spoken, a non-drinker and smoker, he is married to Joan and they have two daughters; Brid and Orla and two sons; Donal and Sean both of whom wore the 'Green and Gold'. He has served his county with honour, dedication and distinction.

An Interview with Mick O'Connell

"He abhorred fouling and negative play," said Mick O'Connell.

Dr. Eamonn O'Sullivan was in his senior years when I first came into contact with him in the 1950s. From then until he retired in 1964 I had many pleasant evenings under his tutorage in Fitzgerald Stadium, Killarney.

In those days Kerry teams did not come together for 'collective training' until the Munster Championship was over and won. Dr. O'Sullivan only then got control of the team and the preparations for semi-finals and finals begun in earnest. I myself trained under him for the All-Ireland semi-final against Derry in August 1958. On a very wet day we lost the game. Following that it was almost a full year before we again trained collectively in August of 1959. So when one considers the limited amount of training he had, he produced some amazing results.

There was no question of Dr. O'Sullivan being expected to nurture the footballing skills of the individual players. With the limited time available to him that would have been impossible. His job was to prepare them mentally and physically for the forthcoming contest and at that he exceeded. His training methods were to replicate the type of movement which would go on in a match situation. He put the players through short bursts of exhaustion and recovery interspersed with a certain amount of mobility training. The long distance slogs around the field lap after lap were not for him. The physical preparation of the team was of course, necessary and important but I think that his ability to mentally condition and focus the players on the game ahead was a huge part of his phenomenal success.

Dr. O'Sullivan had a vision for the game of Gaelic football, (which I simply call 'Gaelic'). He had a theory that players should play their 'own sector of play', which meant that defence was the primary job of a defender, scoring or making of scores that of the attacker and midfielders were expected to be good fielders and ball winners. It was generally misconstrued that he was advocating a very rigid non-mobile sort of game. In my own experience he never discouraged or criticized me for moving far from own position at midfield provided it was for the overall advantage of the team. Contrary to what many might have thought I would say that he was always an advocate of good positional play. In fact he was positive in regard to every aspect of the game. In team talks, which he conducted in a calm and dignified way, he placed the emphasis on the way his own (Kerry) team should play and behave. I never heard him talk or discuss counter-tactics – systems to negative the opposition team or individual players. He abhorred fouling and such negative play. I can remember him issuing all of us with a pre-game card with one of the instructions being 'anti-fouling'.

Kerry football and Gaelic football was, I believe, reaching a peak in the 1930s and early 1940s, when Dr. Eamonn's involvement was at its most influential. Although I came later, from my perspective football at that time was being played as it was first destined to be played by instigators of the game. Good fielding, good kicking and letting the ball do the travelling were at the roots of this successful play. I can remember such magnificent players as Paddy Kennedy; his reputation was mighty. He was a midfielder, the position I myself played in. In my travels people could recall the fielding feats of Paddy Kennedy. I doubt if many of the players of later years will be remembered because of any particular aspect of their play. Maurice Fitzgerald is perhaps one of the few exceptions as one who will be remembered because of his kicking abilities.

Dr. Eamonn O'Sullivan was nurtured and programmed by that type of football and he never wavered from it. When I first came into contact with him the solo run had begun to show its ugly head and became more and more common until it had nearly overcome the game. He always adhered to the best form of football but it would almost be looked down on nowadays.

He was quite a young chap when he began training the county in 1924 and in all those following years he steadfastly gave his services to Kerry football. There is no doubt that he had a great influence on the attitude of all the great Kerry footballers that came to the game during his years of influence. This serves as a great tribute to the man himself.

His name seldom comes up in conversation when I talk football because I suppose he was never a man to put himself forward as the kingpin of the whole thing. He was there to assist. He was a very dignified man. You would never see him in the dressing room banging

Dr. Eamonn's father J.P. O'Sullivan, also known as 'The Champion'. The Laune Rangers GAA grounds in Killorglin are named after him.

Eamonn O'Sullivan as a young man.

Graduate Dr. Eamonn O'Sullivan.

Dr. Eamonn and his wife Marjorie.

Left: Dr. Eamonn O'Sullivan's Wedding Day in Killarney on June 17, 1930.

Dr. Eamonn and Marjorie with their sons (from left to right) Robert, Edward, Anthony and James.

Dr. Eamonn and his wife in their later years.

Dr. Eamonn's son Eddie and his wife with family members on their Wedding Day.

Dr. Eamonn and his wife Marjorie at their home in Lewis Road, Killarney.

Dr. Eamonn O'Sullivan with some Bridge trophies. He served as President, Secretary and Chairman of the Killarney Bridge Club.

Left: *St. Brendan's Seminary, Killarney, 1913. Dr. Eamonn had vivid memories of "the wizard of Gaelic football Dick Fitzgerald" coaching the school teams in the skills of kicking points.*

Right: *Dr. Eamonn was also included in this St. Brendans College hurling team in 1914. Dr. Eamonn is in the front row, second from the left.*

Above: *St. Brendan's College Killarney O'Sullivan Cup Winners, 1926, trained by Dr. Eamonn O'Sullivan. Back Row: M. Carroll, J. Moriarty, D. Brosnan, M. Driscoll, D. Sheehan, E. O'Brien, D. Curran. 3rd Row: D. Cronin, M. Foley, T. O'Sullivan, G. O'Connor, T. McGillycuddy, M. Cronin, M. Murphy, T. Moynihan. 2nd Row: G. O'Sullivan, P. Clifford, Dr. Eamonn O'Sullivan, Canon O'Brien, Fr. David Connor, T. Fitzgerald, Bobby Murphy. Front Row: J. McCarthy, W. MacMahon, Dennis Curtin (Captain), Johnny Walsh, N. Healy.*

Dick Fitzgerald captained Kerry to victory in 1913-1914. Fitzgerald Stadium, Killarney is named after him.

Jack Sheehy was on Dr. Eamonn's 1924 winning side.

Dee O'Connell was trained by Dr. Eamonn for the 1926 win over Kildare. He came on to the Kerry side for the replay.

Jerry 'Pluggy' Moriarty – star of Kerry and the Rock Club in Tralee. Jerry played with The Landers' 'Gawksie' Gorman, 'Gal' Slattery and Bracker Regan. He won All-Irelands and a host of Kerry County Championships.

Five Kerry legends captured for posterity in 1924. Left to right: Denny Curran (1903-1904 winning team), Con Brosnan, 'Small Jer' O'Leary, Paul Russell and Pluggy Moriarty. Jerry O'Leary, a close friend of Dr. Eamonn's, was Chairman of the

Kerry Selection Committee in 1936, 1937, 1938 and 1939 and was involved in the purchase of Jones Road, now Croke Park.

Above: *Dr. Eamonn O'Sullivan and Paul Russell in pensive mood, at a Kerry training session in 1953.*

Left: *Paul Russell won six All-Ireland medals, two of which he got in 1924 and 1926, when he was trained by Dr. Eamonn. He later assisted Dr. Eamonn in training some of his teams.*

Dr. Croke's Senior Football Team, 1927. Dr. Eamonn was Secretary of the Club at this time. Back Row, from left to right: Paddy Dillon, Richard Fitzgerald (President), Johnny Donoghue, Pat Meara, Jimmy Foley, Denis Hurley, Paddy Murphy, Paddy Fleming, John Clifford and Dr. Eamonn O'Sullivan (Hon. Sec.). Middle Row: Johnny Clifford, Jack Buckley, Con Meara, Michael Teahon, Harry Turner, Dermot Meara, Charley Fleming, Paul Regan. Front Row: Paddy Healy, Francis O'Connor, Dick Clifford (Captain), Neilus McCarthy, Paddy Looney.

Dee O'Connor and Con Brosnan were two legends of Kerry football trained by Dr. Eamonn. "Hats off to Brosnan, that midfield wonder. He's par excellence with feet and hands. Where is the Gael can bring down the number of Kerry's idol from Newtownsandes." (Poem by Paddy O'Connor).

Johnny Riordan (left) and Joe Barrett (right). Johnny was Dr. Eamonn's goalie in the 1926 win. He also won medals in 1929 and 1930. Danno Keeffe took over in goals in 1931, while Joe Barrett's son Joe Joe also trained with Dr. Eamonn.

Jackie Ryan was one of the stars of Kerry's 1930 win over Monaghan. Dick Fitzgerald died on the Friday before this final.

Johnny Culloty (left) and Fr. Liam Brosnan (right). They were boyhood friends.

Joe Barrett brings home the first Sam Maguire Trophy, in 1929. Joe was one of the stars of Dr. Eamonn's 1924-1926 winning teams. His son Joe Joe played for Kerry in four All-Ireland finals, winning Senior and Under-21 medals.

John Joe Sheehy. His three sons, Niall, Sean Og and Brian, were all trained by Dr. Eamonn. John Joe was winning Captain in 1926; Sean Og was winning Captain in 1962.

Kerry team on board the St. Louis for the 1931 Tour of America. They won all their matches and over 60,000 watched them beat New York in their opening game. Back Row, left to right: Paul Russell, Jackie Ryan, John Joe Landers, Dan Ryan, Tim O'Donnell, 'Pedler' Sweeney, Miko Doyle, Paddy Whitty and Tim Landers. Second Row: Dee Connor, Bob Stack, Tommy Barrett, John Joe Sheehy, Sean McCarthy, Danno Keeffe, Johnny Riordan. Front Row: Eamonn Fitzgerald (also an Olympic athlete), Jack Walsh, Con Brosnan, Con Geaney. (Note the player with the music box left back).

Right:
1931 trophies held by John J. Sheehy – one of the many Kerry legends trained by Dr. Eamonn.

Above: *Micko Doyle star forward on the Kerry four-in-a-row winning team 1929, 1930, 1931 and 1932.*

Left: *Joe Barrett won six All-Irelands, two Táilteann International Championships, four National Leagues, nine Munster Championships and seven County titles in both hurling and football.*

Members of the Killarney Sports Committee pictured during one of their successful events in the Fitzgerald Stadium in the 1930s. Front Row, left to right: P. O'Leary, P. Malone, J. Murphy, F. O'Connor, Dr. J. O'Connor. Back Row, left to right: P. Murphy, D. Courtney, P. 'Squire' Cronin, Dr. E. O'Sullivan (with his son Eddie), P.O'Shea (Cleeny), Supt. B. Harte, W. McSweeney (Killorglan), J. Keogh, D. Fleming, C. Fleming and J. O'Shea.

Eamonn Fitzgerald was a champion athlete and All-Ireland medal winner. He represented Ireland in the 1932 Los Angeles Olympics and finished 4th.

Dr. Eamonn's Captain, Miko Doyle, on the 1937 winning team. Miko won three All-Ireland medals before he was 21.

Kerry's great goal keeper, Danno Keeffe played in 10 All-Ireland finals winning seven of them. Two of these wins, in 1937 and 1946, were under Dr. Eamonn's coaching.

Bottom left: St. Finan's Hospital Killarney Town Cup Winners 1941 trained by Dr Eamonn. Front Row, left to right: Denny McCarthy, Denny Healy, Paddy Moynihan, Paddy 'Dan Mick' O'Sullivan, Denny McSweeney. Second Row: Tim O'Shea, Paddy O'Donoghue, Darby Moynihan, Gerry O'Mahoney, Noel Breen, Dan O'Callaghan. Back Row: Tim Moriarty (Manager), Billy Landers (Mascot), Dee O'Conner, Paddy Murphy, Michael Moynihan, Bill Landers, Paddy Galvin, Dr. Jack O'Conner, Dr. Eamonn O'Sullivan (Trainer). Not Included: James Casey and Tom Lynch.

the table or saying things like: "Go out and beat the other side." He never spoke to the players in a very public sort of way. He encouraged the team always to play positive football. You would never see him parading up and down the sidelines, showing himself off. He spoke to the team beforehand, prepared them, and he would say: "It is the team's day, so let the team do the work."

Nowadays we see too much thuggery both on and off the field which displeases referees, fellow players and trainers. Perhaps if more note of Dr. Eamonn's criticism of fouling and negative play had been taken, this would not go on today.

It was a marvellous achievement to train eight winning teams especially when you think of the constraints he was under at the time. He only got the team later on in the year, July or August and he was expected to produce a fully fit, well-organized team in a number of weeks and win the All-Ireland. Despite the odds being stacked against him, he did just that! That is indeed the proof of the man.

Dr. Eamonn came from the true blue amateur era. He never complained about the amount of time it entailed. Sport was his pastime, he enjoyed it and the game meant something to him. I think that he was wronged by not being made a selector. He was the person who knew the players better than anyone else and of course he should have had a very strong say in the selection of the team taking the field. Just like the captaincy of teams today – I always advocated that the most reliable permanent player should be Captain and he should have a say in matters.

I am told Fitzgerald Stadium, in Killarney, was the brainchild of Dr. Eamonn O'Sullivan way back in the early 1930s. I have happy memories of training under him there many a fine evening, long ago. He was a friendly and dignified man to us young lads. I am delighted this book is being written because he is not forgotten by some of us who got to know him and liked him. He became a kind of father figure to us. It is very important that he will be remembered like this because he did make a great contribution to Kerry football over a very long period. He was not interested in self glorification. He was interested in glory for his county and her people. He has left his stamp on the county and on hundreds of players.

Owen McCrohan on Dr. Eamonn O'Sullivan

The very mention of his name conjures up golden memories. He was the sideline general who gave Kerry teams an aura of invincibility in a distant age when the GAA world reverberated to the sound of Micheal O'Hehir on dreamy Sunday afternoons.

Planet Earth was then a much safer place than it is today, despite the two world wars that had ravaged Europe. Ireland's neutrality had protected the natives against the grim reality of life in troubled places across the globe, which is not to suggest that everything was perfect close to home. It wasn't.

This was a time of communal hardship when money was a scarce commodity. Pitch and toss schools were often abandoned because of a shortage of currency. Foreign holidays were unheard of and the suntan had not yet become a status symbol. Tuberculosis, the scourge of the 1930s, had decimated the flower of a nation's youth. Emigration was in full spate. The GAA, the Catholic Church and the Fianna Fáil Party, all of them traditional corner-stones of Irish society, were firmly entrenched in positions of power.

Gaelic games provided an outlet that helped keep people sane. Paddy 'Bawn' Brosnan was fishing out of Dingle, occasionally berthing his trawler at far-flung places around the coastline, where he would insist that the only training he needed for football was "a few days on dry land" to stretch his legs. Another fisherman, Bobby Beggs of Skerries who won All-Irelands with both Galway and Dublin, was plying his trade out of Ros a' Mhil. McDonagh's timber yard in Galway attracted some good footballers who wanted to earn a crust as well as improve their chances of winning a Celtic cross medal.

Kerry footballers, as is their habit, were winning frequent All-Irelands. Three-in-a-row and even four-in-a-row was the order. To win two titles back-to-back was scarcely worth a mention. Into this primitive milieu was thrust a man who played a significant part in bringing Kerry to a place of football pre-eminence. That man was Dr. Eamonn O'Sullivan. Dr. Eamonn would revolutionize the way that Kerry teams performed in their quest for All-Ireland glory. He also drove confidence levels among supporters to their highest peaks ever, to the extent that Kerry fans fervently believed their team were capable of winning big games whenever they put their minds to it.

That the esteemed mentor was light years before his time is beyond doubt or question. His training regimen was considered superior to anything that had been tried previously and there were some reputable trainers around over the years, men like; Hughie O'Reilly (Cavan), John Dunne (Galway), Jim Barry (Cork) and Peter O'Reilly (Dublin).

It was also noticeable that on the rare occasions when he took a rest (or when he wasn't wanted) that Kerry teams were vulnerable and beatable. The 1947 All-Ireland Final at the Polo Grounds, New York, is the most obvious example. How and why the Kerry County Board of that time found justification for leaving him at home is beyond comprehension. Without his guiding hand the team performance suffered badly; discipline was lax. Cavan won convincingly after trailing by eight points midway through the first half. Kerry were eclipsed by Mayo in 1948 on a score of 0-13 to 0-3 and Clare beat them at Ennis in the first round of the Munster Championship a year later. Before the 1950 semi-final against Louth, two new trainers had been appointed, namely; Tim 'Roundy' Landers and Johnny Walsh. Again Kerry were beaten.

Dr. Eamonn returned to train the teams that beat Armagh and Dublin respectively in the All-Ireland Finals of 1953 and 1955. The 1954 Final went by default when Jackie Lyne was sensationally dropped. Once again the St. Finan's medical guru had been noticeably absent and watched the game from the Hogan Stand. Travelling home on the train later that evening he confided to a friend that the losing team weren't anywhere near as bad as they looked and that they would return to win the All-Ireland inside 12 months. How right he was! This they did with almost the same personnel but with one very notable addition – the good doctor was back in his usual role.

Having trained eight All-Ireland winning teams across five decades Dr. Eamonn's approach to moulding successful teams had stood the test of time. From 1924 to 1964 inclusive, a span of 41 years, his methods were tested against the very best from other counties. Teams like Kildare, Laois, Roscommon, Cavan, Dublin, Mayo and Galway had failed to break the stranglehold that Kerry exerted in football over that period. The only blip in an otherwise impeccable record was when Down in 1961 and Galway in 1964 succeeded in their quest.

Players who came under the influence of Dr. Eamonn O'Sullivan speak of his orderliness, his way with players, his blackboard tactics, his team talks. As a psychiatrist by profession, he knew how to handle the most diverse and volatile of personalities. When a very famous Kerry player 'reared up' and went home after getting fed up listening to him expound on various theories, the trainer kept his cool. He was much too professional to fly off the handle or get involved in a personality clash. The same player realised his mistake instantly and returned the following night to suppress whatever personal feelings he might have held. Obviously, the man in charge inspired that kind of loyalty. His quiet, refined disposition and even temper served him well. You might not agree with everything he said or did but people respected him and went along with him.

When the Kerry players were mobilised for collective training in the 1930s and 1940s, the one constant was Dr. Eamonn. The team would be billeted in Killarney's Park Place Hotel where three square meals a day were provided at the behest of the County Board. Early morning Mass, long walks, football practice at twice daily intervals and early bed time became the norm. For men who worked mostly in the fields or in manual labour this must have provided a welcome respite from the daily grind, however, Kerry's training regimen during those years was no holiday camp – no siree. This was very serious stuff for the times and discipline was strictly enforced to the extent that when Teddy O'Sullivan wanted to go home for a clean shirt he was refused permission to do so.

As a tactician, Dr. Eamonn knew his business. He had devised a system that worked for the type of game that prevailed during his era. His insistence that individual players operate strictly to their nominal positions might sound archaic in the modern world but these tactics had stood the test of time.

Probably the biggest test of these methods came in the 1955 All-Ireland Final against Dublin. It is no secret that Kerry supporters dreaded the possible outcome between full back Ned Roche and the mercurial Kevin Heffernan, who had destroyed the reputations of several leading full backs right through that campaign, most notably the great Paddy O'Brien of Meath. Roche's instructions were to stay on the square, not to be drawn outfield where his lack of pace would be exposed. The towering bulwark that was John Cronin at centre half would act as an indestructible barrier against any marauding Dublin forwards coming through the centre. It helped that Cronin dominated against Ollie Freaney. It also helped that Heffernan, for reasons best known to himself, played an orthodox full forward role that day. Perhaps, he felt confident of beating Roche on a one-to-one basis close to his natural habitat but none of this happened. What did happen was that Ned Roche, the unsung hero of Kerry's success, had a tremendous game and blotted out the threat of his immediate opponent.

How would Dr. Eamonn's tactical acumen and training methods fare in the modern game? Would the high fielding, long kicking Kerrymen of the 1920s, 1930s, 1940s and 1950s, all superb natural footballers, be able to cope with Owen Mulligan, Peter Canavan, Stephen O'Neill, Oisin McConville, Steven McDonnell and Ronan Clarke? These are relevant questions but there are no easy answers. The game is much faster and more fluid now. Fitness levels have been ratcheted up to the ultimate peak. But given the quality of men who played for Kerry right across those decades one could easily make a compelling case for their survival against anything that might be thrown at them in any era of football. Dr. Eamonn had a passionate belief in these men. More than that, he had an unshakeable faith in traditional Kerry football. His unshakeable faith was rarely misplaced.

After Down won the 1960 All-Ireland Final (Kerry's joint trainers that year were Johnny Walsh and Gerald O'Sullivan), their midfielder Joe Lennon wrote in *The Sunday Press* that Kerry football was "ten years out of date". Maybe it was but Kerry teams always came back as they did in 1962 against Roscommon when Dr. Eamonn was again pulling the strings. Kerry football has survived the evolution of the years and under the guidance of this man there is reason to believe that he would have plotted a survival course no matter what the circumstances and regardless of the times. If anyone would have done it, he would.

Padraig O'Sullivan

A Lasting Monument to Dr. Eamonn

Padraig O'Sullivan is currently the Chairman of the Fitzgerald Stadium Committee. Here he pays tribute to Dr. Eamon O'Sullivan:

Dr. Eamonn O'Sullivan was born in Firies. His father J.P. O'Sullivan popularly known as 'The Champion' was born in Brookhill, Beautfort. J.P. married a member of the Spring family who had a business in Firies, hence Dr. Eamonn's birthplace was Firies. J.P. was a very famous athlete in his day and his name was revered throughout the country. In times past it was the county champions of each county that contested the All-Ireland Championship in football and hurling. J.P. O'Sullivan had the honour of captaining the first Kerry team to contest an All-Ireland Football final. He captained the Laune Rangers, Killorglin, in 1892 against Dublin's Young Islanders. The Dublin men were victorious on the day. The Laune Rangers grounds in Killorglin are named after J.P. O'Sullivan and the Firies grounds are called after his son Dr. Eamonn – surly a unique occurrence.

The building of the massive St. Finan's earthen terrace in the Stadium was also Dr. Eamonn's brainchild. This was completed with voluntary assistance of nurses and staff of the Hospital. This is now known as the Michael O'Connor terrace.

Four years ago a plaque was unveiled in the Stadium to commemorate the work of the patients. In my address as Chairman of the Fitzgerald Stadium Committee I was delighted to pay tribute to Dr. Eamonn in stating that he was a man before his time in introducing this type of Occupational Therapy which hastened the entry of patients back into normal lifestyle and helped their discharge from the Hospital.

In 1910 Kerry and Louth qualified for the All-Ireland Final but due to difficulty with the railway company, Kerry refused to travel and Louth were awarded and accepted the Championship. Their next meeting was in the final of The Croke's Memorial Cup which went to a replay and for this second game the County Board sent for

Paddy Breen, a native of Firies, who was working in the General Post Office in London and who had experience of playing soccer with Tottenham Hotspur. It was Paddy's first half-rasping shot to the net that set Kerry on their winning way. Now the great connection with Dr. Eamonn was, that the afore mentioned Paddy Breen later married Dr. Eamonn's sister Mai O'Sullivan and they resided in Beaufort until their deaths.

The receipts from the tickets sales for the two Kerry versus Louth games, added up to a figure of £1,183 (€1,500). This was a wind fall for the Association and it enabled them to buy out Jones Road – now known as Croke Park. That was done towards the end of 1913 at a cost of £3,641 (€4,500).

When Kerry and Louth met that historic year of 1913 the game was played on a rented pitch with no stands and few facilities for spectators. The late Ger O'Leary of Main Street, Killarney and the Dr. Croke's Club, then a member of the Kerry County Board, was involved in this purchase.

I knew Dr. Eamonn personally and would often meet him at Kerry training sessions. He was always anxious to hear other people's opinions on certain players and their best playing positions. During Eamonn's long association with Fitzgerald Stadium, he was always forward-thinking. He succeeded Eugene O'Sullivan as Second Chairman of the Committee. To this day his connections with the Stadium remain very strong indeed. His son James is Patron of the Stadium and his second cousin Ken O'Sullivan, who now resides in the family home at Brookhill, Beaufort, is the current Secretary of the Fitzgerald Stadium Committee.

During the 1980s the late Michael O'Conner was Chairman and I was Treasurer of the Stadium Committee. Through Lotto funding and interest free loan from the Munster Council of the GAA we completed the building of the O'Sullivan Stand, which I trust will remain as a lasting monument to Dr. Eamonn's powers of training successful winning Kerry teams and his contribution in maintaining Kerry's dominance in the senior football roll of honour.

Dr. Eamonn O'Sullivan was without doubt one of Kerry's most remarkable sons.

An Interview with Pat O'Shea

According to Kerry Football Manager Pat O'Shea: "Dr. Eamonn was one of the greatest Kerry men of all time."

Pat O'Shea of the Dr. Croke's Club, Killarney was appointed Manager of the Kerry Senior Football Team this year, 2007. His appointment was in many ways historic especially in relation to this publication on the life and times of Dr. Eamonn. Eamonn trained his last Kerry team for the final against Galway in 1964. It was the one and only loss he had suffered in nine final appearances. Now 43 years later Pat O'Shea becomes the first Dr. Croke's man since his former legendary club-mate to take over the management of the county side. It must be pointed out of course that in Eamonn's time he was referred to as the 'Trainer'. Pat O'Shea is referred to as the 'Manager'. An outstanding sportsman himself, Pat played a huge part in his club's All-Ireland win in Croke Park in 1992. He was also a prolific hurler and basketball player. So what are his views on his legendary predecessor, Dr. Eamonn O'Sullivan?

In Pat O'Shea's Own Words

I would often have read our club's history and other publications as well as talked to my own father Murt and questioned others about the importance of Dr. Eamonn O'Sullivan in relation to our club and in regards to his training of Kerry as well. He was a hugely iconic figure, especially for younger people like me. A kind of mythical figure to our younger generation, Dr. Eamonn was a man who came and did something unbelievably extraordinary with the successes he had and all his extraordinary achievements. Looking back I suppose only Mick O'Dwyer would have followed in his footsteps. Dr. Eamonn was a powerful man not only in the GAA but also outside it as well. He was very influential I would say in the town of Killarney and in the life in Kerry.

Many people remark that he has been largely forgotten. This must be down to the time in which he trained Kerry and worked here. The lack of newspaper coverage, television coverage or local radio coverage, not to mention, the fact that historical documents were not retained could be factors in this public amnesia. Ireland was a completely different country as well – let's not forget that. We lived in a different time; it was easy to forget people back in those far off days. Today we are very fortunate that you are writing a book on Dr. Eamonn as that will give us all the opportunity to examine his life. There is a lot written about all the present players and managers but this was not so with Dr. Eamonn. Information about him was passed on by word of mouth but not enough was written about him. Perhaps there was information out there but never before has it been assembled to the degree that it will be in this book.

In relation to my own club I must say that the young people have little idea as to what Dr. Eamonn achieved. Now I would know because I would have taken a great interest in his life and our club patron, John Moynihan, would have given us a lot of information about Dr. Eamonn. The late 1920s was a unique time as the formation of the Killarney Legion Club was taking place. This club would soon become the dominant team while The Croke's Club went into decline. John Moynihan told us stories of how difficult it was to keep the show on the road as The Legion were the best and the side everyone wanted to beat. All of this was around the period when Dr. Eamonn was training Kerry. Even though he was the great trainer at that time our club was struggling to keep going and that, to me, was very strange and unusual as well.

The man was obviously ahead of his time (a phrase many times repeated by the people interviewed for this publication) and he appeared to have been very forward thinking in terms of events that were going to happen and facilities that were going to be needed. He was able to look around the community and see what was required. He touched everything, not only the GAA. He set up structures, he started to work with people and I am told he had a unique gift of bringing others with him. At that particular time, back in the early part of the last century, we did not have the magnificent golf courses we have today. There was no football stadium; the GAA here in East Kerry had to play in the local cricket pitch. Now suddenly you had this magnificent Fitzgerald Stadium which could accommodate massive crowds, a golf course that was the envy of the country and with it, Killarney became an even more popular place to come to. I will go as far to say that you could trace the continued growth of tourism back to what Eamonn had developed because people had something different to come to Killarney for. I must also emphasis that he seemed to have an understanding of what was needed. Very few people in life have that amazing ability but Dr. Eamonn had it.

Just imagine if he had not led the drive in building Fitzgerald Stadium – what would have happened? Would we have the great interest in the GAA that we have today? The more you look at achievements such as this, the more you come to admire Dr. Eamonn. I would go as far as to say that if it was not for the building of Fitzgerald Stadium, the GAA here in Killarney and indeed Kerry would not be what we know today. Look at it from the point of footballers training and their training facilities – the ability to be able to train, perform and display the skills of the game on one of the best surfaces in the country and be allowed to utilise that surface at any time was of tremendous benefit to all. Compare this to today, where Kerry still don't have their own exclusive training ground and yet our players are expected to perform at the very highest level.

Look at the premiership clubs in England and the facilities they have now. Don't forget back in the 1930s and 1940s when the Stadium was built and developed, it was the 'Old Trafford' of the time. It was the best stadium in the country and maybe even in Europe. What Eamonn did, with the help of my club and the patient's and staff of the Mental Hospital has had massive repercussions since, making the whole district of East Kerry and the County think differently of Gaelic games. As far as I am aware not one club around here had their own club grounds then and all were allowed to play in the Stadium as much as possible. This helped all clubs develop and grow. If the Stadium had not been built, what would have happened? Yes, clubs would have progressed and eventually developed but it was Eamonn's dream that laid the great foundation for football in East Kerry and beyond.

While there were other people who may have had that dream of building such a magnificent stadium in the heart of Killarney and the county and indeed all of Munster, he was the one person who was capable of making that seemingly impossible dream come true. One must remember always the time that all this work was carried out. There were no bulldozers, no giant excavators, huge lorries, etc, all done by hand. It really was unbelievable.

Eamonn gave a sense of purpose to the community, Occupational Therapy to the patients of St. Finan's and indeed a great pride in his club and county. Without the Stadium Killarney would not be the same place. Today Fitzgerald Stadium is as famous as the Lakes of Killarney and that is saying a lot.

I am conscious that I am the first Dr. Croke's man since Dr. Eamonn to be in charge of a Kerry senior team and it's hugely gratifying to follow in the footsteps of such a person. Obviously I will never fill his shoes because, for one thing, I will not be around as long as he was. From a club perspective it is a great honour to follow in the footsteps of such a legendary man and I am so proud of the fact that I have gotten the opportunity to do that. Let me add that what Dr. Eamonn has achieved no one will be achieving in the future.

I am very conscious of his training methods having read he's wonderful book, *'The Art and Science of Gaelic Football'*. Believe it or not a lot of his philosophy has not changed. Much of his thinking is still in vogue. He brought the teams together for 'collective training' before semi-finals and finals. Now counties are going to Spain and Portugal to do collective training for a week. He instigated this idea of bringing all the players together for a particular length of time. Now it's called 'bonding', and we are told it's more important than the twice nightly sessions. Dr. Eamonn could see all of this way back in his time. He had amazing vision. His whole approach to his players such as, 'rest and recovery' and understanding each player on an individual basis was way ahead of its time. He even talked about a possible link with Australian football in the future. Now it's a reality today.

Despite the fact that I never met him, Dr. Eamonn would have been one of my heroes. I think he stands up there as one of the greatest Kerry people of all time because of what he achieved, not alone in the area of football but what he did outside of it. Most people have tunnel vision regarding what they want to achieve. In contrast, Dr. Eamonn had an array of visions regarding what he hoped to achieve. It must be said that he made everybody's life, regardless of whether you played GAA or not, more enjoyable.

Yes without a shadow of doubt he was a man far, far ahead of his time. He deserves to be remembered forever.

The Story of Phil O'Sullivan

Phil O'Sullivan was Kerry Captain in 1924. A lesser known fact is that he was also responsible for Dr. Eamonn training his first Kerry team.

The story of Phil O'Sullivan and his part in persuading Dr. Eamonn to take over the training of the Kerry team is one that was very nearly lost in the mists of time. Indeed, only for the coming to light of Eamonn's fascinating '*Self-Outline of Biographical Details*' included in this publication and thanks to the generosity of his family, it is extremely doubtful if we would have discovered that it was Phil who was responsible for the single greatest appointment to the Kerry GAA scene. It is my own experience over 50 years or so that practically nobody is aware that it was the man from Tuosist who began Eamonn on his remarkable career as Kerry trainer. The exemplary long-serving Kenmare District Board Chairman, Mick Granville, who did such a magnificent job in the research for the following article on Phil O'Sullivan, was greatly surprised when I informed him of Phil's part in Eamonn's appointment to the post of trainer. And this was even despite the fact that Mick possessed complete detailed knowledge on the life of the 1924 Kerry Captain from Tuosist.

Eamonn wrote of that historic period in 1925 when Phil persuaded him to take over the team: "Qualifying in my final medical examination in March 1925, I had arranged to take out a three month Post Graduate course in the world famous Coombe Gynaecological Hospital. It was immediately prior to this that my old friend, the late 'Phileen' O'Sullivan announced to the Kerry team (who had arranged to play a trial game against Wexford towards the end of March) that I would train them for their 1924 All-Ireland Final against the holders Dublin which was not played until April 1925. Needless to emphasize I thought that Phil was joking, but he soon set me right when I took my residence with both the Senior and Junior teams in O'Grady's Hotel, Ashe Street, Tralee."

Eamonn's career as one of the greatest names in the annals of the Association had commenced thanks to the great foresight of a youthful Kerry footballer. Eamonn was just 28 years old when he trained his first winning Kerry team. This in itself is an amazing statistic and to my knowledge he is the youngest person ever to train an All-Ireland winning senior county team.

Neatly resting at the foot of the Caha Mountains lies Glenmore Lake, on whose south-westerly shore is situated the former local National School, now a youth hostel. It was here that Phil O'Sullivan, one of Kerry's great captains, was born in 1897. His father, John F. O'Sullivan, a man of great strength and athletic ability, was the local school teacher.

According to oral tradition, Phil was a man of exceptional talent that few written records uncover. He was an outstanding footballer and hurler, a great athlete, intelligent, courageous, and a man who had reckless pluck and tenacity. Stories about the lengths to which he went to perfect his skills are legendary, and not all fictitious. The record books of Gaelic football recall the magnificent game he played for Kerry, which he captained in the 1924 All-Ireland against Dublin. Not so well documented, though, is the story of the man who brought fame and honour to his native parish of Tuosist.

It is only natural that a man of such great talents would have reams of stories trailing after his memory about his youthful activities in his own locality and beyond. Doubtless some of these have suffered from exaggeration down through the years, while others have retained their authenticity since their actual occurrence. A few of the latter will be sufficient to expose the true character of the man.

It is said that he could swim the length and breadth of Glenmore Lake, which is nearly a mile long by half-a-mile in width and thanks to Phil's persuasive methods of teaching, the majority of his schoolboy companions were also good swimmers. He would throw them into a deep part of the lake and make them splash their way to safety, while he swam close by in case assistance was required.

In the lake lies the island of 'Oilean a Tighe'. The island was named after a house that is built on it. At that time a contest would be held in the locality from time to time to see who could throw a stone from the mainland and hit the house on the island. Phil O'Sullivan is reputed to have been the only man to accomplish this feat of strength.

Apart from being an outstanding footballer and hurler, he was also a very fine athlete and excelled in the 100 and 220 yard dash, the long jump, the hop-step-and-jump, and weight throwing. On one occasion, at a sports meeting in Adrigole (which he walked to over the Healy Pass as there was no road there at the time), he tied with his opponent in the final of the 100 yards dash. A dispute arose, with both claiming victory. Phil proposed that the prize money be divided, but his opposite number refused to co-operate. Finally it was decided to re-run the race. The contestants were allowed a rest during which time the man from Glenmore went for refreshments, of a strong nature, and in the re-run Phil came in a clear winner.

His fame as a footballer and athlete was known far and wide, but it once nearly cost him his life. In 1921 he was in Johnny Shea's Pub in Glengarriff, now Doc Ryan's, with his brother-in-law, Florry O'Sullivan, a native of Kilgarvan. At that time the Black and Tans had their headquarters in Eccles Hotel and on the same occasion three of them were in O'Shea's Pub.

On the same day some members of the West Cork Flying Column were waiting in ambush outside Glengarriff for a Tan patrol. The ambush was later called off when the patrol failed to turn up. Three members of the Flying Column went into Glengarriff that evening to seek information on the Tans. Whether by design or coincidence, they went into O'Shea's Pub. As they entered one of them saluted Phil O'Sullivan by name. A short time later the Tans left, followed almost immediately by the three members of the Column. Outside the pub a skirmish broke out and in the exchange of fire one Tan was killed, one wounded and one of the Flying Column wounded.

The surviving Tan escaped and raised the alarm at his headquarters. Reinforcements were immediately rushed to O'Shea's Pub where the surviving Tan pointed out Phil O'Sullivan as the one to whom a member of the Column spoke. He was taken outside the door to be shot, which was one of their normal methods of retaliation. Johnny O'Shea insisted that the Column knew him only because of his popularity as a footballer. Had it not been for O'Shea interceding on his behalf and insisting on his innocence, there is no doubt that he would have been shot, as similar incidents happened on numerous occasions throughout Ireland during the Tan War.

During his playing career there were no county or local leagues such as we have today, but many challenge games were played. He played with UCD and Faughs in Dublin during his student days. Later, he played Championship football with Ballymacelligott, where he was employed as a teacher and won the county title in 1923, thus enabling him to become Captain of the Kerry team in the following year. He also played hurling with his native Lauragh in local challenge games.

His main mode of transport was the bicycle and his journey home from Ballymac was done in two stages. He came with his bicycle, by train to Kenmare and cycled from there to Glenmore. However, the return journey to Ballymac was done entirely on the bicycle, a distance of approximately 65 miles. It was usually well past midnight before he set out on his journey, as the day's sporting activities had to be discussed with the locals before leaving. On many occasions he cycled to and from Ballymac, and the journey was not always lacking in adventure. On one of his return journeys one night, he came across a group of Travellers camped on the roadside and Phil, possibly full with more spirits than the spirit of devilment, decided to pay them a visit. He wasn't received with overflowing hospitality and a resulting fight with one of his ungrateful hosts ended in a draw. In later years, Phil said that he was one of the best men he ever met.

However, it is as a footballer that he is best remembered. Carbery in his book *'Famous Captains'* (1947) refers to him as "a muscular man, 5'10", weighing 13 stone. He was an outstanding wing-back, a strong resolute tackler, safe fielder, strong kicker. He beat some of football's finest wingers and was a good hurler as well." His first recorded appearance in the 'Green and Gold' was with the Kerry Juniors in 1915. Kerry and Westmeath met in the final played in Athlone on August 20. The final score was Kerry 0-6, Westmeath 1-2, with Kerry scoring the winning point in the dying moments of the game. In the line-out, Phil O'Sullivan is listed as playing in the right half-back position. He was now 18 years of age and approaching what would be remembered as some of the best years of his playing career.

However, historical events from 1916 onwards seemed to have had an effect on activities on the Kerry playing fields, and it was many years before sporting activities returned to normal in The Kingdom. During this period many Kerry Gaels were interned in different internment camps – Ballykinlar and Frongoch, South Wales, being two of the more notorious ones. This had a weakening effect on GAA activities in Kerry and is evident in the county's absence from the All-Ireland scene from 1915, when Wexford beat them 2-4 to 2-1, until the 1923 Final, which they lost to Dublin, 1-5 to 1-3, played on September 28, 1924.

From the above, it is safe to assume that Phil O'Sullivan would have appeared in the 'Green and Gold' at senior grade long before his recorded appearance in the 1923 All-Ireland Final and possibly would have been the holder of more than two All-Ireland medals, had Ireland enjoyed a more peaceful era between 1916 and 1923.

In the 1923 All-Ireland against Dublin, he played full back, a position he retained for the 1924 All-Ireland semi-final against Mayo – the final score: Kerry 2-4, Mayo 0-1. In the same year, he filled the right full back position for Munster who defeated Leinster in the final.

The most memorable occasion of his playing career was the 1924 All-Ireland Final, played on April 26, 1925, the year he filled the role

of Captain. It was for this match that Phil benefited from the aid of
Eamonn as team trainer. It was a final that aroused great enthusiasm
throughout the country. Croke Park was specially resurfaced and
excursions were arranged from all nooks of Ireland. In addition to the
number who went by road, 3,706 travelled by train from Kerry. The
attendance of 30,000 broke all previous records, with gate receipts
amounting to £2,563.

This was a final which meant something special to the people of
the district of Kenmare, not just to the people of his native Tuosist.
Their spirit glowed with pride and exultation at the thought of their
newly crowned hero leading the men in the 'Green and Gold' onto
Croke Park. That man out there was one of them, and this gave
them a glorious feeling of involvement. Joe Lyne remembers the
momentous occasion quite well: "On the morning of the All-Ireland,
a large contingent of supporters left Lauragh in the early hours of
the morning on the first leg of their journey to Kenmare, where they
boarded the train at 7 o'clock, arriving in Dublin around one. The
round trip cost 10 shillings and 6 pence. This may not seem very
much in our days of rapid inflation, but 10 shillings at that time was
considered a good weekly wage."

As his local supporters waited for the game to commence, victory
or defeat did not matter – it was enough for the moment that their
newly crowned hero was out there leading his men.

'P.F.' (Paddy Foley) in his book, *'Kerry's Football Story'* says the
following about the game: "The 1924 Final was a terrific struggle.
Twenty minutes had gone before Dublin had opened the scoring with
a point. Kerry equalized two minutes later. Again Dublin pointed and
Kerry levelled. A free just before the short whistle put Kerry leading
three points to two … Feature of the match was the sterling play of
Phil O'Sullivan, Joe Barrett and John Murphy in Kingdom's last line
of defence."

The following is a brief extract on the match from *The Cork
Examiner*, Monday, April 27, 1925: "The display of football was
superb, clean and brilliant. To the end almost the issue was in doubt
… To say they [Kerry] deserved it and that Dublin had hard luck is the
best way to pass the compliment. Both teams were game and manly.
They knew the game and played it. The Kerry backs were mainly
responsible for the victory, the defences having been superb. Burke
[from Dublin] was a source of danger, but Phil O'Sullivan responded
with effect."

It is interesting to note that in these two reports on the game that
Phil O'Sullivan is one of the few to be singled out for praise, which is
testimony to the man's playing ability.

In 1925 Kerry were once more on their way to contest the All-Ireland after defeating Cavan in the semi-final at Tralee on August 23. The final score was Kerry 1-7 : Cavan 2-3, a Kerry back having scored one of Cavan's goals. Since there was no broadcasting at that time, some of the Cavan supporters released carrier pigeons from the Tralee sports field to convey the results of the game back home.

Kerry's All-Ireland hopes suffered a severe setback a few days later when the Kerry County Board received a letter from Mr. Fay, Secretary of Cavan County Board. It read as follows: "My committee claim the match on the grounds that Phil O'Sullivan, who played with Kerry, was a suspended player, he already having played with UCD and Faughs in Dublin League Championship in 1925, the necessary transfer not being granted from the former to the latter club."

The question of his legality was considered at a meeting of the Kerry Selection Committee on the Sunday morning before the match. The committee accepted Phil O'Sullivan's version that concluded: "If I am illegal, Smith and Murphy are illegal also." Kerry's contention was that Phil O'Sullivan was playing hurling for Faughs who had no football team, and football for UCD in 1925. However, Cavan maintained that twelve months should have elapsed from the time he played hurling with UCD, before he could play with Faughs. A strong appeal was made to Cavan to withdraw the objection, but the Chairman said he had no doubt Phil O'Sullivan was illegal and upheld the objection. Kerry then lodged a counter objection to J. P. Murphy of Cavan. On a majority vote of the Central Council, Cavan were declared illegal also and ruled out of the Championship.

Needless to say the objection was the main topic of conversation in Kerry GAA circles for some time afterwards. Terrier coursing was popular in the county at that time, and the name 'Cavan's Objection' was given to a well-known Kerry Blue who ran successfully at most of these meetings. Phil O'Sullivan must have regretted he was the cause of Kerry's suspension from the All-Ireland, and also the chance of his colleagues winning an All-Ireland medal.

Still, Kerry were back in the All-Ireland Final the following year, this time against Kildare. He lined out at centre field in this final, an unusual position for a man who played most of his inter-county football in the full back line. But one of his teammates, the late John Joe Sheehy, R.I.P., once said of Phil O'Sullivan: "In any position that Kerry were experiencing difficulties at, all they need do was switch Phil to that position and the problem no longer existed." This, possibly, explains why be was picked at centre field, because in this final, Larry Stanley, who was centre field for Kildare, was more than a handful for any opponent. At half-time Phil O'Sullivan retired with a knee injury.

The game ended in a draw: Kerry 1-3, Kildare 0-6.

Many of the greatest players of these decades lined out in the Tailteann Games of 1924, 1928 and 1932 and the distinction of playing for Ireland in international matches became a prize of great importance for those honoured. Phil O'Sullivan was one of the chosen few. In 1924, together with his Kerry teammates Con Brosnan and Jim Baily, he lined as Ireland beat England.

In 1927 Phil travelled to New York with the Kerry team. It was here he first met Kathleen O'Mahoney, who was playing the piano at a reception for the visiting Kerry team. It was love at first sight and they later married. Kathleen had been born 18 years earlier in Tipperary and emigrated to the USA when orphaned at a young age. Like many exiles at that time Phil spent the greater part of his life in America. He returned to Glenmore on a few occasions and died in America in 1952.

Today Phil O'Sullivan lies at rest in Calvary Cemetery, New York, far from his native Glenmore. His grave is marked by a marble headstone erected by his many friends at home and abroad.

Go nDeanfaid Dia trocaire ar a anam.

In 1965 the Tuosist GAA Club named their sports field 'The Phil O'Sullivan Memorial Park', a fitting tribute to the memory of a great sportsman.

(Our thanks to all those who gave information, no matter how small, to help compile this article, and a special word of thanks to Mr. Joe Lyne and Mr. Dick Smith of Lauragh and Mr. William Cousins, Kenmare. Also, P.F's book *'Kerry's Football Story'* was an invaluable source of reference. In particular thanks to Mick Granville without whose help this tribute would not have been possible.)

A Tribute to Tadghie Lyne

THE PRINCE OF FORWARDS

In 1955 Tadghie Lyne, trained and coached by Eamonn, helped power Kerry to one of their most memorable ever All-Ireland victories over the indestructible Dublin team in a final that is still spoken about to the present day as one of the most unforgettable football finals ever. Tadghie gave one of the greatest ever displays that day and some of his point kicking was equal to and some say even surpassed anything that was ever seen in Croke Park. Maurice Fitzgerald in 1997 was for me reminiscent of that exhibition.

The very mention of his name evokes a multitude of memories. Growing up in Killarney of the 1950s, he was my first real life sporting hero. I can still see him in my mind's eye; superbly fit, tall and rangy, dark hair slicked back, kicking points from all distances and angles. One fleeting glance at the goal posts was all he needed before kicking what seemed like radar controlled high arching points, which was his trade mark. It was a beautifully natural skill that had been perfected over many hours of practice in Fitzgerald Stadium and at his father's garage in High Street. What an honour it was to be requested to act as ball boy and return the one ball available to the great man as he practiced the skills that would propel him to three Senior All-Ireland medals (1953, 1955 and 1959), Kerry's top scorer for three years and a host of other honours.

The all-round sportsman, Tadghie Lyne won an All-Ireland basketball medal with Kerry in 1957. But he was also a star at pitch and putt, snooker, billiards and athletics as well as representing Munster and Ireland in football.

A quiet, shy person, he rarely, if ever, gave interviews, and while he had been in deteriorating health for some time his death at his home on Killarney Road, Castleisland on May 31, 2000 came as a great shock to his family and huge circle of friends and admirers. He was 69 years old.

However, on one lucky occasion Tadghie acquiesced to an interview request. So I found myself in Tadghie's home conducting an interview for my Radio Kerry *Terrace Talk* Show, an interview that is now, in retrospect, a vital documentation in the history of Kerry football. I say this because to the best of my knowledge it is the only available question and answer discussion on record with one of Kerry's greatest ever footballers, the man so fittingly hailed as 'The Prince of Forwards'.

He was born in Sunnyhill, Killarney, one of three boys and two girls. His mother was Nellie Flynn from Firies. She came from a family of seven girls and two boys while his father Jerome was a Kilgarvan man and as Tadghie recalled, "played a bit of hurling."

He attended school at the Presentation Monastery and St. Brendan's College where his early football powers were soon noticed. However he did not get on the Kerry Minor side of his year but he did help The Sem. to win two Dunloe Cups and a Munster Championship.

His boyhood friends in the Killarney of the 1930s and 1940s included; Mickey Doc O'Donoghue, Dan O'Keeffe, Murt O'Shea, Bill Landers, and John O'Connor, and it was his great friend Murt O'Shea who influenced him to join Dr. Croke's Club. He gave great service to Dr. Croke's until he transferred to Castleisland Desmonds in 1960, following his marriage to Mary who hailed from that town. While he was to go on to become one of the greatest forwards in the game, Tadghie began his career in defence.

In this unique interview with the author, Tadghie explains why 1955 was not his fondest memory and he talks at length about the influence Dr. Eamonn O'Sullivan had on him:

"I started playing with the Killarney Minors at left half back, it was okay but I loved the forwards and my favourite position was left half forward. Eamonn was a great trainer and Paul Russell was with him for the 1955 Final. If you were overweight you got a gruelling. Paudie Sheehy and I were always well up in the sprints and we could take it easy for the heavy training. We were staying in St. Brendan's College that year and before the Cavan semi-final a gang of us decided we would go to Puck Fair for the night. About 14 of us went back in a lorry and the following day we got a fierce gruelling. Eamonn was all about sprinting because 'get the ball first' was his motto. 'We all had our own little half acre on the field to mind and we were left with that and if you roamed from your own square he would give out to you. Don't worry about the man next door, there's someone minding him and if you keep to your own half-acre we will keep on winning' – this was Dr. Eamonn's motto.

I was at my peak in 1955; I scored the first point, getting the ball from the late John Dowling. It was great just to beat Dublin alone. However my fondest memory is the first All-Ireland I won in 1953 against Armagh. I was all nerves at the start and wanted to come off but Eamonn told Colm Kennelly and Donie Murphy to play the ball to me and I got a few catches and I settled down. Bill McCorry missed the penalty, I don't remember much more, but that was my favourite memory."

The one characteristic that separated Tadghie from the greats of his era was his magnificently distinctive style of kicking. How can one describe it? It was like Maurice Fitzgerald, Pat Spillane and Mickey Sheehy all rolled into one and in his interview he revealed his fascinating secret. He talks about his father's garage situated at the top of High Street, Killarney, where Andy O'Sullivan's Carpet and Furniture Store now operates. So I put it to him: "How did you become so accurate?"

"Every evening when the garage closed I would hang two footballs off the rafters with ropes about three inches from the ground and hit them with my left and right legs, trapping them as they swung back. I would do that for about an hour every night until I perfected my style. I would have to follow through to precision; it is the follow through that that makes the kick. If you don t follow through, the ball can go anywhere, so that's how I did it. I also practiced putting spin on the ball to the left or right, this is very difficult to do but you get used to it after lots of practice and I used it a lot in my career," the great Tadghie Lyne revealed.

On Sunday September 11, 1955, before a record semi-final attendance of 71,504 people Kerry met Cavan in a replay. On the same day Dublin took on Mayo, also in a replay. Three weeks before Kerry had been extremely fortunate to draw with Cavan and it was in this game that Tadghie Lyne scored the goal that he remembers as maybe not the greatest but certainly the most important he had ever scored for Kerry. Few will argue with his choice, as it was instrumental in Kerry winning the title that year. Tadghie recalls that magic moment thus:

"Peter O'Donoghue was a deadly kicker of points and he had Cavan ahead with five minutes left and they were all over us. Then Johnny Culloty crossed a high ball, I got to it first and sent it to the net. We were a point ahead against the run of play but Keyes scored for them to draw the match. We won the replay easily. Johnny scored a goal in that game when I centred the ball for him. Those two matches brought us on a ton and we were flying for the final against Dublin.

I was in great form that year and in the Munster Final against

Cork, in Killarney, Paudie Sheehy and I scored nine points between us as we won by two points. I loved playing against Cork. Paddy O'Driscoll and Denis Bernard were the two men who used to be looking after me, you knew you were going to get it hard but you took it and gave back the very same. O'Driscoll was one of the best men I ever marked. Of course the Dr. Croke's man knew the Fitzgerald Stadium like the back of his hand and I put it to him that playing at home was a great advantage and he fully agreed with this assertion.

I knew every blade of grass in Killarney and in the 1953 Munster Final I had my best game ever against Cork. I kicked six points that day. This time I knew the pitch like the back of my hand. Tom Ash and Sean Kelly got the two goals. I remember there were 17 special trains to Killarney for the day. Jas Murphy, John Cronin, Jim Brosnan, Donal 'Marcus' O'Neill, Ned Roche and Jackie Lyne were also on that side."

Again the question of how he perfected his magnificent kicking with both left and right legs came up and he revealed another aspect of his secret. I had seen him kicking points from the corner flag while training on his own in the Stadium, 40 years earlier and I have never seen any footballer do likewise with such ease and regularity in all the intervening years. I can vividly recall in the 1958 All-Ireland semi-final in torrential rain against Derry (which Kerry lost), Tadghie racing up the wing on a typical solo run and from the corner flag dropping the rain sodden old pig-skin football with his left leg right on top of the crossbar. This image remains etched in my memory but his answer to my query confirmed that my memories of those far off summer evenings were not figments of my youthful imagination.

"It was all down to practice. I did it with my right leg and with my left leg. I would start on the 21, kicking frees and off my hands. I would then work all the way out to the 50, first in the centre and then to the left and right of the posts. Standing about 40 yards out I would pick a spot on the crossbar, the bit with the dab of paint in the middle, and try to pinpoint that with my kick. You would get more accurate all the time. A few young fellows would then kick the ball back out to me again. Yes I would also practice from the corner flag and perfected this kick also."

Don't forget that the Killarney man was Kerry's top scorer in 1955, 1956 and 1959, while his total for Kerry in 1955 was 5-42 (57 points) in 14 games, and average of 4.07 points per game – fantastic kicking in any man's language. Following such a long and distinguished playing career one fairly obvious question for the Kerry legend was if he had any regrets as he looked back on his career. I certainly did not expect the answered I got, and in fact he left me slightly stunned as he revealed something previously unknown about himself.

"There is one thing I often wonder about. Shortly after the 1953 Final three fellows called to the garage in High Street. They were scouts from Glasgow Celtic and they asked me if I would go to the club for a six months trial. I discussed it with my father, but he was against it and he refused to let me go. Of course, I will forever wonder how it would have worked out for me."

At the height of his greatness Tadghie was chosen three years in a row – 1954, 1955 and 1956, for the Irish team that played the Combined Universities, which was the equivalent of today's All-Stars. He captained them in 1956, and among the galaxy of idols lining out with him were celebrated names such as; Jack Mangan, Bill Casey, Nace O'Dowd, Brian Morgan, Art O'Hagan, Stephen White, Jim Crowley, Dessie Ferguson, Aidan Brady, Paddy Prendergast, Paddy O'Brien, Tom Langan and the great Iggy Jones. He was also a regular on the Munster team during his golden era of the 1950s.

Tadghie had no hesitation recalling his best game ever on the local scene when his exciting talents were first unveiled with the Dick Fitzgerald's team that won the County Championship in 1951. Earlier that season in his favourite stomping ground, Fitzgerald Stadium, he gave a memorable display against Iveragh scoring points from all angles, near and far.

"This was easily my best game at local level and everything I kicked seemed to go over. I was marked by Joe Lennon of Renard who I recognized as a very good footballer. Dan Kavanagh was on that side as was Donal Prendeville, Teddy O'Connor, Connie Riordan, Gerald Teahan and Donal 'Marcus' O'Neill was in goal. We won 3-8 to 2-3 and beat Dingle in the final. I also played in the county hurling final two months later when Crotta beat us. Denis O'Brien, Ben Campion, Jackie Lyne, Joe Boyd and Martin Cleary were on that team. I liked the bit of hurling.

When I was young I would always go up to the field with Billy Myers on his bike and mind his boots for him, back in the 1930s and 1940s. Jackie Lyne was becoming very strong at that time and then you had one of the best backs of all time, Bill Casey. Bill would have made a great athlete, especially over the hurdles as he had a very long loping stride and was a great runner. I thoroughly admired Batt Garvey for his strength and along with Myers and Healy would have made the greatest full back line of all time, I would say.

In my own time then you had great players like Tom Long, John Dowling, Mick O'Connell, Mick O'Dwyer, Johnny Culloty and Paudie Sheehy. Outside of Kerry there was Gerry O'Malley of Roscommon, Jim McKeever, Paddy O'Brien, Kevin Heffernan, Mick Cahill from Tipperary, Mick Tubridy from Clare and my friend in Tyrone Iggy Jones, who for a small man was brilliant.

There was also a little fellow in Killarney and a great friend of mine, Freddie Murphy, from Legion. He was a hard man to shake off and another fellow down in Caherceiveen called the 'Dasher' O'Connor was also very hard to get away from."

On the night the interview was broadcast tributes flowed in for one of Kerry's greatest footballers. Renowned author, journalist, and football historian Owen McCrohan, from Valentia, paid this fitting tribute:-

"Above all others Tadghie was the man who coloured my youthful imagination, and I feel privileged to have seen some of the best moments of his career with club and county. He had an incredible range of pure natural skills, his reading of the game was fabulous and his ball control was flawless. He had a superb deceptive turn of speed, a baffling side step and an intuitive instinct for being in the right place at the right time, and his kicking with left or right was phenomenal. He was an impeccable sportsman and in every facet of the game he lived up to my estimation of a hero."

Basketball began in Killarney in 1951 and Tadghie Lyne became an instant hit, helping Killarney Town to three county titles while his club side 'The United' was one of the very first great Kerry basketball teams. Consisting of John C. Cooper, Danno Keeffe, Murt and Sean O'Shea, John Joe Sheehan, John O'Shea, Liam Brosnan and Sean O'Sullivan, they were practically unbeatable and Tadghie was the star.

He was also a regular on the Kerry side leading them to Munster and All-Ireland titles alongside; Paddy Culligan, Tim Dorgan, Eddie Barry and Jerome O'Shea during those great years of the mid-1950s. Other fond memories of him also involve his years with another legendary side 'The Jokers' in which his late brother Mickey Joe played. Eamon O'Donoghue, Jackie Looney, Jimmy Redpath and Michael Courtney were also involved in that side which got its name following a game of poker in the local Parish Hall.

Tadghie had this unique style of scoring with a long underhand looping throw from the half way line of the now demolished Killarney Town Hall. He was a wonderful basketball player, very strong and an immense rebounder from both baskets. However, he made it very plain that Dr. Eamonn O'Sullivan did not take too kindly to him playing the game. "He taught it was too hard on the feet and that both games did not mix and I was using different muscles for both but fair play to him he did not stop me from playing. It gave footballers great vision on the field and kept us fit in the winter. In 1957 I was on the panel that won the All-Ireland Basketball title, played on the same day as the National League Final against Galway. I had just undergone an appendix operation and should not have played in the football. We lost that day to Galway but won the basketball, but I did not play in that final."

Bishop of Kerry Bill Murphy also paid his tribute to the Kerry great: "If I was picking a team of the best footballers I have seen I would certainly have him on at left half forward. It would be very hard to keep him off any best 15 of Irish footballers. We had great admiration for him when I was in St. Brendan's. He was a real gentleman, he was very quiet and shy and not a show off in any way. He was beautiful to watch at his best, he had such an easy laid back style and he would always get to that ball before his man and he was deadly accurate. He was a model for us youngsters."

Tadghie's great friend and fellow Dr. Croke's clubman Donie Sheehan said: "All the talk these times is about a fellow being one of the all-time greats of the game but I have seen them all and Tadghie was the greatest of them all. I would say, as far as I am concerned, his best game was against Cavan in 1955. I saw both games against Cavan and if Mick O'Dwyer had him in Kildare kicking those great, long range points, he would win a couple of All-Irelands. We had great days in Sneem for Fr. Teehans seven-a-side teams. They all came just to see the great Tadghie. We will never see his like again."

Tadghie Lyne played in five Senior All-Ireland Finals, winning three, and the day before the 1959 Final against Galway he married his sweetheart Mary Brosnan from Castleisland and finished his playing career with the local Desmonds. They had four children, Eileen and Brid, Diarmuid and Brendan. Diarmuid, popularly known as 'Domo', was an outstanding footballer and starred as Desmonds won the 1985 All-Ireland Club Final, scoring 2-2 in the semi-final – surely a chip off the old block!

That doyen of sports journalists, the late Padraig D. Mehigan who wrote under the pen name 'Carbery', summed up Tadghie beautifully following that 1955 Final.

"When everything is said and done the outstanding figure in the whole panorama was Tadghie Lyne. He showed phenomenal speed and when he gripped leather he swung clear in bewildering fashion to swing over those long-legged sailing drives that curled in on the posts as if radar directed. His football was a joy to behold and in my opinion he is the greatest wing forward ever seen at GAA headquarters. Polished, cool and effortless, he has a great swerve, great hands and an unerring kick," Mehigan wrote.

What I have written only scratches the surfaces of Tadghie's career, nevertheless he will always remain in my memory from my teenage years as my first sporting idol. More important than anything else though, 'The Prince of Forwards' was simply a nice person. How fortunate I was to have known him. Dr. Eamonn has coached many great Kerry footballers, however it can be safely said that Tadghie Lyne was as good if not better than most. And he himself paid Eamonn the ultimate tribute when he told me that it is doubtful if he would have achieved the legendary status without the expert guidance of the good Doctor.

An Interview with Tom Long

Eamonn, I suppose, was a very dignified man, very calm. He wasn't the gregarious type. He wasn't the type that you'd meet on the street or in the clubhouse standing up in deep discussion about football. Yet his contribution in a different way to the GAA was enormous. He was very professional. I suppose his contribution to the Fitzgerald Stadium is well-known, he had a major part in the planning of it and seeing that the whole project was successfully completed. He was also instrumental in organising college's and inter-colleges football, putting it on a formal scale. And of course, his book, *The Art and Science of Gaelic Football* was way ahead of his time.

He was an awesome person. I remember as a youngster reading about him in *The Kerryman*. He was such a methodical person. Everything was well-programmed. It was a time of 'collective training' and all the players came together in Killarney. Everything was programmed from the rising in the morning, getting up at 7.30 am, starting with 8 o'clock Mass, until they went to bed at night; every detail was planned. I remember reading that in *The Kerryman* and I also heard afterwards that not alone was there a special time that the players went to bed but there were the occasional check outs by himself personally in the various houses where the players stayed. This was done if he had suspected that the times weren't adhered to.

I'd say that he was a very orderly person. I remember one time he gave us those little cards and on the card were three rules of play. He had obviously put a lot of thought into them. The first one was: 'close continuous coverage' by defenders. The second one then was: 'fear fatal fouling' – that was within the scoring area. The third one was: 'occupy open spaces'. With these simple rules he certainly got his message across. That was the type of person that he was. At that time there was no such thing as a coach. Eamonn was both coach and trainer. Kerry was very, very fortunate to have him in charge of the county team.

Another maxim of his was 'keep your hands quiet when tackling a player' – meaning that the players should only use their body or their shoulder, your hands were for blocking the ball. The pulling and dragging you see today went on in my own time too. That's what he tried to eliminate altogether, because it destroys the game. It's most unattractive. When a player has a ball you see other players, in the pretence of tapping the ball out of his hand, throwing blows at the body, and this is allowed go on.

Now when I spoke of his exactness to detail I can well remember he even had the meal times in the programme at the very same time every day. I remember later on then, he was extolling the medicinal virtues of the tomatoes. Word leaked to the Press seemingly, and the sale of tomatoes escalated for a while. However, when we were defeated in our next game I think there was a sudden drop in the sale of the humble tomato.

Dr. Eamonn was a man really before his time. I'd say his own professional training was a great advantage to him. He had a way about him that made people feel at ease and they found him easy to be around. He had no difficulty in settling down with strangers. No doubt his own profession of dealing with so many types of patients was a great help to him.

His reputation was undeniable for many of us who were beginning our training with Kerry. I had never met him until I was called into training. He was a very quiet, natural type of man. He was always in his collar and tie and he sat on this little stool and he had his umbrella available if it rained. He had his whistle and he had his stopwatch. He always led people to believe that they were improving. Even if they added seconds on, he told them that they were so many seconds better than they were the previous week or the previous evening. Oh I think he will be remembered forever in the story of Kerry football. Jimmy Cullinane immortalised him in a little ballad he wrote. I always remember the last two lines: *"Your name shall be remembered in the Kingdom's hall of fame as a man who always taught us how to play a sporting game."*

He was a very fair person. He always discouraged rough play and fouling. By the same token, I remember we had a pep talk one day as we were playing Cork the following Sunday. There were a few newcomers. Dr. Eamonn said, "It'll be a hard game, lads. Ye'll be hit hard. So ye'll have to hit back. You'll have to hit hard. You'll have to expect that." One of the newcomers took him literally and on the day of the match, there were a few little clouts struck at Cork. You probably remember the game I'm referring to. It was a real battle. There were some missiles coming in and we were sheltering under the net and I got a call to move outfield. I was never so anxious to answer that call. He was very sporting. He always believed in playing the game in a sporting way.

I had such respect for the Doctor that once I even went on strike in support for him. Actually at that time things were different. Kerry was the only team who had a person of that status training them, and you know, he was recognised by the County Board as the trainer. However, once the night of the All-Ireland was over, he was forgotten. There were very few perks that were going at that time for footballers. He was never considered for any trip to the States or anywhere in thanks. It wasn't right! A group of us living in Dublin met and discussed this. We made a complaint to the Kerry County Board. I think Eamonn himself agreed with it. Thus, Eamonn stood down that year. Following this Eamonn was brought to England and America on trips.

Unfortunately all these events coincided with my removal from Dublin to Kerry and I was in a very awkward position, because the boys were training in the Fitzgerald Stadium and I was down in St. Brendan's College field training on my own. But after a few nights the lads came and we discussed it in its entirety. The two trainers Johnny Walsh and Gerald O'Sullivan were great friends of mine and everybody knew that they were. So I came back and trained with the team for that game. We were beaten that year in the final. Eamonn was badly missed.

Was it the first ever strike by a GAA footballers? I wouldn't go as far as to say that now. Ah, it was a little stand. I think we were justified and we proved our point in the end.

He was a very gentle giant in Gaelic football – a very professional person, who always believed in playing the game in the sporting way. He was a man before his time, Weeshie.

The Story of Tom Long

THE MAN WHO WENT ON STRIKE FOR DR. EAMONN

'High, wide and handsome.'

An hour long interview conducted with Tom Long before the Kerry versus Derry All-Ireland semi-final of 2003 resulted in my Radio Kerry programme, *Terrace Talk*, winning a McNamee Award. To the best of my knowledge it is the only in-depth interview given by a man who in many experts opinion was one of the all-time great Kerry footballers.

Quiet, unassuming and reluctant to talk of himself in the interview, Tom documented an era of Kerry football in the 1950s and 1960s when all aspects of the GAA was beginning to undergo massive changes. Changes were noticeable in: style of play, dress, training methods, travel, even match reporting. It was an era of the great Down team, Galway's terrible twins Stockwell and Purcell, Kerry's dramatic loss to Waterford, the first and only players' strike by Kerry players, the great midfield partnership of Mick O'Connell and Seamus Murphy, Dr. Eamonn O'Sullivan and much more.

The legendary Paddy 'Bawn' Brosnan described Tom thus: "Tom Long is my kind of footballer; high, wide and handsome." This beautiful summing up of his West Kerry friend was delivered to Michael Hussey, brother of 1959 All-Ireland medal winner Paddy, on the Dingle Pier many years ago as 'The Bawn' returned from a day's fishing off the Kerry coast. Readers who will have seen Tom in action while at the peak of his powers will realize exactly what the legendary Kerry great was referring to here. It's the first time I have heard this phrase used to describe a Kerry footballer and it sums up Tom Long perfectly.

July 29, 1956 is a day that is firmly etched in my memory in relation to the history of Kerry football. The memories are both good and not so good because it was the first time I had seen a Kerry team beaten on a playing pitch and it was my first Munster Final. I was working my summer holidays in the silver pantry of the Parknasilla Great Southern Hotel under a man named Harry Levens from Louth. I was just 15 years old and the great bug that is Kerry football was beginning to take effect, even at that tender age. I was playing school leagues with the Monastery and palling around with The Killarney Legion lads.

That Sunday I was up at 5.30 am, did my washing and shining for Harry and, after a quick breakfast, headed for the Sneem Road where although cars were as scarce as hen's teeth in those hungry 1950s a thumbed lift to Killarney was quick to arrive. The terrace of Fitzgerald Stadium was a heaving mass of humanity. No crash barriers, no safety regulations, no yellow numbered stewards back then and the only colours to be seen were rosettes or badges sold on the way to the grounds by Killarney entrepreneur Pats Coffey.

What a day to attend your first Munster Final as Kerry had three teams out that afternoon. (Tom Collins from Ardfert played in both junior finals, hurling and football, and was introduced as a substitute in the replayed senior final, creating a record that is unlikely to be equalled in our time.) It was in that replayed Senior Final of 1956 between Kerry and Cork that I first laid eyes on Tom Long. He had made his debut in a first round game against Tipperary in Tralee, as Kerry won 3-7 to 3-2. Jim Brosnan later saved Kerry in the final in Cork with a last minute goal and Donal 'Marcus' O'Neill had brought off some miracle saves in the Kerry net. Cork led at half time, 0-6 to 0-0 and it was described as highway robbery as the game finished in a draw.

I strained to follow the action in the replay jumping up and down in the huge crowd with only a minute to go and the old dilapidated score board reading 1-7 each. The crowd was in frenzy, as it looked like we were heading to overtime. However, it was not to be. Cork Army Captain Niall Fitzgerald picked up a ball around the centre and headed in for the dressing room end goal. On he went, shaking off a series of tackles until he reached the 30 yards mark. I can still see the ball rising high in the sky. It seemed to go on forever until it landed right on top of the Kerry net. The white flag went up and Kerry, who had won that memorably final against Dublin the previous year, were out of the Championship.

Thirty-five years later as I recovered from a hip operation in hospital in Cork feeling sick, sorry, and sore for myself, the man in the bed along side me struck up a conversation. Football was the topic and lo and behold I quickly discovered that my room mate was none other than the aforementioned Niall Fitzgerald. During the next two weeks we spent long hours late into the night talking Cork and Kerry football. A great companion, Niall quickly corrected this often mistaken speculation that Tom Long was marking him when he scored that dramatic last minute point back in 1956.

"No, Tom was not marking me at that time, I had just been moved out to midfield from centre forward when I went on that match winning a solo run and Tom did not follow me. He was one of the best Kerry players I ever saw."

And in our interview Tom was quick to make the very same point in relation to whom and who was not marking Niall. The name of that man is a story for another day. I kept in touch with the army man during the following years and he obliged by coming on *Terrace Talk* one night and clearing up what was a complete misunderstanding.

Born in Ventry, football for the young Tom Long was always going to be a way of life. He was surrounded by some of the greatest names in the county's history – Batt Garvey, Dan Kavanagh, Bill Casey, Bill Dillon and Mick Murphy. And, of course, just up the road Paddy 'Bawn' was at the height of his powers and it was with that legendary player that the 15-year-old from Ventry played his first senior game at corner back.

"We had no team in the Gaeltacht at that time. One day you would have plenty of players but emigration was rife and the following Sunday you might have only the bare fifteen," Long recalls. "When I went to America in 1959 with Kerry I met more Ventry footballers there than were back home. Fr. Jackie McKenna, now Cannon Jackie, was the man behind football there at the time and he did great work for the youth, organizing school leagues and matches between the different areas."

Tom played four years with the West Kerry minors, losing in the final one year to John Mitchell's of Tralee. School days were spent in Coláiste Iosagan in Ballyvourney where it was football morning, noon and night, even in the snow. The school team led by Tom won three Munster championships. From there it was straight on to the Kerry minor teams of 1953 and 1954. Cork beat them the first year, 2-9 to 3-5, and the following year there was absolute heartbreak.

"We were leading Dublin in the final by five points and the game was gone into injury-time. They were awarded two very harsh frees, two goals resulted and we were beaten. We had great players like Brendan Kennelly, Frank O'Leary, Teddy Dowd, Johnny Culloty, Brian Sheehy and Jack Dowling," Long remembers.

Following the dramatic injury-time loss to Dublin in the Minor Final of 1954 Tom Long failed to get the call up to the senior panel for the momentous year of 1955, which turned out to be one of the most glorious All-Ireland victories for the 'Green and Gold'.

Studying in Dublin he lined out with his college and the following Sunday he came home to play with West Kerry in Tralee. There were rumours that he might be illegal and this was probably the reason that the Kerry selectors decided not to include the up-and-coming young star for that season. However, in 1956 Tom got the call for the first round of the Championship against Waterford and the subsequent replay defeat in the Munster Final to Cork in Killarney. His notification was, to say the least, unusual.

As he recalls: "I was attending a dress dance in Dublin when some man decked out in a black suit and dickey bow informed me that I had been selected for Kerry the following Sunday. Needless to say I was delighted."

It was the beginning of a brilliant career, but 1957 was to prove one of the most traumatic years in the annuals of Kerry Championship football, as we will discover. Events that year had begun well as The Kingdom reached the National League Final. Galway were the opponents as the sides squared up on May 18 in Croke Park. Amazingly it was Kerry's first National League final since 1930/31 when Miko Doyle had led his team to victory against Cork in that decider.

Tom's memories of his first Senior National final are vivid. He lined out at midfield partnering Denny O'Shea. Jerome O'Shea was Captain and Donal 'Marcus' O'Neill was in goal, while the following players (all now sadly gone to their eternal reward) were on the starting 15; John Dowling, Tiger Lyons, Tadghie Lyne, Paudie Sheehy, Colm Kennelly, Ned Roche and Dan McAuliffe.

"It was the first time we had met Galway in a league final, we beat Cavan by a point in the semi-final, Gunner Brady was their Captain. Tom Moriarty was superb at centre back for us. We were six points behind at one stage of the second half. I began at midfield with Mick O'Connell and was then moved to the wing. In the final I was again at midfield with Denny O'Shea, we led at half time by a point and with five minutes to go, we were level. Then they got a great goal. Frank Stockwell gave Sean Purcell a beautiful pass, he ran to the corner flag with the ball, drew the defence, centred and Stockwell fisted to the net and Galway were on their way to America. They were two superb footballers, they added a point each and we were beaten 1-8 to 0-6."

This had been the most talked about decider in years with the 1955 All-Ireland champions meeting the 1956 winners though, Mick O'Connell was missing from the Kerry line up. The former Cork player Billy O'Neill was wing forward for Galway, Jack Mahon captained the Tribesmen, and he and Tom later became great friends. They had an emotional meeting at that McNamee Awards night in Dublin. Jack was seriously ill at that time and sadly died shortly afterwards. Stockwell and Purcell were dubbed 'the terrible twins' and were a deadly combination, which they proved with that winning goal.

Two months later on June 2, 1957 in Waterford City, Kerry were to experience their most humiliating defeat of all time as the country were stunned in one of the greatest surprises in the history of the GAA. That game is now part of Kerry folklore. Mick O'Connell was back to partner Tom Long at midfield but Kerry were without Marcus O'Neill, Sean Murphy and Tom Moriarty from their National League Final side. Denny O'Shea, carrying an ankle injury, was the only sub available and to alleviate a desperate situation, John Barrett, a reporter with *The Kerryman* togged out as a sub. Tim Barrett, who had played minor with Kerry, was pressed into service at the last minute in goals. The outcome was considered to be a mere formality. The general opinion was that Waterford would not keep the ball kicked out for Kerry – that is what everybody thought.

Tom's memories of that eventual occasion are vivid: "We were never as fit going into a game, but for various reasons we only just got 15 players together. We were eight points ahead at the beginning of the second half and well in control. Then Noel Power got a soft goal for Waterford, the crowd of around 3,000 were going mad and with four minutes to go Jim Timmons of Killrosantey punched another goal and the scores were level. Then almost on full time Tom Cunningham, their centre back, came up field to kick a great long range point to win the match, and we were beaten 2-5 to 0-10."

So what is the real story behind this historic defeat for Kerry? Owen McCrohan writing in Mick O'Dwyer's excellent biography explains: "Kerry's troubles started well in advance of this match when a dispute over the captaincy of the team was starting to ferment. As county champions the honour automatically went to a South Kerry man. Waterville, as South Kerry champions, would normally be free to name Mick O'Dwyer as Captain. However, he had not established himself on the Kerry team so the captaincy issue was thrown into the lap of Caherceiveen St. Mary's Club who had two recognized members of the Kerry team, Jerome O'Shea and Donal (Marcus) O'Neill playing."

St. Mary's nominated Jerome and Marcus withdrew from that team to play Waterford while as stated two star players; Sean Murphy and Tom Moriarty also did not travel. Whatever about the rights and wrongs of the captaincy issue Marcus was one of the greatest goalkeepers I have ever seen and I base my remarks on having seen him win three County championships with South Kerry in 1955, 1956 and 1958. He also won another with Dick Fitzgerald's in 1951. He was on the losing Killarney side to Castleisland following a replay in 1951, and his displays with Kerry in the 1950s were outstanding. He was undoubtedly one of the great Kerry footballers not to win an All-Ireland Senior medal.

1958 was the dawn of a new year and as always in Kerry, there were hopes of another All-Ireland victory. Tom Long, now 22 years old, was starring in Dublin but he did not figure in the Munster Championship. The great Tadghie Lyne was even an absentee as Kerry beat Cork 2-7 to 0-8. Both men were back for what was expected to be an easy win over an unknown Derry side in the All-Ireland semi-final. The West Kerry man explains his recall to the team for that now historic match. "Kerry played Meath in a challenge game in Tralee the week before the Derry game. I travelled down from Dublin and was happy enough with my display but it was Tadghie who was the star that day. We won 2-14 to 2-6 and he scored 2-6. Both of us were picked for the semi-final and the general opinion in the county was to wait for the final."

Long was chosen at centre foreword and in the programme of the match he was described thus: "A National teacher, Tom returns to the team after a long absence owing to an illness. A star footballer as a minor, he showed glimpses of his best form against Meath recently. A dashing player, a topper overhead and most unselfish in his passing; he is a great distributor of the ball and his presence should add greatly to the attack. Age: 22, Weight: 13st Height: 5ft 11ins."

All was in readiness for the Derry clash but again as he had experienced with the Dublin minors, Cork in 1956, Galway in the league and especially Waterford the previous year, Tom was going to suffer yet another shattering defeat.

On August 24, 1958, I stood under the old Cusack Stand as torrential rain and driving wind lashed Croke Park. Tom Long was picked at centre forward for this All-Ireland semi-final against no hopers Derry. They had won their first ever Ulster Championship and had never before played in Croke Park but what unfolded over the next hour would send shock waves through the GAA world. To the backdrop of that dark and dismal background of rain laden skies what Derry were to achieve would be carved into the folklore of both counties.

The final minutes were heart stopping. The sides were level until Sean O'Connell pointed Derry ahead with six minutes to go. Then one minute later O'Connell got the ball on the right wing from Peter Smith's centre, cut into the middle and cracked the ball low into the Kerry net past the diving Marcus O'Neill. Tadghie Lyne got his second goal with only seconds left, but it came too late, it was now 2-6 to 2-5, and Derry went on to meet and lose to Dublin in the final.

Tom Long recalled that now infamous day for Kerry football: "John Joe Sheehy had been sent to watch Derry play Down in the Ulster Final but his car broke down on the way and when he got there the crowd were leaving the pitch. Paul Russell, writing in a local paper, had warned us that this was a very fit Derry team, as he had attended one of their training sessions. Jim McKeever was a physical training instructor and it must have been the very first time we had met a side trained in this manner. We dominated the game but kicked a litany of wides. P.F., in his match report, berated the forwards and was scathing of the display, saying it was as well [Kerry] were beaten as it saved the county a lot of expense training for the final."

This match is also memorable for the meeting between Mick O'Connell and Jim McKeever. O'Connell was moved to midfield at half time and gave an exhibition on what was the first time the great Valentia man was seen in Croke Park. "The fielding by both men was magnificent and Micko probably got the best of the dual. They would meet many times in the succeeding years in league and Railway cups and give more memorable displays. That Derry game was Tom Moriarty's last in the 'Green and Gold', he broke his leg that day. He had won two All-Irelands with Kerry and a National League with Cork in 1952," Long recalled. The wheel of fortune was about to turn full circle for the Ventry great. On May of the following year he scored an early goal as Kerry won their first National League title since 1932: 2-8, to 1-8. The same Derry side were the final opponents as Tom lined out at centre forward.

To prove his outstanding versatility, he added two more league medals to his collection. Derry were hammered 4-16 to 1-5 in 1961 with Long at centre back, and two years later, playing at full forward, Tom Long scored three spectacular points as the great Down side of that time were defeated 0-9 to 1-5. He had occupied three different vital centre positions while he was equally at home at centrefield. Had any other Kerry player been as versatile in such vital centre positions?

1959 would prove to be a memorable year for the Ventry man. In a classic semi-final Dublin were beaten 1-10 to 2-5 as all attendance records were broken. "Mick O'Connell gave a majestic display at midfield, ably assisted by Seamus Murphy. Both men were outstanding players and one of the best ever partnerships Kerry produced. Seamus was, in my opinion, the most underrated Kerry footballer ever, he was superb," Long maintained.

After that match one scribe wrote of the Kerry centre forward,

"What will one say that will adequately describe Tom Long's magnificent display? Until Sunday Cathal O'Leary was rated the best centre half in the county. Long blitzed that reputation with one of the best displays of his career. I cannot recall him being beaten in even one jump for possession, and one had to marvel at the ease with which he brushed off the tackles of the Dublin defenders."

On September 27, 1959, Tom Long won the first of his two senior All-Ireland medals as Galway were put to the sword by 3-7 to 1-4. While the match will be forever remembered as the Sean Murphy Final, he gave a devastating display that day, Long was not far behind and the experts were lavish in their praise following his move to midfield when Mick O'Connell suffered a knee injury. The late Mitchell Cogley, writing in the *Irish Independent*, was gushing in his praise:

"Tom Long's part in the victory effort was a vital one. In the early stages the Galway midfielders Mattie McDonagh and Frank Evers were exerting what was shaping into being a match winning superiority. Then Kerry's mentors made the astute switch of Long to mark Evers, and it proved a real match winner. Long did not try to match the mighty Evers in high fielding, he used his superior pace to get to the open spaces ahead of his rival and won enough of the ball by those means to curb Galway's hitherto dominance at centrefield. Furthermore, Long's astute distribution led directly to the two Kerry goals in the 15th and 17th minutes of the second half and put The Kingdom firmly on the road to victory, a truly magnificent display."

When questioned about his feelings and memories in relation to winning his first medal, Tom's reply was typical of his wonderful sporting attitude to the game and more importantly where his priorities lay: "Of course I was delighted to win. However, I was working in Dublin and I missed out coming home with the Cup. It was up for school the following morning. Times were different then; not like today. I have two All-Irelands and I think very little of them because the games were really not great. But the two semi-finals of those years were against Dublin and they were outstanding games and you remember good matches rather than winning and losing. At the end of the day what is a medal, it's the memories that matter."

Once again it's well worth recounting Tom's match profile in the run up to that victory.

"Another product of Coláiste Iosagain, Long helped his school win Munster Colleges titles and his performances earned him a midfield position on the Munster colleges teams of 1953-54. He graduated to St. Patrick's Training College in Dublin and there he played with Erin's Hope, helping them to the Dublin title in 1956.

He first appeared on the Kerry Minors in 1952, was chosen again for the next two years and won a Munster medal with them in 1954 at midfield.

"He first played for the senior side in 1956 against Tipperary on the 40 and can play in any of the central areas. Two years ago he was midfield for Munster and after going in as a sub in this year's semi-final he was picked at left half forward for the final. He was 23 years of age in June."

Not a man to court any type of media publicity I was always amazed by the fact that, to the best of my knowledge, Tom Long's achievements and football career was never properly acknowledged. Indeed, I am only scratching the surface of his brilliant career but it's fair to say that what is written here goes some small way to rectifying this omission.

Tom won his first All-Ireland medal as Kerry beat Galway in 1959 and what a year that was for him. Kerry swept all before them capturing all the trophies that were possible for a team to win in the one season – winning the Munster and All-Ireland Championships and the National League.

New York were defeated in Gaelic Park in the St. Brendan's Cup Final: 2-11 to 1-8, and three great Kerry exiles lined out against their native county in that final – Jim Foley, Tom Moriarty and Timmy Moynihan. Following that, Kerry beat an unknown Down side in The Gaelic Weekly's Cuchullan Trophy: 1-11 to 0-9, but little did Tom and his teammates realize then that this Down side would come back over the following two years to haunt them and write themselves into GAA history. (It is also worth noting that the legendary Tadghie Lyne married Mary on the eve of the 1959 Final.)

The ultimate tribute to Long came from the late Joe Sherwood, author of a lovely column on the back page of the now defunct *Evening Press*, when he penned the following tribute on that 1959 Final: "He was in no doubt that close to the final whistle Sean Murphy was in the running to be man of the match. O'Connell's injury was a sore blow to Kerry and Evers up to then was as conspicuous as the Rock of Gibraltar to every seaman who has passed through the Mediterranean. Now I don't pretend to know whose brainwave it was, but I reckon it turned out to be a masterstroke putting Long on Evers. It was the turning point in the match. Came the moment, came the man in Tom Long and Kerry started playing like Kerrymen."

The emergence of Down as a major force is one of the fairytale stories of Gaelic football, it flew in the face of all known tradition. Prior to winning their first Ulster Championship in 1959 Down were never heard of.

"They beat us in April of 1960 in the semi-final of the league in Croke Park, it was our first defeat in over 12 months and when we met them in the All-Ireland Final of that year; worse was to follow. They were the first side to bring the professional look to the game, even the way they dressed was different. They were a great footballing side like the team of Kerry's golden years, but they were spoilers and well-tutored in the art of fouling and breaking the ball at midfield. They had a wonderful half forward line as good as I have ever seen in football, probably the best in the history of the game – Sean O'Neill, James McCartan and Paddy Doherty. Two goals in the second half from James McCartan and a penalty from Paddy Doherty and they beat us: 2-10 to 0-8."

At this period of his football life Tom took a stand against the Kerry County Board which, to say the very least, was ground breaking in its own right. "At that time Dr. Eamonn O'Sullivan, our trainer, was not brought on any trips abroad, to Wembley, London or New York. Some of us based in Dublin thought this was wrong and took a stand against it. Unfortunately for me it coincided with my return to Kerry. I refused to train in the Stadium with the team and trained on my own in St. Brendan's College field in Killarney for that All-Ireland. Eventually things were straightened out and the two men then in charge, great friends of mine, Johnny Walsh and Gerald O'Sullivan came together with me and I returned to the Stadium." This, in my opinion, was probably the very first time in the GAA that a player took such a stand as this and one imagines the media would go to town on it if it happened today.

Tom had great admiration for the legendary Kerry trainer and this was abundantly clear in a press interview following one winning final: "This was a triumph for our trainer Dr. Eamonn O'Sullivan. He had us in wonderful form and we appeared to be much faster than Galway. I would like to thank him for his care and devotion to us in training and I think the major credit for the win must go to him." This is a lovely tribute from a great footballer to his trainer.

1962 saw Tom collect his second All-Ireland medal. He starred at full forward as Dublin were beaten in the semi-final: 2-12 to 0-10. He was now at the height of his power and in the Munster Final and All-Ireland semi-final he bagged decisive goals. A goal in the final against Roscommon by Garry McMahon after just 32 seconds sent Kerry on their way to a comfortable 1-12 to 1-4 victory, with Long on fire at full forward.

The following two years saw the Ventry man on the losing side to an emerging Galway team when a late goal from Pat Donnellan and three Seamus Leydon points shocked The Kingdom: 1-7 to 0-10.

The following year in the final, which would prove to be Tom's last, Galway hammered a very poor Kerry team 0-15 to 0-10. The Kerry selectors came in for plenty of stick following this rout as they had changed the complete team around like a pack of cards, and the day was a disaster. Tom's Inter-County career was now at an end. Now teaching and living in Killarney he joined Dr. Croke's Club helping them to four O'Donoghue Cup wins and his goal scoring feats at this time will probably never be surpassed. In the 1965 O'Donoghue Cup Final he bagged 3-3, and in the 1968 decider he scored 2-2. That same year I was fortunate to captain a great East Kerry side to county honours and in the final against Waterville. Tom Long scored an astonishing 4-1 all from play. To see him up close in training was unforgettable, he had great strength, superb balance, a brilliant fielder and was wonderfully skilful on the ball. He could literally skip around his closest marker and possess a bullet of a shot with both legs. We will never see his likes again, that for me is a certainty.

He also starred with his native West Kerry, winning two County Championships with East Kerry, playing in four finals. He represented Munster for a number of years and in 1960 as a forerunner to the now All-Stars, Tom was picked for a star-studded Ireland team to play the Combined Universities. Among his teammates were some of the all-time legendary names of Gaelic games; Aidan Brady, Pat Rice, Frank Evers, Des Foley, Jim McKeever, Kevin Mussen and Cathal O'Leary. He was picked in his favourite position at centre forward.

Now enjoying a quite retirement with his wife Brid in Fossa, as his family have spread their wings, he enjoys his daily walks in the nearby Kenmare Estate. He calls to that great GAA pub in Killarney, Jimmy O'Brien's, where his great knowledge of the game is so appreciated.

Mick O'Connell in his excellent book, *'A Kerry Footballer'*, pays tribute to Long during that era: "Tom Long, Mick O'Dwyer, Paudie Sheehy and Seamus Murphy were consistently good throughout, and in fact I can think of no other four contemporaries of mine to have given greater service to the county."

So how good was Tom Long? Denis P. O'Sullivan of Kilgarvan, that exemplary long serving Kerry GAA activist who knows his hurling and football better than most, summed him up for me when he said: "Without a shadow of doubt he was one of the 20 best footballers this great county has ever produced."

Sean Murphy of Camp

THE GREATEST RIGHT HALF-BACK OF THE CENTURY

When talking of his native Camp, Sean Murphy exudes pride in his own place. When speaking of Gaelic football and its greatest exponents, the man who was selected as one of the 15 greatest Gaelic footballers of the century, is equally enthusiastic. The 1959 All-Ireland Final is a game that became known as 'The Sean Murphy's Final'. His exhibition of Gaelic football was reckoned by many to have been the finest ever seen in Croke Park. It resulted in his winning the Texaco Award. The Award had been introduced the previous year and Sean was the first Kerryman to win it. Jack Mahon, centre half-back for Galway in that game, described Murphy's performance as, "Kerry football in all its glory, effortlessly executed by a master."

In Sean's own words:
Camp is an unusual place. It has a population of about 200 people. Tim O'Donnell, Charlie Sullivan, Denis Shea, Seamus Murphy, Padraig Murphy, Tom Murphy and I all came from Camp. They won a lot of All-Irelands between them. I inherited the skills in Camp. It was all round me. In a community so small, where Gaelic football had such a high profile, it would be difficult not to become interested and involved. Tim O'Donnell was my idol. I had not seen him play but the stories of his games filled my early years. My father, Jackie Murphy, played football for Kerry. He was originally from Ballydavid, in West Kerry. They were mostly half-backs and midfielders. Mainly they were 'catch and kick' footballers – that was the type of football they played. They never over ran with the ball. They got the ball, looked around and kicked towards a forward running into position.

Camp won the West Kerry League in 1929, this was an extraordinary achievement when you consider the small number of players available. John Kerry O'Donnell and Tim O'Donnell were on this team. There were powerful footballers in Camp, who would hold their own with anyone. There were also Driscolls; Pa and Michael, who played for the Kerry Juniors, John Dunne and Micheál O'Leary, who played for the juniors and the minors. There were local leagues and school competitions.

It might be difficult to get the small area and the small population of Camp into perspective. Valentia would be like a city compared to Camp. Camp is only Camp Cross, there is Ashe's Pub, Barry's Pub and O'Shea's. Lower Camp, where there is only one house, is a half a mile away. In order to play the game of football, the practice was to rent a field from a farmer, whatever field he did not want in that year. The local school played an important part in fostering football. That is where I went to school, Camp National School. It is also where my mother and my father, who died in 1946, taught.

I fine-honed my knowledge of the skills of the game at Ballyvourney College. We won the Munster Colleges for the first time ever in 1949. I played for the Kerry Minors in 1949 and we were beaten by Armagh in the final. Among my teammates were; Johnny Foley, Paudie Sheehy, Brendan Galvin, Bobby Miller, Michael Kerins, Colm Kennelly, Mick Galway and Dinny Falvey. Based on the minor series of games, I was chosen for the juniors and won a junior All-Ireland in 1949 with Mixi Palmer, Tom Long, J.C. Cooper, Liam Fitzgerald and John Dowling. I was young enough to play minor again the following year, and by beating Wexford, 3-6 to 1-4, in the final, I won a Minor All-Ireland medal in 1950. That memorable day, I lined out with Donal 'Marcus' O'Neill, Mick Galway, Pop Fitzgerald, Colm Kennelly, Mick Brosnan, Joe Kerins, Con O'Riordan and Tom Lawler.

The great teams who took Kerry up to mid-1940s when the winning of All-Irelands stopped were linked with the teams of the 1950s by a few players, who more or less handed over the baton. I played against Danno Keeffe. He played for Strand Road against Castlegregory when I was about 16. I also played against Joe Keohane, and I played with Paddy 'Bawn' Brosnan in 1951. I trained with Paddy 'Bawn' and Thomas Ashe of Dingle, at Ballyheigue. In that year, I played my first game in the Senior Championship against Louth when I was co-opted from the Kerry Juniors to the senior side.

A lot of university students were playing College football through the winter, and were able to get places on the Kerry team as fellows who were farmers and fisherman hadn't the time to play. I was playing club football with Castlegregory and with Dingle. In Dublin, I played with UCD and Geraldine's. In spite of playing with good club teams in both counties, I never won a club championship. The nearest I came to it was when West Kerry was defeated by John Mitchels in a replay in 1960. Some of my teammates were Dinny Falvey, Jack and Pat Dowling, Paddy Hussey, Tom McKenna, Gearoid Cronin was the Captain. Mitchels went on to make it five-in-a-row county championship wins.

Essentially I played at right half-back for most of my career. In 1953, I started off for Kerry, as a sub against Clare. My first playing position was centre-half forward against Cork whom we defeated in the 1953 Munster Final. I was taken out of that position to play left half-back against Louth in the semi-final and I was switched to midfield, with Dermot Hanafin as my partner against Armagh in the All-Ireland Final. Jas Murphy was delighted to take the well earned Sam Maguire. We won 0-13 to 1-6.

In 1954 we lost the final to Meath 1-13 to 1-7. Kerry, captained by the young John Dowling, were hot favourites. In 1955, I collected my second Senior All-Ireland medal, when Kerry won 0-12 to 1-6, a victory that shocked Dublin.

Kerry was in the doldrums from 1956 to 1958 but in 1959 they came back. Only four of us survived from the 1953 team – John Dowling, Paudie Sheehy, Jerome O'Shea and myself. We beat Galway in the final 3-7 to 1-4. Mick O'Connell was Captain. We came up against a great Down team in the 1960 Final. They won and took the Sam Maguire over the border for the first time. In 1961 Down again beat Kerry in the semi-final. It was the last of my 10 years in Inter-County football.

As I came from Camp, I hadn't a club pushing for me. Most of the other players had. Without the club influence, a player was used for filling in the positions that they didn't have anyone for. Eventually, the day came when they couldn't afford to pick the team without you. Matches were tough – you were technically semi-confined to a sector, and then you had an opposing footballer who was in close contact with you the whole time. Everything was a tussle, a lot of effort went into acquiring every ball, and it had to be fought for and won.

I played from 1949 to 1961 and I was never warned by a referee or assaulted on the field. I never saw the footballers I knew engage in fisticuffs. I can't honestly remember a fight.

The best teams I played against were Down of 1960 and the Galway team of 1959. Over my career period, Cork were always a good team. They played very good football and they were very difficult to beat. We had a theory then that any time you beat Cork you could win an All-Ireland. They were always good enough to test you. We had the advantage of meeting very good teams in the league and other matches. Carlow beat Kerry at Tralee. Waterford also beat Kerry in 1957 in the Munster Championship; this was one of the greatest shocks of all time. We were really tested by teams such as; Galway, Mayo, Cavan, Roscommon, Down and Tyrone. Wexford was also a good team. Dublin, Lough and Meath were great teams to play against, so we had plenty of good competition. Any of the teams I have named could have gone on to win an All-Ireland in those days.

One of the footballers who stands out in my memory as giving the greatest sporting pleasure to his teammates, the opposition and the spectators was Paddy Doherty of Down. As a back, he was the best player that I ever played against. Another who I rate as first class was Sean Purcell of Galway. He was the best player on the field in my time. There was a saying about the young Jack Dempsey that he was *nonpareil*. I can equally say that Sean Purcell of Galway had no equal. Other players who left a lasting impression were: Enda Colleran (Galway); he was one of the very great right full backs, Jack Mahon (Galway), Dan McCartan (Down), Con McGrath (Cork), Sean O'Neill (Down), Paddy O'Brien and Michael Grace (Meath), Jack Kenna (Laois), Sean Flanagan, (Mayo); an inspiring footballer, John Nallen (Mayo), Padraig Kearney (Mayo), Jim Crowley (Dublin), Brian Smith (Meath), Peter McDermot (Meath), Bill Goodison (Wexford), Andy Murphy (Carlow), Gerry O'Malley (Roscommon) and Pakie McGarty (Leitrim).

Of the Kerry teams, any list of the greatest must include: Paddy Kennedy, Mikey Sheehy, Jack O'Shea, Mick O'Connell, Jim Brosnan, Tadghie Lyne, Paddy 'Bawn' Brosnan, Mick O'Dwyer, Tommy Doyle and Paudie Shea. Yes, you could say that these were the best. Paudie Sheehy was a splendid footballer. He didn't have the physique, but he was a very accurate, good free-taker, with a great football brain. He integrated well with the rest of the team. He was very fit and had a great spirit.

The modern game depends a lot on running. I think they will have to get back to the older type of football. There has to be more 'catch-and-high' fielding. The game needs more kicking effectively towards a player. Forwards are less accurate today. They tend to move closer into the goals and rather to go for goals more than points. If they could marry the present smooth running game with more of the traditional one it would make a better game. I would eliminate the hand pass, in any shape or form; it is ruining the game. It lends itself more to basketball. It is very difficult for the referee to be near enough to players to identify whether they palmed or fielded or fisted the ball. I would like to see the return of the old method of picking the ball off the ground, which was the flick up. This would prevent bending for the ball. This year's All-Ireland should end the type of football that caused the problems. Holding on to the ball is the biggest problem in football today. If you hold the ball long enough, you are enticing someone to physically take it from you. In the older days we let the ball go a lot quicker. Fair shouldering is a thing of the past. The rules should be designed to get rid of fouling.

The Whit Sunday Game in London and the American Football Tour were tremendous stimulants for the county players of the winning All-Ireland team of my time. The role that John Kerry O'Donnell played in giving Gaelic football an international image and reality has not been generally appreciated. The GAA is enormously in his debt.

I like the international dimension that Australian football can give to Gaelic football. There is a golden opportunity today to make the game international. Circumstances have given Ireland emigrant communities in Australia, America and England. You could have international Gaelic football, but the difficulty is to try and figure how you can marry Australian football with Gaelic football without destroying the identity of each of the games. I think it could be done. The professionalism of the Australians will always be a problem. They are always fully fit.

When playing any sport, you must consider whether there are demands on you to turn up for your job on Monday morning. If that is the case, you will have to think about injuries. I had the experience of being the Medical Officer of the Scunthorpe United Team in England. They were a third Division team. My job was to go along and see the injuries on a Monday. The physiotherapist seemed to be the key person to getting these people back on the field. Medical officers in clubs today should be better trained. Players should warm up before games. In any big final, it would be more effective if they spent a few minutes exercising and kicking the ball around, rather than having to meet the President and march around after bands. I can't understand all the injuries of today – ankle injuries are the most common. Better training could prevent these, it would strengthen the muscles around the joint.

The role of sponsorship in the future of the GAA is a big subject of debate these days. It has a useful role. I was one of the first advocates of it. I think it can be of great value, but sponsors should not demand too much.

I am very pleased to see the change in rules that now protect the goalkeeper from injury. In my playing days, a goalkeeper didn't have a chance. He presented the soft frontal part of his body to aid in rushing knees or shoulders. The risk of serious injury was too great.

The greatest tribute paid to Sean Murphy's prowess was being honoured as a member of the Team of the Century in the anniversary year of the GAA. It was chosen by a panel, after the readers of the *Sunday Independent* had submitted nominations.

In the book, *'My Own Story'*, published by Gaelic sports commentator Sean Óg O'Callaghan, he also includes Sean Murphy in the best team since 1950 and says: "Sean Murphy (Kerry) was an automatic choice for the position of right half-back. When other heads were dropping around him he was the stylist able to kick equally well with both feet. Sean Murphy was a marshalling force."

The Murphy's of Camp

The parish of Camp lies a few miles west of Tralee in the shadow of the Slieve Mish Mountains at the entrance to the Dingle Peninsula. This parish has produced great Gaelic footballers over the years such as; Tim O'Donnell, Charlie O'Sullivan, Denny O'Shea, the Murphy's, the Driscoll's, and the Doyle's. It was here in the 1920s that Jackie and Hannah Murphy; both school teachers, settled down and reared a family of seven; four boys and three girls. Jackie won a junior All-Ireland with Kerry in the early 1920s and led the famous Camp team (which also included Tim and John 'Kerry' O'Donnell) to victory in the West Kerry league of 1928. The four boys; Padraig, Sean, Tomas and Séamus were imbued with the love of Gaelic football, and with the great encouragement of their father, no spare moment was wasted, as they practised the great skills of their heroes; the majestic Paddy Kennedy, Tim O'Donnell and Charlie O'Sullivan. Padraig and Sean, having finished the National School went on to Coláiste Íosagáin, Ballyvourney where in 1949, Padraig as Captain and Sean as midfielder helped the college to win Corn Uí Mhuirí for the first time. The two brothers also won Cork County Minor Championship medals with Macroom and were selected on the Kerry Junior team that won the Ireland of 1949, while Sean also played on the Kerry Minor team. In 1950 Sean was on the victorious Kerry Minor team that won the All-Ireland, so has the rare distinction of winning a Junior All-Ireland before he won a Minor. Tomas and Seamus followed the older brothers to Coláiste Íosagáin and both won Corn Uí Mhuirí; Tomas in 1951 and Seamus in 1954, which is a unique achievement for four brothers.

Sean went on to St. Patrick's Drumcondra and UCD, where he qualified as a teacher and later as a medical doctor. He won three Sigerson Cups with UCD, Dublin Leagues with Erin's Hopes and Geraldine's, and also started his fabulous career with the Kerry Senior team. He won his first Senior All-Ireland medal in 1953. His second was the historic 1955 victory over Dublin and his third in 1959, where his display against Galway is rated as the greatest ever given by a defender in an All-Ireland Final. Sean Murphy has the rare and unique distinction of winning All-Ireland medals with three different brothers; a junior with Padraig in 1949, a minor with Tomas in 1950, and a senior with Seamus in 1959. He also captained the combined universities to victory over the rest of Ireland in 1958. A Texaco Award in 1959, A Gael Linn all-time great in 1961, selection on 'The Centenary Team' and also the Millennium Team bears ample testimony to his prowess as a supreme Gaelic footballer – a legend in his own lifetime.

Séamus joined Sean to win his first All-Ireland Senior medal in 1959, and went on to win three more in 1962, 1969 and 1970. So Séamus won All-Ireland medals in three decades also won four National Leagues, two Sigerson Cups, one St. Brendan's Cup and also has the rare distinction of never playing on a losing Kerry team in 11 Munster Senior Football finals. Séamus was also a gifted athlete; the long jump being his speciality. He qualified as an agriculture scientist in UCD and taught in Warrenstown, County Meath – the great Sean Boylan of Meath fame being among his pupils.

Tomas Murphy qualified as an engineer in UCC where he won two Sigerson Cups as well as an All-Ireland Minor medal with Kerry in 1950. Padraig won a junior All-Ireland medal with Kerry in 1949, played with Erin's Hope and Geraldine's and won Dublin Leagues with them where he was a teacher. He is now Honorary President of na Gael Club in Tralee.

In 1991 when Kerry defeated London to win the All-Ireland Junior title, a certain Joe Murphy (son of Padraig) was a member of that team. So the continuity goes on – from Jackie in the early 1920s to Joe in 1991.

The Murphy's of Camp have given unselfish service, impeccable sportsmanship and complete commitment to the great game of Gaelic football.

The Lynes of Cleeney

The Lynes of Cleeney are a legendary Kerry football family. Denny Lyne, who captained Kerry in the historic New York Polo Grounds Final of 1947, in his last ever interview, told me that if Dr. Eamonn had been brought to New York, Kerry would have won that final. "How I regret that decision," Denny Lyne said.

What better way to remember Dr. Eamonn O'Sullivan than to recall and pay tribute to one of the most famous and forgotten GAA families this county has ever produced? Following the 1946 All-Ireland victory by Kerry over Roscommon Eamonn remarked to friends that, "The Lyne family should never be forgotten for the long and distinguished service they had given to the Green and Gold of our county." Indeed it is remarkable in itself that three of the brothers at one time or another came under the guidance of the good Doctor in his preparation of Kerry sides.

The same applied to the legendary Sheehy family from Tralee. Their story is even more remarkable, as Eamonn trained teams on which both father and sons won Celtic crosses.

Sixty long years ago, in 1946, my club Killarney Legion won their one and only Kerry Senior Football County Championship and without the Lynes of Cleeney this momentous achievement would not have happened. The story of the Lynes is the story of one of the great traditions of this County. They touched my football life in many ways. So this is my tribute to that Legion family – all now sadly departed.

When Denny Lyne died on November 29, 2001, it brought to an end a unique family association with Kerry football – a family connection that stretched back to the early 1930s. The six brothers in the family all played with their local club – Killarney Legion. Four of the boys went on to win All-Ireland medals with Kerry in some grade and in fact, four of the boys played together on the Kerry Junior team that won the 1941 All-Ireland title.

Their story is similar to that of many other great Kerry families who, through the decades, played a massive part in building the great

Fitzgerald Stadium Committee, 1940. Back Row: N. McCarthy, T. O'Meara, C. Foley, C. Fleming, P. Fleming, D. Doona. Middle Row: M. Hogan, T. O'Shea, T. Brosnan, B. Landers, S. Cooper, P. O'Shea, P. O' Leary. Front Row: M. F. O'Leary, P. O'Mahony, Dr. E. O'Sullivan, E. O'Sullivan, J. Clifford, M. O'Riada, J. Hallahan.

Patients from St. Finan's Hospital laying the sods for the new stadium in 1935.

A previously unpublished photo of Dr. Eamonn in his white coat with a group of St. Finans' patients during construction of the Stadium. Note the unfinished wall in the background and the arch for the little entry gate Dr. Eamonn included for the benefit of the hospital patients.

Dr. Michael O'Brien, Bishop of Kerry, blesses the Fitzgerald Stadium on May 31, 1936. Dr. Eamonn is on the extreme right.

1936 poster for the official opening of the Fitzgerald Stadium.

Ten Kerry greats of the past are captured here in 1940. Front Row, left to right: 'Roundy' Landers, John Joe Landers, Dan Spring, 'Bracker' Regan and Johnny Walsh. Back Row, left to right: Con Geaney, Dan Ryan, Bill Kinnerk, Tim O'Donnell and Michael O'Ruairc.

Above: *Paddy Burke's goals against Roscommon in the drawn game and replay helped Dr. Eamonn's Kerry team of 1946 to a memorable win.*

Above: *Paddy Kennedy proudly displays the Sam Maguire Cup after the 1946 All-Ireland Final. Dr. Eamonn once remarked that Paddy Kennedy was one of the "greatest ever mid-fielders".*

Left: *Batt Garvey scored a brilliant goal for Kerry in the 1947 defeat by Cavan in the Polo Grounds, New York.*

Marching into battle – Captain Gus Cremins leads out the Kerry team against Roscommon in the drawn All-Ireland Final of 1946. Kerry got two dramatic late goals to draw that match. Dr. Eamonn trained the side for the replay, as Kerry won their 16th title. Left to right: Gus Cremins, Joe Keohane, Bruddy O'Donnell, Danno Keeffe, Bill Casey, Paddy Kennedy, Jackie Lyne, Teddy O'Connor, Paddy 'Bawn' Brosnan, Batt Garvey, Eddie Walsh, Paddy Burke, Dan Kavanagh, Denny Lyne, Tom 'Gegga' O'Connor. The little mascot holding the hand of Gus is Donal O'Keeffe.

Kerry Team in training – skipping to Dr. Eamonn's whistle.

Kerry selectors: Jackie Lyne, John Joe Sheehy, Johnny Walsh and Mike O'Shea in reflective mood at Fitzgerald Stadium.

Famous players (left to right): Bobby Buckley, Ned Fitzgerald, Gerald O'Sullivan, Jerome O'Shea and Tadghie Lyne at a training session.

Tadghie Lyne – 'The Prince of Forwards'.

Tom Long – 'High, Wide and Handsome'.

Paudie Sheehy, the long point-kicking forward, was on the winning teams of 1955, 1959 and 1962.

Left: Kerry Players in training. From left to right: Seán Kelly, John Joe Sheehan, Donie Murphy and Tadghie Lyne.

Sean Murphy.

Kerry Trainer, Paul Russell using Dr. Eamonn's blackboard methods to prepare the Kerry panel for the game ahead.

Killarney/Kerry Senior Football County Champions 1949. Trained by Dr. E. O'Sullivan. Back Row: P. O'Meara (Sec), M. Moynihan, J. Lyne, J. O'Donoghue, D. Kavanagh, G. O'Sullivan, J. Murphy, D. Brosnan, D. O'Leary, Fr. J. Murphy (Chairman), L. McMonagle and T. O'Connor. Front Row: T. Cooper, F. Meaney, F. Murphy, D. Lyne, T. Healy (Capt.), J. Boyd, P. Batt Shannahan, T. Lyne, J. C. Cooper, P. Moynihan and B. O'Donoghue.

Left: Dr. Jim Brosnan and Dr. Eamonn O'Sullivan pictured here talking together. Jim, son of the legendary Con Brosnan, trained Kerry in the mid-1960s. Once again Dr. Eamonn trained father and then son to All-Ireland glory.

Right: *Dr. Eamonn with a group of visitors to the Mental Hospital in the 1940s. Included back left is Dr. Desmond Hayes (back row, extreme left) whose interview shortly before his death is included in this book.*

Left: *Dr. Eamonn, in classic pose as he watches his men in training. Left to right: Dave Geaney, Mick O'Donoghue, Tom Long, Jerome O'Shea, Tim 'Tiger' Lyons, Dan McAuliffe, Paudie Sheehy and Sean Murphy. Rising for the ball are Kevin Coffey and Pat Ahern.*

Above: *Bonfires blaze – a traditional Kerry homecoming for one of Dr. Eamonn's triumphant teams. The happy faces speak a thousand words.*

Left: *1953 Kerry Parade – Dr. Eamonn sends his men into battle for the 1953 win over Armagh. Note the superb physical fitness of each and every player. Players on the day: Jas Murphy, Jackie Lyne, Johnny Foley, Sean Murphy, Jim Brosnan, Mixi Palmer, John Cronin, Ned Roche, Dermot Hannifin, Donie Murphy, Sean Kelly, John Joe Sheehan, Colm Kennelly, Tadghie Lyne and Tom Ash.*

Right: *The 1953 celebrations at the Great Southern Hotel, Killarney. John Joe Sheehy addresses the gathering. Also included are Frank Sheehy (County Board Chairman), Con Brosnan and Sean O'Siochan. Standing at the back with Dickey Bow is Jimmy Cullinane, who wrote many beautiful verses on Kerry football.*

Left: *Dr. Eamonn's rope training in the 1950s. From left to right: Mick O'Dwyer, Mick O'Donoghue and Paudie Sheehy.*

Right: *Dr. Eamonn (centre) as Chairman at an NACA athletic meeting in the Glebe Hotel Killarney in the 1950s. Left to right: Tadge Crowley, Tom Donnellan, Martin Cleary and Sean Russell.*

Left: *Kerry in training for the 1953 All-Ireland Final against Armagh, with St. Finan's Hospital in the background. Left to right: Johnny Foley (in goal), Jackie Lyne, Mick Murphy, Ned Roche, Sean Kelly, Donie Murphy and Tom Ash.*

Jerome O'Shea – star of the 1955 Final comes from St. Mary's Caherceiveen Club, as did Jack O'Shea, Maurice Fitzgerald and Donal 'Marcus' O'Neill.

John Culloty in 1955. John played corner forward that memorable day. Then in 1959 and 1962 he was in goal for those successful teams trained by Dr. Eamonn.

Mick Murphy – Kerry's dashing full forward who played on Dr. Eamonn's greatest winning team in 1955.

Right: *The Fitzgerald Stadium in its entire splendour during the 1955 Munster Final. Kerry goalkeeper Garry O'Mahoney was beaten by a Cork goal. The Cork player on the right is Jim O'Donovan. Kerry won and went on to win the All-Ireland. Note the packed terrace and the line of supporters sitting high on the boundary wall.*

Kerry tradition. And I choose this Lyne family from the town land of Cleeney, one mile outside the town of Killarney on the Tralee road, as my family topic simply because they were the men who were instrumental in the building of my club, previously mentioned Killarney Legion.

I was fortunate to know most of them on a personal basis and it was from them that I first heard of the training powers of Dr. Eamonn. Denny Lyne had captioned Kerry in that historic Polo Grounds Final in New York in 1947. Before he died, I visited him and he kindly gave me what was to be the very last interview recounting his and his family's life which as he himself said "was dominated by Kerry football".

Their father had bought the Cleeney farm early in the nineteenth century and Denny had vivid memories of travelling to Castletownbeare to buy cattle and then walking home to Killarney, driving the herd before them and finally landing home tired and weary. The longest journey undertaken by the cattle dealing family was to Roscommon. Once again on foot, they sold cattle to the local farmers along the way. This Denny recalled "took a couple of weeks and these long stamina-sapping journeys was to stand to us in the succeeding years as we lined out against the greatest names in Gaelic football at that time, we were naturally fit."

Mickey the eldest boy in the family was, arguably the most stylish forward Killarney has ever produced, although Tadghie Lyne (no relation), Johnny Culloty, and Timmy O'Leary, in a career dogged by illness, had possibly an equal claim. And today Colm 'Gooch' Cooper has all the attributes to join this pantheon of greats.

Studying for the priesthood, Mickey's football career was confined to his holidays from college because of the prevailing playing conditions on clerical students. Mickey Lyne never kicked a ball in the National League with Kerry and amazingly he, the oldest of the Cleeney brothers went on to win All-Ireland medals with The Kingdom in Minor (1933), Junior (1941), and Senior (1937), all in a 12 year playing span with Kerry.

The renowned Kerryman GAA reporter P.F. (Paddy Foley) tells this lovely story in his book *'Kerry's Football Story'*. Writing about the counties All-Ireland Junior win of 1941, he recalls: "Our juniors followed in the footsteps of the seniors by winning All-Ireland honours. They started off with a draw against Cork in Tralee in the Munster Championship. For the replay in Macoom a young man travelled as a spectator, was invited to play and to such good effect that he was largely responsible for Kerry's victory: 2-10 to 2-7. He was Father Michael Lyne, Killarney, now in Glasgow."

1937 was the 50th year of the All-Ireland Championships, and a memorable year it proved for Kerry, as Mickey Lyne kicked a point for his county that year which would remain forever etched in his memory. Following a draw against Laois in the All-Ireland semi-final in Cork the replay took place in Waterford City. In a match which abounded with thrills from start to finish the sides were level at seven points, each with five minutes remaining in the hour. Then in stepped the Legion man, fielding beautifully he rounded his marker and sent the leather high and true between the posts and Kerry were in the final.

In that final Kerry defeated Cavan following a replay, but due to his clerical duties Mickey missed that game. However his club mate Timmy O'Leary came in and helped Kerry to a 4-4 to 1-7 victory. O'Leary scoring two great goals. This was the youngest Kerry team at the time to win the Championship. Mickey Lyne won his second senior medal in 1941 when he came on as a substitute in the second half of that final as Kerry beat Galway 1-8 to 0-7. Playing for Galway that day was Dan Kavanagh a West Kerry man who was an engineer in that county. Dan would go on and star for Kerry five years later when The Kingdom defeated Roscommon in 1946.

Mickey Lyne later became Canon Lyne and ministered in Glasgow for over 40 years where he was also Chaplin to the Glasgow Celtic Football Club. In a forward to our club history *'A Legion of Memories'* Lyne wrote as Club President: "My first game for The Legion had a disastrous beginning. I slipped out of St. Brendan's Seminary Killarney to play with my club, and this led to my expulsion from the College. In the eyes of many I had brought disgrace and shame on my family and friends, a complete failure. Today I am proud to say that expulsion from The Seminary was my salvation. I went back as a day boy, worked harder than ever, passed all my examinations, entered All Hallows College in 1935 and was ordained in 1941. This year (1979) I have completed 38 years of active service work in the Archdiocese of Glasgow," Lyne said.

I remember Canon Mickey Lyne as a man of great leadership, tremendous drive and great passion – both on and off the field. Being the oldest of the family he must have definitely had a massive influence on the brothers that would play with both club and county in the succeeding years following his departure to minister in Glasgow.

Donie Lyne, the quiet man of the family was probably the most dedicated of the boys to the service of his club Killarney Legion, not having the distraction of playing either with St. Brendan's or any Kerry team. He served his club only, and served them faithfully and well. Declan Horgan writing in the club history recalls, "One still has pleasant memories of Donie with his short mincing steps, jacket unbuttoned, and boots held behind his back arriving at the gates of Fitzgerald Stadium. He was always an early arrival. Denny Casey might be mending a puncture at the foot of Tiernaboul. Jimmy Fleming might be laughing his way down a slow pint in Pat O'Mares. Mickey O'Sullivan, the postman, might be seen going down New Street the wrong way as our poor secretary Jack O'Shea jotted down the names of the late arrivals to the background of the referees insistent whistle. But Donie Lyne was togged and eagerly waiting to take up his half back position, where no man in Kerry played with more spirit or enjoyment. It was a pleasure to share Donie's cheerful smile and even temper as a team-mate," Horgan added. He might not have been as famous as his brothers, however Donie typified all that is great in a club player and it must be said that his contribution to the Lyne tradition was immense.

Teddy, the third of the Lyne boys, was the stormy petrel of the family. With Teddy around the expression "hard knocks were given and taken" was hardly a cliché. He was always in the tick of the action and many shrewd judges, even today, swear that he was the hardest of all the boys. A butcher by trade Teddy won Munster and All-Ireland Junior medals with Kerry in 1941, and Kerry Senior County Championship medals with his club in 1946 and later with Killarney in 1949.

The brief but brilliant career of Tom Lyne was cut short when he died in 1942, in his early 20s. He had shown great promise as an aggressive half back, but sadly his great potential was never fully realized. God took him in his prime, a sad blow to a family so closely knit.

The fifth of the brothers was Denny. He outlived the rest of the boys and so his death in November 2001 following a long illness brought down the curtain on a proud family who had served club and county with loyalty, passion, dignity and full commitment. I was fortunate to have known him better than the rest of the boys and indeed I would visit him at his home in Cleeney until shortly before his death. Together we would chat about the boys and his own football career in particular.

I have vivid memories of one beautiful August evening just four months before his death. This meeting remains etched in my mind. We sat inside the window of his front room looking out as the sun set, casting a golden glow on the lush green fields which front the farm house. As Denny talked, recalling in wonderful detail his families sporting history, I recorded the memories of his life and times, both as a farmer and Kerry footballer.

As we spoke and drank together it was clearly evident that one aspect of this exemplary man's sporting life had left some very painful memories – Kerry's defeat by Cavan in the 1947 All-Ireland Senior Football Final. The Final had been played for the first and only time in history in the Polo Grounds, New York. By virtue of the fact that our club had won the 1946 County Championship Denny had assumed the mantle of captaincy as is the rule in Kerry. And now 54 years later I listened in captivated silence as he stated publicly for the first time his version of why Kerry had lost that historic 1947 Final.

"It was one of the biggest mistakes of my life; I should have insisted, insisted that our great trainer Dr. Eamonn O'Sullivan would be brought to America for that game. We did little or no training for that final, Eamonn had been brought back the year before and trained us to win that 1946 Final against Roscommon, without him we would not have won and if he had come to America with us I am utterly convinced that Cavan would not have beaten us. Dan Kavanagh, Teddy O'Connor, Jackie and I often spoke about this and I repeat we should have insisted that he be brought. He was probably too good to the players, if you had anything at all wrong with you (expense for medical bills was no problem) and they did not want him because of this, that's what I believe.

Many people blame the referee from Wexford, Martin O'Neill for that defeat. I'll tell you a story now: A few years ago I met a man from Wexford in Charlie Foley's Pub in Killarney. He knew Martin O'Neill and he told me that O'Neill asked him; if you meet Denny Lyne in Killarney tell him that I said they were robbed of that All-Ireland in New York. What he meant by that remark, you can guess for yourself."

Full backs in football played with effect rather than with style during Denny's era, as the defensive nature of the position leaves little room for the stylist. However this was not the case with the fifth of the Lyne brothers. Denny combined a graceful elegance with the normal solid defensive play of a full back as his secure fielding and stylish, lengthy clearances more than compensated for his lack of inches. Indeed it is of interest to recall that Kerry selected him as a corner forward in the 1944 All-Ireland Final which Kerry lost to Roscommon because of his stylish football.

He later played at corner back in the 1946 and 1947 Finals and one of his greatest memories is winning his All-Ireland medal in 1946 with his brother Jackie staring at right half back, just in front of him. The memories of the home coming, thousands gathering at Killarney Railway Station and especially the massive bonfire lighting up the dark

September sky at the Cleeney home as the two brothers arrived with the Sam Maguire Cup, were impossible to forget.

My final meeting that summers evening at the Cleeney farm which Denny worked all his life is one of my fondest sporting memories. Despite his great career that loss in The Polo Grounds New York, in 1947, when he captained that star studded Kerry team, I believe, haunted him right up to the time of my final interview with him. Denis, one of Denny's four sons, now runs the farm at Cleeney.

Jackie the sixth of the Lyne boys was the best known. Indeed in tracing his career it must be said that he was one of the all-time greats of Kerry football. His record speaks for itself. His playing career spanned 20 years in Cork, Dublin and Kerry. When he hung up his boots he went on and served the county both as a selector and later as a most successful trainer, guiding Kerry to two Senior All-Ireland wins in 1969 and 1970. Jackie was the most versatile of the family, gaining All-Ireland medals with Kerry both as a back and forward, a rare feat indeed. Despite gaining almost every national honour he was, before all else, a dedicated club man. He wore the 'Green and White' of his beloved Legion for 18 consecutive years. Surely a club record at the time.

Like his brothers Jackie began school at the local Presentation Monastery. He then moved across the road to the famed football nursery, St. Brendan's College, and here his great football talents began to flourish and grow. He helped The Seminary to win the Dunloe Cup, The Kerry Colleges Cup and the Kerry Colleges Senior Hurling title. Thus began a career which would see The Legion man travel the world both as a player and ambassador for his county.

Jackie played for the Kerry Minors in 1941 and Roscommon beat them in the semi-final. His direct opponent that day was the great Bill Carlos. Following his time in the Sem., he helped UCC to a Sigerson Cup victory. The previous year however, in the autumn of 1943, he donned the county jersey for the first time in a tournament against Roscommon and later recalled, "I caught the first ball cleanly that came my way and put it over the bar." It was clear that a new star had burst onto the Kerry GAA stage.

The year 1944 saw the fair-haired, low-sized, and built-like-a-tank Jackie win his first Munster medal with legendary names such as; Danno Keeffe, Joe Keohane, and the great Paddy Kennedy. 1945 saw Kerry beaten by Cork. 1946 was to prove unforgettable for the Lyne family, as Jackie won his first All-Ireland medal beating Roscommon in the final with brother Denny behind him at corner back. His opponent that day in 1946 was Donal Keenan who was later to become President of the GAA. Jackie later admitted just how lucky they were in the drawn game against Roscommon. "I was sure we were gone that day and then Paddy Burke and 'Gega' Connor got two late goals to save the day and we won the replay 2-9 to 0-10." While Jackie was winning his first Celtic Cross, Danno Keeffe was winning his then record seventh medal in goal for Kerry.

The next year, 1947, saw The Legion man march behind his brother in that famous New York Polo Grounds Final and the bitter disappointment of defeat that followed. Another Munster medal in 1948 and interestingly the ball was thrown in that day by Monsignor Hugh O'Flaherty who is known world-wide for his exploits in Rome during the Second World War when he defied the German forces and saved many Allied lives. The Killarney priest lies buried in Caherceiveen. Kerry proved no match for Mayo in the semi-final that year.

Clare sensationally beat Kerry in 1949 but missing from that team, for family reasons, were Jackie and brother Denny. Now starring at centre back, 1950 saw the Cleeney man proudly captain his beloved Kingdom to another Munster win with Teddy O'Sullivan, Dan Kavanagh and Jim Brosnan, as teammates. In the All-Ireland semi-final Louth scored a surprise 1-7 to 0-8 victory. Yet another Munster medal in 1951 with Paddy 'Bawn' Brosnan as the star defender. However following a draw against Mayo there was more heart break for Jackie as the Connaght men won the replay 2-4 to 1-5. Cork were too good in 1952 in Cork as Kerry goalie Donal 'Marcus' O'Neill and Paddy 'Bawn' prevented a rout.

The following year 1953 would be extra special for the Cleeney man as Kerry won the Jubilee All-Ireland beating Armagh in a dramatic final. The moment of greatest suspense came in the second half when Kerry were leading by two points and Armagh were awarded a penalty. Years later Jackie spoke to me of the drama surrounding that moment in time. "There we stood helplessly, as Bill McCorry ran up to take the kick faced by our goalkeeper Johnny Foley. My line of vision to the goal was obscured by players, but when I saw the Kerry men jumping with delight in the air I knew he had failed to score. Yes Weeshie, there might be truth in the story that McCorry was obstructed by some of our lads as he ran to kick the ball." Jackie and J.J. Sheehan added points and another All-Ireland was on its way to the farmhouse in Cleeney. Years later Jackie recalled, "I have been playing All-Irelands since 1944 and I was the only link with the boys who won the last title in 1946, the spirit was tremendous and the training under Dr. Eamonn and Paul Russell was the best we ever had and it was extra special for me as I had my club mates Mixi Palmer, Donie Murphy, J.J.

Sheehan, and Gerald O'Sullivan with me. Dr. Eamonn played a huge part in my career and later when I became Kerry trainer I put into practice many of the skills I had learned from him."

The year after this saw the end of Jackie Lynes Inter-County career and it ended in a storm of controversy. Kerry qualified to meet Meath in that year's Final, 'collective training' was banned and the selectors dropped a bombshell when they failed to include Lyne in the starting 15. Raymond Smith in has excellent book, *The Football Immortals* summed up the prevailing mood in the county at the time: "The Kerry selectors made a huge blunder by dropping Jackie Lyne, although approaching the veteran stage he was confidently expected to land a goal or two."

"The attack lost much of its sting by his absence. His heart was set on winning a third medal before he retired. Kerry turned in one of their worst ever performances in that Final and Meath won easily. He was however too big a man to let personal regrets effect his loyalty to his beloved county and despite the disappointment of being denied the honour of a third medal he continued his association with the senior team and he was a member of the selection committee when Kerry beat Dublin in that historic 1955 final," added Smith.

The last time Jackie Lyne wore the 'Green and Gold' was in a tournament game in Tralee in 1954. His final kick shook the Mayo net! He lined out for Munster from 1945 to 1954, missing out just once while he also had the honour of captaining his providence to a Railway Cup win in 1948. He represented Ireland twice against the Combined Universities, a fore-runner to the present All Stars. Jackie gave 18 consecutive years to our club. Along with his brothers, they were the heart and soul of The Legion and, at the height of his career, he was the star as he led his club to County Championship victory.

Without doubt 1946 was the big year – Mickey Lyne was Captain while Teddy lined out at mid-field and Denny in defence. The bonfires blazed again in Cleeney that evening as the boys brought home the Cup. Lining out with Teddy at mid-field that day was Tom Spillane. He later married Maura, one of the boys' sisters and they had three sons; Pat, Mick and Tom who went on to become Kerry stars with Mick O'Dwyer's great side.

With Kerry football going through a periodic crisis in the middle 1960s, the County turned to Jackie. He accepted the position of trainer and the rest is history. He built a marvellous Kerry side, and while they lost to Down in 1968 Jackie's team went on to win the All-Irelands in 1969 and 1970. Training under him was a revelation. He knew how to get the best out of each individual. Paud O'Donoghue, Tom Prendergast, Liam Higgins, Mick Morris and D.J. Crowley blossomed under his guidance. He also succeeded in pulling a master stroke as he coaxed some Kerry legends out of Inter-County retirement to help his cause – Mick O'Connell, Johnny Culloty, Seamus Murphy, and Mick O'Dwyer all made a come-back when approached by the Cleeney legend, and without them Kerry would be minus two titles. The win in 1969 was special for our club, as not alone did Jackie train the side, but Johnny Culloty was Captain and goalkeeper. I was lucky enough to be Johnny's understudy that memorable day. It was Kerry's 21st All-Ireland victory. They had lost the 1966 and 1967 Munster Finals to Cork and the County was in big trouble. What would have happened if Jackie Lyne had not taken over as trainer at that point of Kerry's history, we can only speculate.

Jackie's contribution to the GAA was huge in all facets. He refereed many games including the 1957 Munster Final between Cork and Waterford as well as a Kerry Senior Football final. He was a good hurler and helped establish basketball in Killarney in the early 1950s.

In 1982 he retired from his job as a rep for Guinness with whom he worked for 18 years. Fishing on the magnificent Killarney lakes and mountain walking then became his favourite past times – a far cry from the roar of the crowds on which he grew up. It was here he was happiest.

Jackie Lyne strode the fields of Kerry, Munster, and Ireland like a colossus. Looking back through the mists of time it is, in my opinion, safe to say that this member of the Cleeney family was as good as any of the great players before or after him.

Jackie Lyne died unexpectedly on Wednesday December 15, 1993 and lies buried in Aghadoe Cemetery overlooking the lakes and mountains of Killarney.

Strangely enough, Con the seventh and youngest Lyne brother, never played football, but his brothers often told me that he knew more about the game than all of them put together and they were never in a rush home to face the sharp lash of Con's tongue following a defeat for either club or county.

Rarely can a single family have served club and county so loyally as did the Lyne family of Cleeney. I became involved in The Legion around the mid-50s and got to know six of the boys. Their passion and dedication to the game was to me, in my young days, frightening at times. Families such as the Lynes scattered all around the country are the backbone of the Gaelic Athletic Association. We may never see their likes again. Dr. Eamonn O'Sullivan was an integral part of their lives and they in return served him with loyalty, dedication and great passion through the 1930s, 1940s and 1950s.

Dr. Eamonn and the Legend of The Sheehy Family

When it comes to marquee names in football they don't come much bigger than the late John Joe Sheehy who distinguished himself as a Kerry footballer par excellence over a span of 12 years from 1918 to 1930. Those years saw him scale the dizzy heights of fame when he played 35 senior knockout Championship games for his county, four senior All-Ireland medals, twice Captain of All-Ireland winning teams, Captain of National League and Munster Championship winning teams, seven All-Ireland final appearances, club honours in both hurling and football. He also played hurling with Munster in the Railway Cup and was considered as good a hurler as he was a footballer. All of this and more tells only part of the story of John Joe Sheehy.

Away from the playing field he was an uncompromising Irish nationalist who suffered imprisonment for his beliefs at a time when the open wounds of the Civil War and the atrocities that it provoked were still fresh in the minds of the people. This was no easy option for somebody who had young children to rear, when times were hard and who could have been safely ensconced at home in the bosom of his family rather than staring at the flatlands of the Curragh through the bars of his prison cell.

His enthusiasm for all things Irish was ingrained into his persona and this love affair often found expression at county conventions when his trenchant denunciation of any truck with "foreign games" became par for the course. When his former playing colleague Bob Stack proposed at one such assembly that the so-called "Ban" (Rule 26) be deleted from the rule book, he got a withering look from a man who had nailed his colours to the mast on that particular issue from a long way back. Sheehy proposed "a direct negative to safeguard the ideals of the Association" and the Ballybunion motion didn't even get a seconder.

Times change and people change but John Joe Sheehy would never alter his views on this subject no matter what the circumstances. He was unchanging and unchangeable. The coming of soccer and rugby to Croke Park with the Union Jack flying over the stadium, the very place where he and his kind had shed blood, sweat and tears to win glory for their county would have left him outraged and betrayed – you can be sure of that.

After Kerry had won the All-Ireland Final replay against Kildare in 1926 a headline in *The Kerryman* read: TRALEE REJOICES.

Here a short paragraph described how the news was received in the county capital: "Wireless sets were in great demand and anyone who had one was invaded by friends and besieged by anxious crowds. The reception was rendered difficult due to interference that was malicious in its persistence."

It is said that when the result became known a torchlight procession headed by the band of the British Legion paraded the town and serenaded the homes of the various players in turn. This provided a surreal touch as several of the Tralee men on the winning team, most notably; Sheehy, Barrett, Riordan, Moriarty, Slattery and Ryan were unrepentant nationalists and rebels who detested the British presence in Ireland. How they felt when patronized by the British Legion is unknown.

The 1926 Final (draw and replay) marked the zenith of John Joe Sheehy's career in the Kerry jersey. A short synopsis of his achievements in *The Kerry Sentinel* described him as "a man of vast leadership qualities, 28 years old, prolific score getter, brilliant hands, splendid physique, fast, agile and utterly fearless in his approach".

That would appear to have been a fair summation of his outstanding talents but in those far-off days it was the local ballad-maker who did most to immortalise their local heroes. A man who signed himself P.C. did the honours (P.C. was a writer and poet who contributed regularly to Kerry newspapers – the late Micheal O Ruairc once told me that P.C. was a Kilkenny man who worked at the Tralee Railway Station):

I'll luck's dark veil had vanished
And a bright one came instead.
For John Joe playing in winning vein,
Some brilliant charges led.
And Pluggy famed at centre-half,
Each fierce attack repelled.
While Bailey's feats on Gorman's left,
Will never be excelled.

As a County Selector and president of the County Board, Treasurer of the Munster Council, delegate to the Munster Council from 1936 to 1973 as well as holding numerous other offices, John Joe Sheehy remained a father figure to the GAA in Kerry up to the day he died at the Bons Secours Hospital, Tralee on January 13, 1980.

His sons, Paudie (RIP), Niall, Sean Óg and Brian kept the family name to the forefront throughout their distinguished playing careers both in the inter-county arena with Kerry and, equally important in their scale of priorities, with their beloved Boherbee John Mitchels. Paudie, the supreme stylist whose sudden death at the age of 36 shocked all who knew him as one of the fittest men on the Kerry team, won three senior All-Ireland medals (1953, 1959, 1962). He was singularly unlucky to have been omitted from the team that beat Armagh in 1953 when he was Captain after giving a stunning performance in that year's Munster Final against Cork in Killarney.

However, the Sam Maguire Cup was merely delayed from entering the family home at Ballymullen. That happened in 1962 when Sean Óg captained the side that beat Roscommon. Niall was an indestructible presence at full back for about ten years and will always be remembered for his obliteration of Frank Stockwell of Galway in 1959. This was a key factor in Kerry's success. Brian won junior and National League medals with the county and was a sterling midfielder on the Mitchels' side that garnered five successive county titles.

Playing for Mitchels brought out the very best in the Sheehy's. Niall often switched from full back to full forward where he would invariably wreak havoc on the opposition while Paudie, Sean Óg and Brian gave everything they had for the jersey. The indomitable spirit of the clan was epitomized by the way they encouraged each other on the field. There was no holding back. Pride of place and pride in their club were obviously huge motivating factors.

Paudie and John Joe are long gone but their names will endure in the hearts and minds of Kerry people who love and appreciate their footballers.

The legend of the Sheehy's, father and sons, has been deeply ingrained in the lore of Kerry football and it must be added that Dr. Eamonn O'Sullivan played a vital part in fostering that legend. To train a father and four sons in pursuit of Kerry glory is very special indeed. But what would you expect but something special from Eamonn – the man who shaped the sporting fortunes of so many great Kerry families.

Ar dheis lamh De go raibh a n-anamacha.

Interview with John Kelly

John Kelly was a community worker for 27 years and in this interview he gives a vivid insight into Dr. Eamonn, the Resident Medical Superintendent (R.M.S.), away from the cheering thousands of Croke Park on All-Ireland Final day.

My earliest introduction to Dr. Eamonn O'Sullivan and the Kerry football team was on a mid-September morning in 1946. I was then an eleven-year-old schoolboy completing a milk sales round in Killarney Town and on dropping in to the Franciscan Church with my father to say a morning prayer a group of 22 very athletic looking men were leaving after morning Mass and on their way to the nearby Scott's Hotel, for breakfast.

My father exchanged brief greetings with two of the group namely; Denny Lyne from Cleeney also a milk vender and Gerald Teahan who owned a licensed premises in the town. He wished them well in the up-coming All-Ireland Final against Roscommon. Turning to me he said: "They are the Kerry football team and that's their great trainer Dr. Eamonn O'Sullivan and they're in collective training for the final against Roscommon." My life long passion and love for Kerry football was born there and then on the steps leading to the Friary.

Nine years later, Saturday, April 22, 1955, I joined the staff of St. Finan's Psychiatric Hospital and it was here I was to meet the man who gained legendary status on many occasions both as a psychiatrist and a sports personality. St. Finan's then had a patient population in excess of 1,100 (it is now down to under 100), with many of those unfortunate people having been admitted there during the era of the economic war and the hungry 1940s when Ireland and Kerry were in a state of economic stagnation. The outside world had little to offer them and so the Hospital became their home.

E.C.T. or Electro Convulsive Therapy (still administered sparingly), combined with a small amount of other medication was used to treat most disorders in the early days. These treatments are in sharp contrast with modern day procedures such as; psychotherapy, counselling and a wide range of medication to treat the various disorders like depression, schizophrenia and anxiety states.

In that far off era the R.M.S. of a psychiatric hospital enjoyed a status on par with a county manager and was rewarded on the basis of the patient population of the hospital that he administered a service to. He was also entitled to accommodation and supplies from the hospital farm and garden.

On taking over the position of R.M.S., following the resignation of his father-in-law Dr. Griffin in 1933, Eamonn took up residence in a large apartment overlooking the entrance of the Hospital. The Hospital had first opened its doors to the mentally ill in 1896. Despite the fact that he took over an administrative role in the worst possible stage in the economic life of the country and when the rate-payers simply could not afford the extra revenue required to improve the standard of care in the Killarney Hospital, Dr. Eamonn O'Sullivan must be given major credit for the manner in which he improvised to deliver a reasonable service of care for those less privileged members of society.

A year after his appointment he prepared an elaborate plan of improvement for the Hospital which he deemed necessary for the welfare of the patients and staff which included; a dental and general surgery, a proper regeneration plant for the storage of food, a modern occupational department and workshops, as well as recreational facilities to include; a hand ball court, billiard tables and tennis courts. He provided a recreational room for the staff, extra land for the hospital farm, new furniture and decorations, a proper house telephone system, laundry equipment and new bathing facilities all at a total cost of £21,000 (€25,000). He recommended that this be submitted to the Irish Hospital Sweepstake which, at that time, funded improvements in health care. Having secured some funding to defray the cost of the aforementioned expenditure he again made a further application to the visiting committee for the appointment of a third doctor. However, due to the economic climate this application met with strenuous opposition and a further number of years elapsed before such an appointment was passed.

In that Victorian era when any worthwhile form of treatment was a distant dream and the risk of patients becoming chronically institutionalised was very high, Dr. Eamonn's main focus was on what became known as Occupational Therapy ('O.T.') to help to rehabilitate patients. He subsequently went on to write a book on the subject. His main objective was to adopt a programme of therapy suitable for each individual whether it was the workshops, garden or farm and products from the hospital workshops were sold to retailers as far away as Cork City. Such a programme of O.T. was extended to the development of Killarney Fitzgerald Stadium, which today stands proudly as a memorial to his vision of having a top class GAA stadium in Killarney. The Stadium is also a monument to the combined contribution of staff and patients from St. Finan's.

It was little wonder that the group of us nurses who arrived to St. Finan's in 1955 viewed this man Dr. Eamonn O'Sullivan somewhat as a legendary figure. Over the previous 20 years he had made an enormous contribution to the development of facilities in the Hospital and helped develop sporting facilities such as the Stadium and the Killarney Golf Course at O'Mahoney's Point.

1955 was the year Kerry scored a magnificent victory over Dublin in the All-Ireland Football Final, a victory with which the name of Dr. Eamonn will be forever associated. In essence, while 'collective training' had been banned by Central Council in 1954 Dr. Eamonn, as trainer, still managed to have a major share of the players arrange leave from work to train regularly during the day and obtain adequate rest. Having watched many Kerry teams preparing for finals in the interim period I feel that the system of collective training combined with adequate rest and diet was possibly the nearest to what English professional soccer clubs have in operation today. Dr. Eamonn was years ahead of his time in matters of preparing players for matches.

Dr. Eamonn operated in the role of trainer, manager, coach, sports psychologist, dietician and sports injury specialist, all at the same time. Nowadays such back room facilities are provided by various people specializing in these roles. He made the hospital facilities available on a regular basis for changing, showering and the treatment of sports injuries to Kerry teams, as they prepared for big matches. This was one man's contribution to the county team, a contribution which now costs the County Boards in excess of €200,000 per annum. Yet when Kerry played Cavan in the historic Polo Grounds Final in New York in 1947 the Kerry County Board would not include Dr. Eamonn in the travelling party and again in 1960 when his ticket allocation was cut to a minimum. It was a decision which provoked a strike by some of the players prior to the final, a game Kerry lost to Down as Eamonn had stepped down from the training of the team.

The mid-1950s marked the arrival of a group of young trainee sports-minded nurses to St. Finan's Hospital and, despite being in the twilight of his career, Dr. Eamonn fully immersed himself in the formation of a hospital GAA club, a rowing club and basketball club and he took great pride in their success during the years following their foundation. I can still vividly recall him travelling in his Morris Oxford car to support patients and staff teams. He was also the man who trained the hospital team that won the All-Ireland Connolly Cup in Croke Park in 1959. On that memorable day for his hospital he later remarked to me how he had marvelled at the skill displayed by county player Johnny Culloty, who scored St. Finan's total of 1-6 on a day of torrential rain. Around the same period he was instrumental in the formation of a patient's football team.

His record in Croke Park was phenomenal. He loved the big occasion and the challenge of training men and preparing them both mentally and physically for major games in Croke Park.

I can recall a special occasion in 1958 when St. Finan's won the Premier Race, the Senior Sixes, at the Annual Killarney Regatta because two weeks later the entire crew and their trainer Dr. Jack O'Conner were summoned by Eamonn to the hospital boardroom where he presented each with specially inscribed gold medals as a memento of their achievement. Other special events I can recall were the weekly dances and the Halloween and Christmas socials, which again were the brainchild of one of the most remarkable men I had the privilege of working with.

The late 1950s marked the advent of modern treatments that resulted in many patients being discharged from hospital to the community. Once again Dr. Eamonn was to the fore in the development of a community care programme. This involved the appointment of extra psychiatrists and community nurses and the development of out patient's clinics in the major towns of Tralee, Killarney and Listowel – a service that was later extended to Kenmare, Dingle and Caherceiveen.

Dr. Eamonn was one of the great Kerrymen of the last century. He left a major legacy to our county in the areas of psychiatry and sport. He touched and greatly benefited the lives of thousands of people. His funeral was one of the largest seen in Kerry for many years and was attended by officers of the GAA, N.A.C.A.I., The Gaelic League and Comhaltas Ceoltóirí Eireann from many counties. The guard of honour was composed of members of the Dr. Croke's Club, Killarney, past and present, members of the Kerry teams and the Laune Rangers Club, Killorglin; his father's old club.

This publication in his memory is long, long overdue.

Well-known Killarney poet Jimmy Cullinane penned the following verse in his honour:

God rest you, Dr. Eamonn,
you made us all feel proud,
While we say a silent Ave,
or sing your praises loud,
Your name shall be remembered
in the Kingdom's hall of fame,
As the one who always taught us
to play a sporting game.

An Interview with James O'Donoghue

"Every Kerryman is a tiller of the soil and
football comes natural to them," Dr. Eamonn.

James O'Donoghue spent the whole of his working life as a psychiatric
nurse in St. Finan's Hospital, Killarney. Due to his great love for
Gaelic football he became very close to Dr. Eamonn. In this interview,
Jameso, outlined yet another perspective of what life was like working
under Dr. Eamonn in St. Finan's and the massive contribution that
the Doctor made to the life of the patients who lived there.

Dr. Eamonn had a huge interest in all sports, he was a man far ahead
of his time and he was a sporting man through and through. He had a
handball court constructed specially for the patients, and this sport of
course is part of the GAA. Dr. Eamonn was very interested in it and
he encouraged the patients to play handball with the staff. We also
played football in the airing court. This was a big green area closed
in on all sides, the patients would be walked out there morning and
evening where the nursing staff would help them pick teams and play
for long periods. That was the big recreation – playing football with
the patients in the airing court. And we'd take them down to a game
on the Sunday in Fitzgerald Stadium. We had a special door to the
Stadium strictly for the patients.

The door was put there because it was the patients of St. Finan's
that built Fitzgerald Stadium with the backing and organisation of
the Dr. Croke's Club. This fact is beyond repute. The patients assisted
Eugene O'Connor. They toiled with shovels and with hand-barrows
and they removed a massive hill. They worked and worked. And as
recognition Dr. Eamonn put in the green door as an entry to the
Stadium in the hospital grounds exclusively for patients, with a special
key that was kept in the hall porter's room of the Hospital. The nurses

could then take the patients down to any of the big games played in Fitzgerald Stadium on a Sunday. That patients' door was there until the 1970s and eventually, as I'm sure those who know the Stadium intimately will recollect, it was closed up. In my opinion it should not have been bricked up. If Eamonn was around I'm sure he would have insisted that it remain. He was a very thoughtful person and the patients' better welfare was always his first priority. He was always searching for new means of occupational therapy that assisted the patients' recovery more quickly. He was a man of great foresight introducing all of this before anyone else in the country.

There were lots of patients interested in sport because they had played with their own clubs, and remember – they came from all parts of Kerry. Eamonn saw this connection with football as a tremendous opportunity to motivate the patients under his care. He often remarked to me that, "Kerrymen, football and the land are synonymous with each other." He was of course completely correct, and the same applies even today.

Then there was the nursing staff from all the various football clubs, Kilcummin men who played senior football with their club, and they came from Listry including Tom Lynch whose sons Brendan and Paudie became great Kerry footballers. Brendan is now the R.M.S. of St. Finan's. You also had Mike Moynihan and Paddy Moynihan of Headford, legendary names in Gaelic football in Kerry. They included some lads from the town also, naturally, who played with Killarney Legion or Dr. Croke's Club. Johnny Culloty the legendary Kerry player did great work with the patients through his football career not to mention John Kelly from Spa and John Cahill from Glenflesk. They all played with their own clubs. Eamonn encouraged all the staff to play on our hospital team and we were also allowed to play men like Kerry All-Ireland medal winners Donie O'Sullivan and Mick Gleeson, despite the fact that they were not employed by the Hospital.

Dr. Eamonn's influence on football in the Hospital was immense and with his urging and backing we formed our own club. It was founded at a meeting in the Hospital on February 22, 1956. The great Kerry footballer Bill Landers was our first President and Eamonn was appointed as Vice President. We entered the East Kerry League and Championship and competed very well. Then in 1959 we had our first ever All-Ireland win when we won the Connolly Cup, competed for each year by the psychiatric hospitals of Ireland. And once again it was down to our trainer, Dr. Eamonn. Despite his hectic schedule that year, as he guided Kerry to another title, he devoted his spare time to his hospital side and we had a historic win in Croke Park as we defeated Castlebar in the final.

I had the great privilege of training under the great man and it was an unforgettable experience. He was quietly spoken, never got excited and this rubbed off on the players, with the result that you were always relaxed going into a match. He had this special way about him and he fully understood every player; their needs, their weaknesses, their strengths and their moods. I can now, on reflection, look back and fully understand why he was so successful during all those years as Kerry trainer. Dr. Eamonn was special. We will never see his likes again. He even allowed the players limited time off for training during his term as trainer of the hospital team. I suppose you could say that we were the first of the semi-professional players.

Dr. Eamonn had a hugely positive effect on the patients and directed his efforts into getting them to play football. He maintained that it was the ideal form of Occupational Therapy. He got us jerseys. He got us boots, stockings and togs. No expense was spared. And when we went off to play other hospitals the Secretary at the time, Mr. Bill Walsh, would give me a blank cheque going off in the bus. We used to have the 'Knight of the Road' bus and we'd carry patients; the best of them. We had great patients. We had fine footballers from the Dingle peninsula and everywhere and together they helped us get as far as the All-Ireland Final. This was played in Clonmel. We would have a great time on the journey home and the patients looked forward to those outings so much. I'm fully convinced that a number of them were discharged later from the Hospital due to the football outings organised by Dr. Eamonn. It certainly got them out of those long-stay wards and helped them mix with the outside world. It was the ideal therapy.

On one of those outings we stopped at a little village pub in Tipperary and ordered 24 pints of porter and many minerals. And the first thing the owner had to do, poor man, was go out to some other place and get a loan of glasses. He didn't understand us at all. Donal, one of our patients called me aside and said: "Come here Jameso, I want you," and posted inside on the back door was a motto written (there were mottos everywhere) and it said: "You don't have to be mad to work here, but it helps," and Donie said to me with a hearty laugh, "How well the so and so knew the lads from the Mental Hospital were coming." Dr. Eamonn would follow us in his own car to whatever venue we were playing and after the match all the patients from the two teams would sit down to a big meal together and Dr. Eamonn and the R.M.S. of the local hospital would give a talk to the gathering and you could see how proud the patients were. He always praised their efforts and they responded to that in a very positive way. Once again Dr. Eamonn was well ahead of everyone else in psychiatry at that particular time. You won't see any initiatives like that anywhere today. He was a great man in every sense of the word.

He was a fanatic in so far as strictness was concerned. One time he handed me two footballs and said they were not pumped correctly and the pressure in them was incorrect. I pumped them again for him. He took one of the footballs and he put it up on the boardroom table. It turned a bit sideways. It didn't stay on the table and his immediate response was to tell me to deflate it again and pump it right. He was a perfectionist and he demanded that you always perform the task that he set you correctly. He made the whole observation dormitory of the Hospital available for the Cork team when they came down for the Munster Final while the Kerry team also togged out in the Hospital.

When training the Kerry team he was able to put weight on some players and with others he could get them to shed weight. He could judge each individual player to perfection. I can't explain his methodology but he was a great judge of players in that respect. He would instruct me to weigh all the players on the hospital scales. I would record all their weights on a monthly basis and hand them over to Dr. Eamonn. I remember weighing all the lads in 1946 before the All-Ireland against Roscommon.

He trained Killarney to win the Senior Football County Championship in 1949. On the Thursday night before the final we finished training in the Stadium. We were all along a line sitting down. Dr. Eamonn walked along the line to us and said: "I won't see ye now till Sunday lads and I want everybody in bed early and I want no drink," but he weighed back and he continued, "but Denny Lyne, it would be detrimental to you not to have a drink; you're used to a few pints." Denny's response was to shout hurray, he stood up happy in the knowledge that had got permission to drink a few pints. Unfortunately the rest of were not allowed near it. Dr. Eamonn knew his man and a few pints would help Denny relax. He went on to play a blinder in the final. Once again we saw the genius of Dr. Eamonn, his intimate knowledge of each individual's psyche was amazing.

Because he was a fanatic, people listened to him. And he knew the rule book inside out. He caught me out several times. I would referee the matches at that time, when he'd be training the Kerry team, the juniors versus the seniors and so forth. And he'd often correct me when I'd penalise fellas for something. He'd tell me that rule isn't in the book at all.

Dr. Eamonn was a fanatical Irishman and GAA man. And then you see, Dr. Hayes was the opposite; he was a rugby man. He was second in command in St. Finan's at one time and they had an argument in the boardroom one day and Dr. Hayes said to Dr. Eamonn: "You go back playing golf." "Isn't that a foreign game, GAA men should not be playing foreign games?" "Ah not at all," replied Dr. Eamonn, "It was golf Cú Chulainn played!" He was a strict man. There was nothing humorous about him. He never mixed with the staff or anything like that, just went along his own way and came to you when he needed you. He was a very private individual in many ways.

He was the daddy of them all. He had the basics that nobody has today; it is only all running and fitness nowadays. How would he perform in today's football world? I believe he'd be out there. He'd be ahead of all of them. In my opinion he'd be light miles ahead of them because he had the ideas, he knew the whole thing inside out. He was unique in many ways. With his psychiatric background, dealing with people every day of his life and his great family tradition of sporting greatness, he had a great understanding of the human mind. He was the great communicator, dealing with people and knowing how to motivate others. Now you tell me one person in all of the GAA today who has a record in all facets of the game and life that Dr. Eamonn had. There is no one there with Dr. Eamonn's life record and I am delighted that his life is being documented in this way. What a tragedy it would be if he was completely forgotten.

My fondest sporting memories would be the big games in the park, where we had to organise some way of getting down if we were on duty. It was a trade in itself to get out either with patients or get out under some guise or another. I remember Dr. Eamonn sending me down one time with chairs. Another time incidentally I was Chairman of the East Kerry Board; I was in charge of the sideline for the Munster Final. The sideline that time had a cycle track. It was not a sideline as such and for a week before it, we started building it up for the people coming. Cork and Kerry were playing. Billy Bird gave me his lorry to draw planks and concrete blocks and everything and we built up the whole place. Dr. Jim Brosnan was Chairman of the County Board at the time. It was a scorching day in the park and he said to me before the game started, "In the name of God, James, tell him to lock the gate coming into the sideline. Because we'll be all killed. We'll be all murdered with the crowd coming in." They registered 10,000 people on the sideline on the day and all that money went to the Fitzgerald Stadium.

Behind it all Dr. Eamonn was a very soft person and easily hurt. One year, I believe it was in the early 1960s, we were beaten in an All-Ireland semi-final and Dr. Eamonn was very low in the estimation of the County Board and the followers. Some things never change in Kerry. He had made a big deal of including tomatoes in the diet of the team; all the papers reported it. It became a bit a joke but would you believe the sale of tomatoes in the county went sky high. The team was beaten and he was ridiculed in some quarters about all of this and I could see it hurt him greatly.

It was Dr. Eamonn who was responsible solely for the football played by staff and patients in St. Finan's during my years there. He had two obsessions – football and the Hospital. He sent every patient out in the garden working because he said: "Every Kerryman was a tiller of the soil." And he added, "Secondly, the one sport that the patients will appreciate and will come natural to them, is football, because, it's natural to Kerry." So that was the way it worked. The football was there, there was no problem. He would often come to me, after the Kerry team training, with a practically new football for the patients. "There's a football there Jameso for the patients, see after them.

He was an amazing man Weeshie, and without a shadow of doubt he was well before his time.

An Interview with Dr. Des Hayes (RIP)

FORMER SENIOR ASSISTANT MEDICAL OFFICER (A.M.O.)
AT ST. FINAN'S

The following interview with Dr. Desmond Hayes was conducted by Weeshie Fogarty in May 2001. Dr. Hayes became Senior Assistant Medical Officer at St. Finan's Hospital in 1938. There he remained until 1962 when he took up the position of R.M.S. at St. Canice's in Kilkenny. Dr. Hayes was a founding member of St. Finan's Rowing Club and also served as Captain of Killarney Golf and Fishing Club and Killarney Rugby Club respectively. Here he illustrates quite clearly the substandard conditions prevalent in the Hospital during the 1930s and 1940s. Dr. Desmond Hayes died on September 28, 2001, five months after this interview.

Upbringing and Education

Well I was born in England, but my parents were Irish of course. I was only six months of age when my parents came back to Ireland and I grew up in Cork until the age of ten and from there I went to Bray. After school I went to University. In those days you didn't have to get points to get into university. My father was a civil servant, and he wanted me to do accountancy, but I discovered early on that I wasn't very good at it, so I asked him could I change over to medicine. You could do that in those days. So I turned over to medicine because some of my friends from school were also doing medicine. I went to Trinity College because in those days there were night courses there, and my father thought it would be a good place to go if you wanted to do accountancy.

Arrival at St. Finan's

I qualified with a Medical Doctorate in 1936. I worked in Baggot Street

Hospital and qualified from there. Later on I was a House Surgeon in Baggot Street Hospital, and after that I held various local positions around Dublin. Then I applied for the post in the Mental Hospital and I got it. I came in 1938 and I arrived in Killarney to take up my post. Dr. Eamonn was the man in charge. In those times it wasn't psychiatry at all, you were just a doctor in the Mental Hospital. There were a thousand patients there and conditions were pretty rough. I hadn't been in the Mental Hospital before, but at the same time I had some experience in Dublin before I came down, so I wasn't taken aback. I settled down. At that time myself and Dr. Eamonn were the only doctors in the Hospital.

Treatments in the 1930s and 1940s
Dr. Eamonn had already started occupational treatment and he had already set up Ross Products when I went there. I'm glad to say that Ross Products is still there, which I would regard as a great monument or memorial to Dr. Eamonn. That was very forward thinking in those days. That was the only sort of treatment outside of talking to people and advising them. You talked to patients and comforted them – that sort of thing. Of course a lot of it was ordinary medicine. I was very much involved in that. I was like a general practitioner because there were so many people ill from time to time, that most of your work was in doing that.

Patients in the Hospital
Dr. Eamonn was a big man and a very pleasant man. I got on very well with him generally. Now I was there a long time, and at times we didn't always agree. As I say when I came to Killarney he had already started Ross Products; that was a big advance in those days, one of the first to do it, in Ireland anyhow. Of course in those days, the patients worked in various departments in the Hospital; female patients might work in the laundry, some of the men might work on the farm and around the grounds and so on. Of course when people were admitted, they were incarcerated. Nonetheless you treated them as kindly as you could. Most of them didn't run away, anyhow you understand. But the conditions were not very good for anybody in those days. Things were rough for most people.

Dr. Eamonn's Initiatives
Of course he talked to me about his interest in Occupational Therapy, and I was involved in that with him. He was very keen and very interested and did it very meticulously. He had all sorts of occupations going. He had them weaving, making ink, and paper

work and envelopes and all these sorts of things. These patients were under the help of the staff. That went on then and developed and developed. He kept that up all the time. Of course he was a great man for the GAA and he was heavily involved in that. I was different in that way – I was a rugby person. But we got on quite well. The Stadium had been started before I came here and it was partly done. He went on improving it then. But that was all done in those days by pick and shovel and so on. An amazing thing to do – to build the Stadium up on that site, and a magnificent site it turned out to be. It was an extraordinary thing to do. Now he had some of the patients working there, but not all of them, some of the strong male patients worked there, helped by the staff of course who looked after them. That's how it was.

New Treatments

Well of course it's so different now. The modern treatment did come in while I was in Killarney. We got an extra Medical Officer, a new doctor there – Dr. Robert McCarthy. With extra medical help we tried other treatments. When they started Electric Convulsive Therapy (E.C.T.), Bob McCarthy and myself got very interested in it and we used that quite a bit. We were one of the first to use it. That caused a lot of controversy afterwards, but in my estimation at the time, it was a treatment that worked in depression and still works in depression. And then one time we had what you called a 'straight' which put the patient half asleep and relaxed him, and it had the same result. People would lose their memory for a short time afterwards, but it came back quite well. It led to a lot of controversy because of that. But now it is still being used quite often. Other treatments have also come in now – mood changing medicine – which we didn't have then.

Conditions at St. Finan's

Of course in those days once you got into the Hospital you didn't get out very often. Most people were either of unsound mind or temporary patients. There were no voluntary patients earlier on, then voluntary patients came (with the passing of the 1945 Mental Treatment Act), but they weren't completely voluntary. You had to allow them to leave but if you didn't think they were fit you could get them certified. I can tell you that, in the earlier part, the amount of money being spent on mental hospitals was atrocious altogether. They weren't funded at all. Everything was being done on the cheap. Then they closed a ward and all that. The patients weren't able to wear their own clothes; they had to wear hospital clothes. And the clothes weren't good – they were the cheapest you could get as far as I could see. Dr. Eamonn worked very hard to get extra staff, particularly extra medical staff. He fought very hard for that, and he got a lot of criticism for that too. Remember the farmers were protesting against us saying we had to do with what we had. Those were the times that were in it alright.

Children at the Hospital

Dr. Eamonn was a man that had his own ideas and you couldn't change him from that. But he was a kindly man and treated patients very kindly. I remember the children. Of course in those days there were a lot of children around the Mental Hospital. I remember, even my own children, and Michael O'Shea and also people in the stores that had families, and Peter O'Leary he was there – God be good to him – he was very good as well. Peter would be trying to keep the children out of the way, but of course he couldn't. Dr. Eamonn would come along; you see he suffered from diabetes, and so always had sweets in his pocket, and all the children would be after him. Peter, and Ann the Matron – a Miss O'Neill, and they would be saying "Go away now and leave the Doctor alone". But Dr. Eamonn of course would be giving them the sweets.

John Kelly was Community Psychiatric Nurse and is a member of St. Finan's Historical Society. Here he comments on the interview the author had with Dr. Desmond Hayes:

The text of this interview conducted by Weeshie Fogarty with Dr. Desmond Hayes, Senior A.M.O. at St. Finan's from 1938 to 1962, clearly and concisely illustrates the laissez-faire attitude which then prevailed in the Mental Hospital during that distant era.

The grossly overcrowded conditions referred to contributed to the widespread prevalence of tuberculosis among the hospital population with both patients and staff alike becoming infected regularly with what was then a dreaded disease.

As Dr. Hayes quite rightly states, all efforts by concerned members to confront such undesirable conditions, and to bring about change, were met with outright opposition by the ratepayers of the county. Indeed it is on record that when a motion was submitted to a hospital committee meeting in the 1940s seeking the appointment of a third medical officer to help improve the lot of the patients therein, over 100 farmers paraded to the meeting on horseback to oppose such an appointment, on the grounds that this would be a further burden on the ratepayers of Kerry. Possibly this action could be explained by the economic stagnation which prevailed in that era. A lack of resources in the area of the mental health services would remain a serious source of concern for a further 20 years, before this unacceptable state of affairs was finally addressed in the 1950s. The term 'closure' was rarely heard from the lips of a department official or county manager, and I should imagine that instantaneous dismissal would be the fate of the official courageous enough to suggest it.

The children referred to as playing on the Hospital grounds were the families of the Medical Officers and Land Steward, who resided within the Hospital complex. The Medical Officers Dr. Hayes and Dr. O'Connor occupied the area where the offices are now situated, including the upstairs area, which was later converted into a nurse's home for female staff residing in the Hospital. Dr. Eamonn O'Sullivan moved to a new residence in Lewis Road in the late 1940s. The Land Steward Michael O'Shea and his family resided in accommodation adjacent to the old Occupational Therapy Workshop.

While the Trade Union movement continued to legislate for an improvement in staff conditions, it was left entirely to concerned medical and nursing staff to cajole various departments locally and at central government level to address the unacceptable level of care which then prevailed in St. Finan's Hospital.

When I arrived on the scene in 1955 however, the winds of change were finally beginning to blow through the corridors of St. Finan's.

A Man of Vision

Dr. Eamonn The Psychiatrist

On April 1, 1933, Dr. Eamonn M. O'Sullivan, A.M.O. wrote in Irish and English:

"I beg to apply for the vacant post of resident Medical Superintendent of the Killarney Mental Hospital, being qualified for the position in accordance with Section 5 (1) of the Local Authority (Officers and Employees) Act, 1926, being a pensionable officer of the Killarney Mental Hospital Committee of Management under the Asylum Officers' Superannuation Act of 1909. I am a Registered Medical Practitioner of over seven years' standing, being registered on the April 20, 1925, and have served for almost eight years as Assistant Medical Officer in the Killarney Mental Hospital, being appointed to the latter post in September, 1925. I am also registered as a Medical Practitioner in the Medical Register for Saorstat Eireann. Regarding special qualifications, I secured the B.A. degree in Latin, Irish and Philosophy (including Psychology) in the National University in 1918; the M.B.B.Ch. and B.A.O. degrees in the N.U.I. in 1929.

In addition, I studied Psychology – an important branch of mental work – in Maynooth College, University College, Cork and Propaganda University, Rome. I desire to state that I have a competent and fluent knowledge of the national language, having become a member of An Fáinne (The Irish-speaking organization) in 1917, and can speak, read and write the Irish language with ease. Finally, I beg to state that I have given satisfactory service as an M.O. in the Hospital since my appointment, as the retiring Resident Medical Superintendent (R.M.S.) will testify. In addition to my ordinary medical duties I have taken a special interest in providing suitable amusements for the patients, establishing the Patients Comforts Fund, which has to date realized close on £400 (€500). If the committee will pay me the honour of appointing me in the responsible position of Resident Medical Superintendent (R.M.S.) I will leave no stone unturned in maintaining the high reputation for administration which this Hospital holds among the public institutions of the country."

The hospital committee met to ratify the appointment and a member of the group Miss Breen spoke: "I propose that we send Dr. Eamonn O'Sullivan's application to the Minister, and ask him to sanction his appointment. It gives me great pleasure in doing so, because everyone knows Dr. O'Sullivan's worth from an Irish-Ireland point of view, as well as being a competent officer in this institution for a number of years. He has done his duty without objection from anybody."

Mr. O'Sullivan seconded the proposition, which was passed unanimously.

While Dr. Eamonn devoted a major portion of his life to the development of sport and sporting facilities in Kerry he also made a huge contribution to the development of psychiatry at St. Finan's Hospital Killarney during his 37 years of service there. It must be stressed that following his arrival in 1925 the range of available treatments to the mentally ill was very restricted and during that era Electric Convulsive Therapy, (E.C.T.) was widely used for most psychiatric illnesses.

There was also much emphasis on the promotion of Occupational Therapy to activate long stay residents of the Hospital. While many patients made a partial or full recovery from their illness only a small percentage returned home with the result that many became institutionalised within the wall of this vast Hospital. Eamonn soon got to work to redress this undesirable situation and became utterly convinced of the need for a programme of rehabilitation for the entire patient population of St. Finan's.

It must be recorded that during this time the population of the Hospital was marginally short of the 1,000 mark. In 2006 this figure has been reduced dramatically to less than 100.

Following the decline in the rate of infectious diseases and the opening of the new extension for the treatment of tuberculosis in 1938 the unit which had been previously been used for this purpose was soon converted into an Occupational Therapy unit where various crafts were cultivated by staff members skilled in this area.

The hospital farm and gardens were better developed and farm and garden produce were used for hospital consumption. Dr. Eamonn had a basement area developed for the production of concrete blocks and over the next 25 years Occupational Therapy became very much the norm. Products from the hospital workshop were sent to retailers as far away as Cork City. Rolls of diamond wire were sold to sporting organizations and household equipment such as mats and baskets were in much demand. It is fair to say that many a Kerry footballer spent much of their baby years sleeping in one of the beautifully handmade hospital wicker baskets. These were in huge demand right up to the early 1980s.

A modern printing press was installed to cater for all the printing and office requirements of St. Finan's: self-sufficiency at it's best. And then of course another major Occupational Therapy outlet for the patients was the building of Fitzgerald Stadium. Following the untimely death of Dick Fitzgerald in 1930 a committee of the Dr. Croke's GAA Club was set up under the ever guiding hands of Dr. Eamonn, Eugene O'Sullivan, John Clifford and others. They set about developing the new stadium in Fitzgerald's memory and the long stay patients in the Hospital played a major role in the work. It must be pointed out that these patients would probably have spent their days locked in a ward deprived of the freedom that the work afforded them. Now they were able to spend their days happy in the knowledge that they were needed and appreciated by others. Dr. Eamonn always argued that a Kerryman had a great natural bond with football and the land, therefore working on the stadium project was what can be loosely described as natural occupational therapy.

On October 21, 2001, 65 years after the official opening of the Stadium, the contribution made by staff and residents of St. Finan's Hospital was rather belatedly acknowledged. Past and present staff members together with members of the Stadium Committee, Dr. Croke's Club, and a large gathering from around the county attended a special mass in the Hospital and later unveiled a limestone plaque on the wall of the press box in the Stadium. It bore the inscription, "Erected in Appreciation of the Contribution of Staff and Patients of St. Finan's Hospital to the Development of Fitzgerald's Stadium 1930-1936." Glowing tributes were paid to all involved in this historic development during that period of deep economic depression and all the various speakers referred to Dr. Eamonn's massive contribution. This plaque was the direct result of the great foresight and work of former staff members. Dr. Eamonn and those patients he had devoted his life to were at last properly remembered and commemorated.

Following the War of Independence and the Civil War, the new Free State continued to be plagued by political turmoil. Issues such as neutrality and the use of Irish ports by Great Britain resulted in Britain placing an embargo on the export of our own farm produce. The result of this was that the country was plunged into a depression known as the 'Economic War'. Unlike our current booming economy boosted by European funding, the Irish Health Services were funded from local rates with the business and farming sectors as the major contributors. The reality was that, with farming in a general state of stagnation, the farms of Kerry simply did not have the resources to fund the health services, including the local Mental Hospital, now St. Finan's.

Undaunted by all of this Dr. Eamonn continued to be a harbinger of positive change. He still saw fit to present a report to the Hospital Committee in 1934 recommending a number of improvements such as a dental and general surgery, a refrigerator plant and a more modern Occupational Therapy Department. He went further and looked for more patients facilities such as; handball court, (which still stands today), tennis courts, billiard/snooker tables, a recreation room for staff, more furniture and decorations for various wards, a house telephone, laundry equipment, swimming baths and extra farm machinery. All of this was at an estimated cost of £20,000 (€25,000) – quite a sizeable sum in the 1930s.

Naturally the Hospital Committee envisaged a difficulty in securing this amount from the ratepayers of the county. Dr. Eamonn would not be put off and made an approached to the Irish Hospital Sweepstake (similar to today's national Lottery), a group who then rose funding for the health services. Back then the money was raised through the medium of the sale of Sweepstake tickets with very attractive prize money. Dr. Eamonn's request was successful and funding was made available for the provision of the required facilities. Once again Dr. Eamonn's persistence and persuasive powers together with his cry for help for the mentally ill of the county triumphed.

When Dr. Eamonn considered two medical officers completely inadequate to cater for the physical and mental health of a patient population in excess of 1,000 he again made a further request to the Hospital Committee for the appointment of a third medical officer at an added cost to the already overburdened ratepayers of Kerry. In April 1940 members of the Kerry Farmer's Association assembled in High Street Killarney and marched as a body to the Mental Hospital to protest against such an appointment.

The Kerryman newspaper report of the meeting reads as follows: "The boardroom of Killarney Mental Hospital was invaded on Tuesday by upwards of one hundred farmers who attended to protest against the appointment of a third doctor to the Hospital. Their visit however proved fruitless as the meeting was adjourned after transacting urgent business."

The members of the Farmer's Association according to *The Kerryman* report continued to protest at subsequent committee meetings with members of the Gardaí being summoned to the Hospital on one occasion to restore order. Eventually a motion recommending the appointment of a third doctor was narrowly passed and the appointment was duly made. Eamonn had won the day against huge odds.

During the 1940s and 1950s there was very much a laissez-faire attitude towards mental illness, with little development in the area of improved treatment methods. With limited resources at their disposal, the medical and nursing staff worked towards making conditions as comfortable as possible for the residents. Weekly dances and film shows were provided and Dr. Eamonn had a football pitch laid out in the large "airing" court with many patients becoming interested in football and handball. Once again Dr. Eamonn saw an opportunity to add to the Hospital's Occupational Therapy outlet. He worked with staff to organize a hospital football team from the hospital population and this was entered with great success in a specially organized Mental Hospital league.

It was a regular and uplifting sight to see a bus load of patients set out complete with playing gear to oppose teams from rival hospitals such as Cork, Clonmel or Kilkenny. Eamonn often accompanied the team and offered advice to selectors James O'Donoghue and Paul O'Sullivan. Even looking back today, this sporting initiative was an extraordinary accomplishment and it must be doubtful if one would witness such an event in any other country in relation to mental illness. Once again it proves without a shadow of doubt Dr. Eamonn's unique gift of introducing new occupational methods and leading others to follow through with his ideas.

Since it first opened its doors for the treatment of persons suffering from mental illness the Hospital's emphasis over the decades was on custodial care. Due to the absence of any worthwhile form of treatment the number of patients at St. Finan's continued to increase and in the early 1950s this figure was in excess of 1,100.

However, the winds of change were beginning to blow through the vast complex that was then known as the Killarney Mental Hospital and Dr. Eamonn was to the forefront of these historic changes. Treatments such as Insulin Therapy, Electro Convulsive Therapy (E.C.T.), and Paraldehyde were gradually being replaced by more modern treatments such as drug therapy, psychotherapy and counselling. Patients thankfully responded to such treatments and for the first time in decades they were gradually being discharged to their homes. Under the ever-guiding hand of Dr. Eamonn, outpatient clinics were established in all the major towns in Kerry. This enabled referrals from local general practitioners to avail of the improved treatments and discharged patients were monitored through the outgoing treatment programme. Dr. Eamonn continued to adapt to the changing times in the area of psychiatry and, as in the area of sport, he took much pride in what was being achieved.

The changing scene also called for better training for nursing staff and in 1961 he invited the establishment of a training school under a trained nurse tutor. Life in a large psychiatric hospital in that far distant era could be mundane for both patients and staff and this fact was borne out in the following passage from a nursing charter of the early 1950's: "The development of suitable hobbies and recreation will help to maintain the stability and good humour that are necessary personal qualities for nursing. The nurse must avoid becoming self-centred or narrow in interests and should keep in touch with current events not only in nursing but the world in general."

Conscious of the recommendations of the charter Dr. Eamonn greatly encouraged the establishment of a very successful hospital rowing club which won many honours at local regattas for both women and men. This was followed by the establishment of a hospital football team that won the hospital All-Ireland Connolly Cup on several occasions. The first great success in 1959 occurred in Croke Park and Dr. Eamonn himself was the victorious trainer of the side. Later, a basketball club, that also won many honours at local and national level, was founded.

In his capacity as R.M.S. at St. Finan's Dr. Eamonn extended his full support to all these organizations and held the honoured position of President of both the rowing and football clubs. Of course, he took great pride in all their achievements.

On his retirement in July 1962 the clubs made presentations to him in recognition of his great contribution. His untimely death in 1966 was deeply regretted by all staff members and there is no doubt that he laid the foundations for modern day development in the complicated area of psychiatry.

Dr. Eamonn O'Sullivan's vast contribution to Kerry, St. Finan's and psychiatry in general has been immense and until now, unrecognized. While the massive structure that is St. Finan's Hospital, Killarney is facing eminent closure, Dr. Eamonn's memory is still revered along its hallowed corridors. He was certainly a giant of his time.

Articles on *The Art and Science of Gaelic Football*

BY Dr. Eamonn O'Sullivan

A Press Release from 1955 Announcing the Arrival of Dr. Eamonn's 'The Art and Science of Gaelic Football'

'A fine book on Gaelic football by the best man fitted to write it.'

Dr. Eamonn O'Sullivan was born and reared in a Kerry 'moonlighting' parish. As a young lad he must have been thrilled to hear the stories of his father's team – the Killorglin Laune Rangers – who blazed the trail to Kerry's football glory and of his father, the immortal 'J.P.'s prowess in the athletic arena. As he grew up, 'the 1903 men' wrote the name of Kerry imperishably in the records of Gaelic football. Nurtured in such an atmosphere, it is no wonder that love for the game and for athletics has remained with Dr. O'Sullivan through life.

In his student days Dr. O'Sullivan was prominent in Gaelic football and athletics. On his return as a young doctor, to Killarney, he became active in the promotion of both. He infused new life into the Dr. Croke's Club in Killarney. He was an executive of the Kerry County Board, Munster and Central Councils, as well as organising Kerry schools and colleges competitions in hurling and football and later for the All-Irelands.

Following the 'Troubled Times' (as the war years were known), in 1923, the playing of the games was once more resumed in Kerry. That year the jails and internment camps were thrown open and hundreds of young Kerrymen were released. They quickly made their mark on the Gaelic fields and reached the All-Ireland.

They were beaten by Dublin, but were back for next year's final (played in April 1925). The young doctor was invited to act as trainer.

In his new role, Dr. O'Sullivan proved remarkably successful as Kerry beat Dublin. It was the first of Dr. O'Sullivan's training triumphs. Dr. Eamonn went on to train eight winning Kerry sides, not counting semi-finals. The only loss under Dr. Eamonn's tutorage was the 1964 All-Ireland Final against Galway – surely a remarkable achievement.

'Collective training' was initiated by Louth for their Croke Memorial Relay with Kerry in 1913. Kerry followed the 'Wee County' example, with Jerry Collins in charge of preparation. Jerry trained the winning Kerry team also against Wexford in that the All-Ireland of that year and the one following. When the Dublin based civil servant was unable to devote the necessary time to do the job; Dr. O'Sullivan later stepped into Jerry's shoes.

Well-Equipped

'Dr. Eamonn' as he is best known to us all has now written a book: *The Art and Science of Gaelic Football'*. From the brief sketch of his background, it is evident that the author is singularly well-equipped for the task. As athlete, player, administrator and organiser he has the widest high-class experience – no man in Ireland more. A previous book by Dr. O'Sullivan, won for him the highest encomiums in academic circles and shows that authorship is yet another of the doctor's gifts.

A Pioneer

'Carbery' (the pseudonym of Padraig D. Mehigan), the eminent sportswriter, has already written a book on Gaelic football. However Dr. O'Sullivan treats the subject from a completely different facet. It is, in fact, a pioneer undertaking – a journey through a territory hitherto unexplored. From the lengthy list of authorities quoted, treating of ball games the world over, their origin and history, it is clear Dr. Eamonn carried out extensive researches and delved deeply into his subject. These matters are covered in the early chapters of absorbing interest.

Many fondly cherished beliefs in this country will be debunked, as for instance, the idea that Gaelic football is something invented by Michael Cusack in the 1880s and that in point of antiquity it does not compare with hurling.

If this publication carried a subtitle, it would probably be: *How to play Gaelic Football'* – to borrow the name of the book by Dick Fitzgerald which appeared in 1914. *The Art and Science of Gaelic Football'* gives valuable advice on teamwork; each position on the playing field is dealt with, from goal man to full forward; the tactics each should employ; hints on catching, kicking and other fundamentals of the game; hand-passing, hand-to-toe and pick-up. References are made to the innovations in the code down the years and the author illustrates his points by recalling notable games and teams of the past. It is those chapters, which make the book a 'must' for anybody charged with the training of teams, especially juveniles in the schools and colleges.

While each section of the book has its own appeal, according to the taste of the individual reader, it is the chapters devoted to training, which I found of special interest. Here the author deals thoroughly with the psychological side as distinct from the purely physical; how the working of the mind affects bodily fitness and prowess in the player. This has long been stressed in the USA and stories have been told of devices employed by John L. Sullivan to demoralise opponents in the ring, or of the tricks used by Kaute Hockney to gain a win for his team.

The Psychology of Sport
This aspect of sport is largely unknown through the country and treating the subject from this angle, Dr. O'Sullivan breaks new Irish ground. None but a medical man could write in this way, in particular, one whose speciality is psychiatry.

On the matter of training football teams Dr. O'Sullivan can speak from an experience and with an authority that few, if any, in Ireland possess. He devotes two entire chapters to this subject. He goes whole-hog for the full-time 'collective method'. In his own words: "What has been described as whole-time collective training is the ideal form to guarantee optimum results." After dealing with other aspects he goes on: "Those points of great importance explain the vast difference in values between the whole-time collective training method and any other modified part-time system. They are of such importance that the latter can never be a satisfactory substitute. This was proved in the preparation of the Kerry football team for the 1955 Final. It took three bouts of part-time or evening collective training (drawn game and replay versus Cavan and semi-final and the final, Dublin), to bring the team to the peak of fitness, which was necessary to succeed against a well-finished and well-trained Dublin team. Such a standard of fitness would normally have been achieved after one long period of the full-time collective method."

These opinions of crystal clarity, coming from one in the position of Dr. O'Sullivan, will cause quite a flutter in Gaelic devotees. He has made an unanswerable case in favour of the system which Congress, in its wisdom or folly, has seen fit to ban.

The injustice done to Kerry has been exposed and the County Board would be well advised to send a copy of the book to every

County Secretary in Ireland (if they have not one already) as it would help to alter their ideas should they be open to conviction and might lead to 'conversions'. There was a training schedule which Kerry teams followed in the past, with much signal success that if it were adopted by some of the counties, it would rebound to their advantage!

All Phases Covered
There is no phase of football from early recorded historic times, till our own day, which the author has not covered; evolution down the years to the coming of the GAA and the improvement of the code until it reached its present standard of efficiency.

It is a pardonable source of pride to all Kerrymen that a son of the The Kingdom should have written this book. This county has played no small part in the development of the Gaelic cause. Gaeldom is further indebted to Kerry for making available *The Art and Science of Gaelic Football'*.

I bespeak for it a wide demand not only from Irishmen at home but among followers of the game in England, America and Australia. This is a book that will be, as it deserved to be, talked about. I would like to congratulate an old and esteemed friend on undertaking this work, in the face of many difficulties.

(A most interesting foreword contributed by Carbery, as distinguished Irish sports writer, of *The Art and Science of Gaelic Football'*. Has been printed and published by *The Kerryman*, Tralee obtainable from all booksellers, price 5/-, or from publishers 5/4 including postage.)

Carbery's Introduction to *The Art And Science Of Gaelic Football* by Dr. Eamonn O'Sullivan

This ninety page book was printed by *The Kerryman* in 1958. It cost five shillings to buy and it was not the first book on the game written by a member of Eamonn's club Dr. Croke's. In 1914 the legendary Dick Fitzgerald had published his book, *How to Play Gaelic Football*. Fitzgerald had captained Kerry to All-Ireland victory and won his five Celtic Crosses in 1903, 1904, 1909, 1913 and 1914. This was a remarkable achievement by this great player. It was the first book of its kind on the game and probably inspired Dr. Eamonn to follow up with his own publication 44 years later.

In a wonderful introduction, 'Carbery' (Padraig Mehigan), paid glowing tributes to Dr. Eamonn and welcomes the monumental work on training and coaching. He best summons up Dr. Eamonn's career and input to Irish life up to that period more than anyone else. Mehigan's writings in the foreword are in my estimation easily the most enlightening on the career of Dr. Eamonn. In his conclusion he states, "I must congratulate my old and honoured friend." These words show his great knowledge of this exemplary man. This fascinating publication is now a collectors item and many of his theories are today as relevant, if not more so, than any time in the Association's history.

I have chosen to include some chapters of Dr. Eamonn's book to give readers a little insight into his ideas, his ambitions on training and the famous daily training schedule which many of his players speak about. The foreword to *The Art and Science of Gaelic Football* was written by the then nationally known Gaelic games correspondent Padraig Mehigan, who wrote under the pen name 'Carbery'.

Here it is in full:-

Having read and re-read Dr. Eamonn O'Sullivan's fine work with ever increasing interest, my main reaction was a personal one – human nature of course! I was left with two rather staggering queries. Firstly, how did I ever reach inter-county standards in Gaelic football without having read such a book as this? Secondly, what heights of football skill and championship achievement would I have attained, had I, in my youth, read and studied this book in all its deep wisdom and intimate minute detail? I was left with bitter, nostalgic regret for all that I had missed! This envious feeling passed quickly however, when I thought of all the good the book did and will continue to do.

No man in the whole of Ireland is better equipped to write such a work as this to the present and future generations, than this widely-known Kerry man. Gaelic football and athletics were in his blood and they were the breath of life to him since infancy. His late distinguished father, J.P. O'Sullivan, Killorglin, was not alone All-Round Athletic Champion of Ireland, but as Captain of the famous Laune Rangers, was one of the outstanding Gaelic footballers of his generation. The well-known footballer of the Dublin Young-Ireland Club, the late Dick Curtis (winner of three All-Irelands), once told me that J.P. O'Sullivan was the greatest footballer he had ever played against. He commented that, "O'Sullivan was equal to any three men."

As a student, the author played splendid football and won many athletic prizes, before his professional studies and duties claimed him. In my opinion, his medical attainments, particularly in the psychological field, were an invaluable aid in compiling the detailed work he has given us. He never lost his love for Gaelic games and spent a number of years organising the provincial college championships in hurling, football and handball. In the late 1920s, he was an active President of the National Athletic and Cycling Association of Ireland for two years.

He played for Kerry in a number of inter-county football games, and was a member of the unexpectedly victorious Munster football team in the Tailteann Games Final versus Leinster in Croke Park, Dublin, in 1924.

His Kerry colleagues were not slow in discerning his ability to get a team into the best football condition. It was in 1925 that he was called on to train the Kerry football team for the 1924 Championship Final. Thanks to his leadership skills – Kerry won. This was his first and successful effort, and was followed by a phenomenal series of 100% successes as trainer and coach of numerous Kerry All-Ireland finalists. He also trained Kerry for their replay final against Kildare in 1926. Kerry won in what was perhaps the finest hour of Gaelic football ever seen at Croke Park.

In 1937 Dr. O'Sullivan was again called on. He was taken from his busy professional duties and had to sacrifice his annual holidays. This time it was the replay final against Cavan and Kerry were again victorious.

Once more he was invited to come to the rescue for the 1946 replay final versus Roscommon – another great final and Kerry were, once again, successful. Next, he was earnestly requested to help his county men in the 1953 Final against Armagh, resulting in another Kerry win. His final brilliant training success was in the 1955 All-Ireland, when he trained Kerry against Cavan (drawn game and replayed semi-finals) and played Dublin in the final. Here we have details of Dr. O'Sullivan's remarkable 100% successes in All-Ireland Finals – surely an unimpeachable authority for writing this text.

Gaelic football is easily one of the most widespread and popular games in Ireland. The wonder is that the subject has not already attracted some competent writers who would enquire into the history, present the principles and rules of play, as well as advice and instruct all ambitious young footballers on the way to develop skill and stamina. Dr. O'Sullivan has done all this and more.

He spent years of research in the sports literature of many countries. He sought authority in many libraries. He gave us a most comprehensive and fascinating work, which is certain of a wide and growing circulation not only in Ireland, but wherever the children of the Gael have found a home.

The first five chapters of the book are devoted to the historical study of the game – a thorough and satisfying research. The evolution of Gaelic football is closely followed and considerable attention is given to what the author calls 'Principles of Play'. He tells us of the advantages of quick-thinking in all ball-games, and goes thoroughly into the subject of fielding, combination and general skill. He is very severe on the 'selfish footballer', who sacrifices his team to win individual praise.

The main object of the book is training and coaching, and in this regard the book is most helpful and instructive. Dr. O'Sullivan makes a strong case for whole-time 'collective training' before semi-finals and finals. He believes that it is only in this way that the public will be given a game to be proud of and a game which will retain gripping interest to the end.

'Team-spirit' is one of the virtues, which the author seeks to extol; each player has his duties and aims. From goal out, every man has a part to play in one strong united team. He advises on tactics and planning in advance.

A regular daily routine of training is laid down in clear detail. Dr. O'Sullivan specialised in psychiatric medicine and wrote one well-known book on the subject. He uses his knowledge of the mental as well as the physical well-being of his trainees. I have often heard of how happy a group these very fit young men were, who had spent a time in training under Dr. O'Sullivan's watchful, yet friendly eye. One man told me, "My training spell in Killarney was the happiest time in my life and 'twas the same with some of the lads."

That was the author's secret of success – he made the players happy by devoting individual attention to every player. He was very aware of the fact that players differ both in constitution and temperament, and approached each accordingly.

Other aspects of the game which were dealt with in the book were; the punched score, the punt, the drop-kick and the hand-to-toe movement. The toe-lift, which has brought so much controversy, comes in for special attention. Fielding of the ball has a chapter to itself. Ball-control, timing, placing, the fly-kick and above all, the need for understanding and control of tempers are covered. Fouling of all kinds is condemned in no uncertain terms. Nothing is forgotten or slurred over – all is thorough.

I must congratulate my old and honoured friend, Dr. Eamonn O'Sullivan, on a monumental work. Every clubroom should have a copy and each player of hope and ambition will achieve his peak by owning this book – the most scholarly work yet published by a Gael for Gaels.

Carbery (Padraig D. Mehigan).

Dr. Eamonn O'Sullivan's Introduction To *The Art and Science of Gaelic Football*

Gaelic football, since its codification towards the end of the nineteenth century and, more particularly, in the present century, has reached a very high standard of general popularity throughout the length and breadth of Ireland. This vogue of popular approval has also been extending overseas to the USA, Britain, the Australian Continent, South Africa and other centres, and this patronage is not confined exclusively to those of Irish birth or descent.

Sports columnists, both American and cross-channel, have paid unsolicited tribute to the many special qualities of the game, including its technical and sporting aspects. They have emphasised its original and contrasting features with the football games of other countries. Some non-native writers have even gone so far as to say that Gaelic football possesses all the better and some of the finer qualities of the American football game, as well as of English Rugby and Soccer. They have expressed the opinion that the scientific side of English Soccer and the physique-demanding qualities of the American and Rugby codes are both a prominent feature of Gaelic football at its best.

Writing on the 1953 Kerry versus Armagh Final, Harry Sunderland, *The Sunday Dispatch* Rugby League expert and former Australian World Tour Manager, described the game as 'superb Gaelic', as follows: "Having seen ever so many Test match series in 40 years of football, seen Notre Dame and the Army at 'grid-iron' football in New York's Yankee Stadium, a Melbourne football final and both Soccer and Rugby League finals at Wembley, I wanted to see the setting and atmosphere of a Gaelic final in Dublin's Croke Park.

This great game was a revelation to me in good sportsmanship in vim and vigour, without viciousness and in an atmosphere of stimulating enthusiasm that blotted out anything I have seen before in any of the world stadiums I have visited.

I saw for the first time, in its true setting the game from which Australian Rules, the game that is so popular in Melbourne and Adelaide, 'borrowed' the basis of their code.

Any game well-played is a good game. But Gaelic football, as I saw it played by Kerry and Armagh, and enthused over by that great Croke Park crowd is undoubtedly a superb game!"

This tribute from such a well-known authority, seeing possibly his first Gaelic football match, is ample proof, if such were needed, of its pre-eminence as a football game. Incidentally, it is of interest to note that the football played under the Australian Rules is almost 95% identical with Gaelic, and incorporates only a few minor features of other codes, the chief one being the oval-shaped ball. It will be accepted with pardonable national pride that the early Irish pioneers, who made homes 'Down Under', played their part in the establishment of the over-riding Gaelic features of this Australian game. It would be a unique contest to stage an international fixture between exponents of both games. The overall similarity in both sets of rules should facilitate such a competition on an annual or biennial basis.

Of necessity, there is a certain element of similarity in the science and techniques of all ball games. There are definite fixed principles of play underlying all ball games, no matter how dissimilar otherwise, running from handball, baseball, tennis, billiards, basketball, etc., to all types of football. It is only natural, therefore, that additional principles have a common basis in all the different football codes. Further, Gaelic football, in its specialised development, distinguishing it from all other football games, has created its own individual principles, additional to those of common application. It has been attempted, in this original treatise, to classify and elaborate on all these pertinent principles, with a view to closing the wide gap between the art and science of our national game.

There is, unfortunately, a complete dearth of books dealing with our national games, particularly from the training and coaching aspect. This has imposed a great handicap to their full development, at least on the technical side. It is sincerely trusted that this attempt, no matter what inadequacies or shortcomings it may possess, will, if not meet this deficiency, at least encourage others, better equipped, to blaze its first impetus from that peerless Gaelic footballer, the late Dick Fitzgerald (ar dheis Dé go raibh a anam). His book on Gaelic football, published in 1914, was a splendid pioneer effort. The author treasures probably one of the very few autographed copies of this booklet, which bears on an inside-cover page, the following: 'Dickeen, April 16, 1929.'

In the Preface, he expressed the hope that his book "will have the effect of exciting a more lively and intelligent interest among all followers of the game," and that all players will benefit by "making themselves more and more expert in the science of the code." He also referred to the book's usefulness for "Gaelic hurlers", as both games "go hand in hand" and "are played according to the same rules" as "the various movements in them are evolved in much the same manner."

The same sentiments can appropriately be expressed for this treatise. Though dealing almost exclusively with Gaelic football, practically every point made throughout the work is of relevant application to hurling, camogie and even handball, mutata mutandis where necessary. Methods of training have a common operational basis and those in agreement with the underlying principles will have little difficulty in applying them to hurling. Many of the hints on points of play and general procedures for both the individual players and for teams as a unit, will, it is hoped, prove of interest and, indeed, of practical application, to hurling and camogie.

(With a view to keeping the purchase price of the book as low as printing costs will permit, photographs and drawings have been deliberately dispensed with, in the text. As detailed in the last chapter, the mass production of special sound and action film shots will provide a much more satisfactory substitute.)

The first four chapters give a condensed history of football through the ages, showing how the 'Mass-Football' type of game was prevalent in many of the European countries from early times and designated in Ireland as 'Rough-and-Tumble' football. From this 'Mass-Football' game is traced the evolution of the various modern types of football, including Gaelic football.

Attention has been drawn to the possible Celtic origin of football from the very earliest times. Evidence is also recorded in these chapters disproving the oft-expressed fallacy that English Rugby football originated in Ireland.

The remaining chapters deal purely with the technical side of the game. They outline the various principles of play and skills associated with Gaelic football and give details as to general and special training procedures, with a final chapter on coaching.

Finally, I wish to record my deep indebtedness to my great friend, Paddy Mehigan ('Carbery'), for his kindness and assistance in reading over the text. I am more than grateful to him for the very encouraging and flattering references in his foreword, and I wish to thank him for the personal and general encomiums expressed therein. His experiences as a well-known footballer and his lengthy journalistic associations with Gaelic games, covering a period of over 50 years, have constituted him a pre-eminent authority in Gaelic football lore. Accordingly, his reassuring commendations provide a most auspicious herald for the book.

I wish also to thank my wife and family for their help and encouragement, as well as the very many friends and well-wishers who gave assistance in various ways. Lastly, I wish to record my sincere gratitude to Messrs. Dan Nolan, Paddy Foley and the other directors of *The Kerryman* Ltd., Tralee, for their ready co-operation in undertaking the printing and publication of the [original] text.

Viri validis viribus luctant. – Ennius
Eamon Naomh Micheál O'Súilleabháin
"Áirdín,"
Bóthar Lughais,
Cill Áirne, Co. Ciarraidhe.

Training –
A Chapter From Dr.
Eamonn O'Sullivan's *The Art And Science Of Gaelic Football*

To achieve the best team results with the maximum individual contribution and the minimum of effort, each individual member of a team must undergo a course of training to acquire the necessary physical fitness. The general fitness of a team is the composite fitness of all its members. Training, therefore, is both a team and individual matter, but ultimate fitness is definitely based on a team training arrangement.

Training has been defined as the science of bringing an individual or group of individuals to a peak condition of psycho-physical fitness for an athletic event or contest. Individual training by members of a team or in small isolated groups ignores team principles and requirements and tends more to individualistic achievement at the expense of team unison and harmony. A sprinter does not train one leg separately from the other and the rest of the body. Nobody would recommend such a procedure, though it has occasionally been erroneously suggested that team fitness can be acquired on an individual basis apart from any form of group training, large or small. Team training is, therefore, essentially a collective matter, whether we agree or disagree on the type of collective training to be approved.

What has been described as 'wholetime collective training' is the ideal form to guarantee optimum results. This is constituted in a special training camp, where the entire team and substitutes are subjected to a daily 24-hour schedule of alternating exercise, tuition, rest and play.

Notwithstanding its apparently regimented nature, as detailed further on, it can, with the injection of the right spirit, develop a pleasant holiday atmosphere. This has been our experience in Kerry, whether the training be domicile, urban or seaside. Training, however, for whatever purpose, is essentially a period of sacrifice, where willing self-denial in many directions is compensated for by the ensuing beneficial feeling of vigorous well-being and by all the pleasantries associated with good companionship and the friendly banter in the camp. This element of sacrifice varies for each member of the team. Excesses in alcohol, tobacco, food, etc., will have to be curbed substantially. Contrary to popular opinion, complete abstention from alcohol and tobacco is not desirable as sudden total deprivation crates a state of irritability and subconscious bitterness, which prevents the individual concerned from achieving the necessary physical fitness. Excesses of any kind whatsoever in this life impose a definite mental and bodily strain, which is to be eschewed, if a proper standard of general health is to be maintained. Apart from any form of physical training, this is equally true in health promotion for all humans, and, in particular, for those approaching middle-age or later in life.

Personal Hygiene

The necessity for health standards in other directions is also essential in conditioning players, so as to acquire the fitness peak which is the aim of any training procedure. The human machine, as with any machine, requires constant attention and checking-up, so as to maintain the highest standards of health, which is a sine qua non for each player in training. The human body has been described as 'the most delicate and wonderful machine on earth'. It has, by a most unique system of metabolism, the capacity for continuous repair of bodily cells, by a constant building-up (anabolism) and breaking-down (catabolism) of these cells. It has the power of adjusting itself automatically to the different conditions to which it is being continually subjected.

This process of repair and adaptation goes on unceasingly and unnoticed until it is subjected to strains, when signals of fatigue, insomnia, possibly headaches and other distress signs flood into consciousness. The normal health sensation of well-being (euphoria) is consequently replaced by a feeling of inertia, lassitude and a consciousness that something is amiss. The individual athlete must, therefore, appreciate the importance of understanding and applying normal health standards by the exercise of discretion and personal control. He must, by a sensible system of adaptation and self-denial, keep the body tuned up, as it were, to concert pitch. His mental control must over-ride harmful health tendencies, whether instinctive or acquired. It is this attitude of mind that must be cultivated to steer the body between the extremes of hypochondria (an exaggerated form of health-consciousness) and the health-indifference that is often associated with the buoyant adolescent period.

The hypochondriac, popularly termed the 'neurotic', must develop a correct attitude of mind towards his self-exaggerated and usually groundless complaints of bodily ill-health, if he is to achieve proper physical condition as a player. Many a brilliant hurling and football career has undergone an early and rapid shipwreck because of failure to adapt a proper mental orientation towards imaginary health complaints. The ravages caused by an over-developed and over-fertile imagination, for want of an early and stern checking, must be seen to be believed. There is no room in the training camp for an established hypochondriac, whose disordered and overactive imagination will stifle any amount of football ability and craft that may be naturally present and will impede training progress to an inordinate extent.

The other extreme of health indifference, which is a natural commonplace attitude of youth, poses a similar problem in reverse. The average healthy young man does not realise or possibly believe that his training should be related to any system of health restrictions. His natural feeling of well-being does not, he imagines, admit the necessity for any form of health guidance. No matter how well one feels, attention must be paid to health requirements, whether these have a preventive motive or are designed towards further improvement. The raising, as well as the maintenance of health standards, is an important function of the training regime.

All the scheduled daily arrangements in the training curriculum tend towards the building up of the general health of each individual member and not the least of these are the regular hours for both sleep and food. It is not, in fact, fully appreciated how important is the contribution, which a system of regular hours makes to the general uplift in physical fitness of reach trainee. Successful conditioning of the body is as much dependent on a system of time regularity and repetition as on the actual physical exercises and field manoeuvred of the training schedule. It is a well-known medical fact that the creation of conditioned reflexes, which form the basis of all habit formation, is governed almost exclusively by time factors and repetition.

These points of great importance explain the vast difference in values between the wholetime collective training method and any other modified part-time system. They are of such importance that the latter can never be a satisfactory substitute. This was proved in the preparation of the Kerry football team for the 1955 Final. It took three bouts of part-time or evening collective training (drawn game and replay versus Cavan in the semi-final and the final v Dublin) to bring the team to that peak of fitness which was necessary to succeed against a very finished and well-trained Dublin team. Such a standard of fitness would normally have been achieved after one full period of the full-time collective method.

Food Requirements

There is nothing, concerning training procedures, as subject to fallacious reasoning as that of food requirements. It is a commonplace, but most delusive view that the athlete must partake of special supplements and some of these in most unusual quantities. Such is recorded of the late Denis Horgan, of Banteer, Co. Cork, that prince of shot-putters who in his day was in a class all his own, breaking the then world record in 1897 with a putt of 48 feet 2 inches. Denis, apart from other weight events, won the Irish 16 lbs. Shot Championship 17 times, the English Championship 13 times and the American championship in 1900, when he defeated, amidst great excitement, the subsequent world-record holder, Wesley Coe of Boston, with a putt of 46 feet 1 ¼ inches. It is recorded by William Dooley that Denis seldom trained in any sort of systematic way, but he is reputed to include, as a routine preparation, the daily ingestion of one dozen raw eggs. This could scarcely be recommended for the average or even the majority of athletes. That it apparently had no ill-effects in Horgan's case is merely a tribute to the iron constitution of a most phenomenal athlete – ar dheis Dé go raibh a anam.

There is not, in fact, a necessity for adopting a special training diet, apart from the presence of individual bodily disorders, calling for special food requirements, as in cases of diabetes, alimentary tract ulcers, etc. Such conditions, however, are rarely encountered among adolescent athletes. Meals, which must be at regular times daily, without exception, should consist of good, wholesome food, with suitable variety and exclude any items that may not have personal appeal due to individual idiosyncrasies. The most important considerations are that meals must consist of fresh, well-cooked foods and must each be consumed at set, definite hours daily. The training value of these two points is of tremendous importance and, combined with a similar regularity in sleeping hours, their joint contribution to the acquisition of physical fitness is incalculable.

Psychological Considerations

The mental attitude of the athlete in training is of paramount importance if full benefit is to be derived. Freedom from personal anxieties or worries is an essential condition for training. The proverbial 'off day', which is an occasional feature in the life of every footballer and hurler, whether of high or average rating, is generally explained by the lack of full physical fitness, due, in many cases, to some personal mental preoccupation. One's mind must be solely concentrated on the purpose of training and must, consequently, be free from any inhibitions or worries that tend to impede smooth psycho-physical functioning.

Individual confidence is an essential prerequisite in the mental approach towards the requirements and objects of the training schedule, and all players should reinforce this feeling by securing the necessary self-assurance, following a full medical check-up. This will eliminate any doubts as to physical suitability to undergo the rigours of training. No athlete can adjust himself to the demands of a training programme if he should ever have the idea or the feeling that his heart or any important organ is not functioning satisfactorily. Doubts of this nature will lay the foundations for a phobia or fear, which would dispel personal confidence. Apart from the psychological danger arising from the development of such a condition of mind, there is no room for it in the mental make-up of any player undergoing a course of physical fitness. He cannot do himself justice, particularly for the big occasions.

One cannot enter enthusiastically into the spirit of training if there is any element, mental or physical, which might alter one's attitude towards the work on hand. The joie de vivre, which should permeate every training camp, is merely a reflection of the general carefree spirit of all the trainees. It depicts that freedom from worry, which enables each player to reduce his personal sacrifice to that of a 'labour of love'.

It may be countered that the mental handicaps referred to are a complete rarity. We have, however, experienced such conditions in some footballers of first class rank and their 'off-day' performances in the big games were popularly accepted as due to 'nerves' or stage-fright. The so-called 'nerves' in these cases were obvious during training and could only be explained by the underlying, if hidden, disturbance and preoccupation of mind. Training must, therefore, be undertaken always in a spirit of light heartedness and freedom from worry and ennui, which will automatically pave the way for the development of full psycho-physical fitness.

The Training Schedule

The schedule of training detailed here, as stated already, is of the collective, full-time type and is the only form that is recommended. Any part-time method of training can, of its very essence, only lead to fitness of a restricted, partial type and is, consequently, an unsatisfactory substitute for the fuller type of training.

There are those who are opposed to any form of special team preparation and, in many cases, the objection is based on alleged professionalism. The generally accepted definition of a professional is one who makes his profession or living from the game or sport concerned. It is inconceivable that any hurler or footballer, under the manner in which the Gaelic Athletic Association functions, could fully qualify as a professional Gaelic player. We are, however, only concerned here, in approving of the full-time method of collective training, from the purely technical point of view. We are, accordingly, fully satisfied that the best results are achieved only under the latter system.

Schedule Details

The full-time programme of training is based on a 24-hour schedule, drawn up in a deliberate manner, so as to preserve a proper time balance between exercise, tuition, recreation, rest and sleep. Each of these latter divisions of the schedule makes an equally important contribution towards the development of physical fitness. The following are the details:-

8.00 a.m.	Arise.
8.30 a.m.	All assemble for short walk before breakfast.
9.00 a.m.	Breakfast.
9.30 a.m.to 10.30 a.m.	Complete relaxation.
11.00 a.m.	All assemble at training ground for short lecture and field manoeuvres in full togs.
1.30 p.m.	Lunch.
2.00 p.m. to 3.30 p.m.	Complete rest and relaxation after this chief meal.
4.00 p.m.	All assemble at training ground for short lecture and further exercises.
6.00 p.m.	Evening meal.
6.30 p.m. to 8.00 p.m.	Complete relaxation.
8.00 p.m. to 10.30 p.m.	Walks, recreations, etc.
10.30 p.m.	Supper meal.
11.30 p.m.	Retire.
12 midnight	Lights out.

The times listed may permit of very slight variation to a limit of 30 minutes in each case, in order to meet local conditions, necessitating such alterations. Irrespective of such changes, stress must be laid on the over-riding importance of strict regularity during the entire period of training, for reasons already enunciated.

Each day is, therefore, a generally busy and active day, which should maintain the sleep habit, even in a strange and possibly unusual environment. All players will arise refreshed at 8.00 a.m. each morning with zest and appetite for the day's work. Intervening Sundays will lead to some minor changes, though schedule times and, particularly, meal periods remain unaltered. Sunday afternoons are generally availed of for important match try-outs and the Sunday preceding the big event usually features a final trial match. This gives an opportunity to assess the fitness of those in training, as a pointer to final team selection.

If training is carried out for the ultimate stages of the All-Ireland Championship or other important events, many of the players will probably commence preparation with some measure of physical fitness. Nevertheless, although there is some fitness variation from player to player, it is advisable to introduce the field and other tactical exercises with a modified tempo, developing towards a gradual intensity, keeping in watch the individual responses to the progressive expenditure of muscular effort.

Following a night's sleep of 7-8 hours, each player arises at the scheduled time each morning. After a brief period of stretching and breathing exercises and completion of dressing, all players assemble for a short 15-20 minutes' walk before partaking of the breakfast meal. This consists mainly of porridge or cereals, followed by a suitable fry, substituted by fish or eggs on Fridays, with tea and toast. For individual idiosyncrasies, this diet can be varied under medical advice. Following breakfast, all members undergo, at least, one hour's complete relaxation, preferably reclining or at rest in easy chairs.

At 11.00 a.m., all players attend in a suitable, if improvised lecture room, which should be equipped with blackboard and accessories. This room ought to be adjacent to the training ground, if this can be arranged. Each lecture or talk, delivered by the coach or his deputy, should be of the short, 15-minute type and generally should only deal with one or two principles or points of play. One can achieve a more successful result by restricting thus the scope of the lecture. Players will be less retentive and readily become more tired and bored if too many points, involving a lengthy discourse, are dealt with. One important point covered in a brief talk will make a more lasting and abiding impression than trying to bring home too much in too long a period. A short, snappy talk will be listened to with greater attention and interest and, consequently, with better results.

This lecture will be followed immediately by about 50-60 minutes of practical training in full togs on the playing pitch. All players will introduce each of these training bouts with a group run over, at an easy trotting pace, of a circuit of the grounds, covering a distance of, approximately, 450-500 yards, commencing and finishing this jog at the same trotting speed. This limbers up all flexor and extensor muscles in preparation for the more vigorous exercises of the field training schedule.

The training exercises will usually include demonstration of the points elaborated in the preceding lecture and repetition exercises will include practice in these points to establish facility in accomplishment and the development of skills. In this respect, it must be appreciated that all habits of performance only acquire full dexterity by a long, continuous process of repetition. The skill or habit of cycling, for instance, is only achieved in this manner. Everybody will have had experience of the initial puny efforts to secure balance and control in remaining upright on a bicycle and the persistence necessary to secure the normal, final control.

The author, in his: *'Text Book of Occupational Therapy'*, published in 1955 by Messrs. C.H. Lewis & Co. Ltd., London, dealing with the rules in habit formation, pages 107-111, emphasises this as follows:-

"Gruender states that a 'neural organisation' is acquired by the mere repetition of an action. In proportion as this 'neural organisation' reaches perfection, the less voluntary attention to the external actions of the developing habit is exercised, until a stage is reached when the will to perform the details of the movement disappears, as occurs, for instance, when acquiring the skill or habit of cycling. When the latter becomes a purely habitual action the mind can become engrossed in thoughts of an entirely different character, without having to concentrate on the movements associated with steering and pedalling. This explains the necessity for the sense of sight in the early stages, when acquiring the skill of cycling, as most beginners fail to cycle in the dark in the early developing stage of the habit. Scholastic-Psychologists have defined habit ('habitually voluntary' action) as one that is due to a past action of will ('imperium voluntatis') to which, however, we no longer pay any attention. They must distinguish it from an 'actual voluntary' act and recognised between the two as end stages many transitional stages which they designated as the 'gradual mechanisation of voluntary actions'. This is a very apt and intelligible description of the method of procedure in habit-formation and offers a very sensible rationale in the development of re-educational treatment."

This emphasises that the development of skills, as in football or any game, is merely the creation of new 'motor' (as opposed to 'sensory') habits by a process of repetition which, in football parlance, is merely constant practising and thus one of the primary purposes of training. Physiologists describe this technically as conditioning or the development of conditioned reflexes.

One of the most important rules in habit-formation shows a further application of those principles of guidance in training procedures, as those outlined further in the author's textbook referred to above on p.110 thus:-

"Secondly, habit-formation is also governed by the frequency and number of learning periods. Psychological experiments with animals have demonstrated that it requires a certain number of days with one trial each day to train an animal to develop a particular skill, while another animal, allowed two trials each day, will acquire the same habit in somewhat more than half the time. In the second case, the number of trials are actually increased and the rest intervals are reduced. It is evident, therefore, that short training sessions, with definite free intervals, increase the rapidity of habit acquirement."

Reduced down to practical considerations, all this demonstrates that football or other skills are acquired by a method of constant repetition (practice) and that this is affected by a system of two short training periods daily, separated by rest intervals. Each player can, therefore, be so trained to overcome any weaknesses in performance, as well as to acquire new skills. The so-called one-footed footballer can develop the weaker foot and gradually improve the latter's performance by painstaking and persistent periods of practice. It is thus that the 'ciotóg' (left hander) acquires the skill of right-hand penmanship. This method of removing weaknesses or acquiring additional skills must be a more or less all-the-year-round training procedure, so as to reach the greatest standard of achievement in any particular skill. This indicates that practice to acquire improvement of skills must be carried beyond any special training periods and must be a regular feature of all work-out periods. The old apothem that 'practice makes perfect' has a perennial application here.

This arrangement of a short lecture, followed by active training exercises, will be repeated in the afternoon, after a post-lunch period of complete relaxation. This latter period is scheduled for, at least 90 minutes (2.00 p.m. to 3.30 p.m.). There are definite physiological reasons for such an extended rest arrangement. This follows the main meal of the day, which leads to a concentration of blood in the abdominal region during the active processes of digestion. Any form of mental or physical activity during this period will tend to divert the blood flow to the brain or muscularly active parts of the body.

Such imposed interference with natural functioning processes must be unhealthy and, consequently, must be strictly avoided.

Likewise, the evening meal at 6.00 p.m. is followed by complete rest and relaxation 'till 8.00 p.m. The subsequent evening periods from 8.00 p.m. to 10.30 p.m. (approximately) are of a varied recreational nature, consisting of walks, concerts, cinema and other shows, etc. These periods play a most important part in building up and maintaining morale and should be placed on a regular well-planned organisational basis.

A light supper meal should be provided at 10.30 p.m., generally consisting of milk and biscuits, but may be varied to suit individual tastes, when necessary. After a short period of relaxation, all members of the training group retire to bed at 11.30 p.m. Twelve, midnight, ushers in lights-out period, so as to secure 7 to 8 hours of sleep and complete rest.

This ensures that all players will respond to the reveille at 8.00 a.m., full of animation with increased zest for the days' activities. It is of supreme importance that each player should have uninterrupted sleep nightly. The nightly recuperative processes, affecting every organ and part of the body, should proceed unhindered by the deterrent activities of consciousness, whether imposed or otherwise.

This training schedule has been drafted and arranged in its present form following a personal experience of over 30 years and has been successfully operated in the preparation of many Kerry county teams for their All-Ireland Final engagements. Its originality, in many of its aspects, may detract from its general acceptance as a form of training procedure. It is, however, recommended as providing a suitable basis of group preparation towards the achievement of the complete fitness, so necessary for a successful outcome in team engagements, in hurling, football and kindred games. Above all, it has proved successful.

Articles on 'Textbook Of Occupational Therapy'

BY DR. EAMONN O'SULLIVAN

Foreword Of 'Textbook Of Occupational Therapy'

By William Rush Dunton

Having been privileged to read the manuscript on Occupational Therapy by Dr. Eamonn N.M. O'Sullivan, it seems proper to express my opinion of this work.

It is pleasant to be able to say that I know of no other work on the subject, hitherto seen, which is so complete and specific. One cannot fail to admire the diligence of the author in his research and in the use of the material he has gathered. His conclusions appear to be most orthodox and in keeping with the opinion expressed by other writers on Occupational Therapy.

These are presented in a clear, most readable style, which makes perusal of the work a pleasure rather than a task. There is never doubt in the reader's mind that the author is expressing his opinions in a manner that permits no misinterpretation of them.

Dr. O'Sullivan has admirably epitomised the subject of mental disorders and given hints for occupational treatment of such patients, but throughout the book emphasises the importance of consideration of the individual in prescribing Occupational Therapy for mental patients.

While the author has written primarily for those who are connected with mental hospitals, there are numerous references to general, surgical, orthopaedic and other special hospitals. Therefore, there is much in the book, which will be informative and stimulating to all who are interested in Occupational Therapy.

The book should be of value to administrative officers who are contemplating the inauguration of an Occupational Therapy department under their charge, but also those who have been familiar with, or have been prescribing or practising Occupational Therapy for a number of years, will gain much inspiration and knowledge from its pages.

The chapters on the organisation of a department of Occupational Therapy in a large mental hospital are admirable in their specificity and should prove of great assistance to those to whom such a duty might fall, but there is one warning which must be given the reader in order to emphasise what the author has already said. In detailing the requirements for equipment and materials, lists are given which are utopian in scope. While the author states that such plans must be gradually put into operation. I feel this should be emphasised more emphatically.

I have pleasure in recommending the text to all those interested in or concerned with the development of Occupational Therapy.

William Rush Dunton

Definition and History – From Dr. Eamonn's 'Textbook Of Occupational Therapy'

'Occupational Therapy', as the term itself conveys, is merely treatment by means of suitable occupation – the word 'therapy' being derived from the Greek word 'Therapeia' which means curing or medical treatment. It will be noted that the word 'therapy' occupies the position of maximum importance in the title and is merely qualified by the word 'occupational' to indicate the type of treatment. This distinguishes it immediately from the use of occupations for any purpose other than therapeutic. In many mental hospitals, especially prior to the 1914-1918 War, occupations were considered more from the economic than the curative aspect. Patients were detailed for work in the farm, garden, kitchen, laundry, tradesmen's shops, etc., often with the emphasis on reducing hospital costs and sometimes without due regard for the prognosis in each individual case.

The term 'Ergotherapy' has also been used, which simply means 'work' therapy, but the restrictive nature of this title, which does not embrace any reference to many occupational activities, apart from work proper, such as: recreations, hobbies, etc., renders it unacceptable and the more suitable term 'Occupational Therapy' is now universally approved. The term 'Diversional Therapy' has also been used, but is not sufficiently explicit and merely characterises one of the main sections of Occupational Therapy.

Various definitions of Occupational Therapy have been given, some of a most comprehensive nature and exceeding all the canons laid down for a logical definition, but, as they are descriptive and most informative, some of them are quoted. The Walter Reed General Hospital, Washington, USA, gives the following:-

'Occupational Therapy' is a term now applied to that form of remedial treatment consisting of various forms of activity, mental or physical, which relieve a patient temporarily, or which either contribute to or hasten recovery from disease or injury. This activity under medical supervision or guidance is consciously motivated.'

The board of Control in England, in its memorandum of 1933, has the following definition:-

'Occupational Therapy is the treatment, under medical direction of physical or mental disorders by the application of occupation and recreation, with the object of promoting recovery, of creating new habits and of preventing deterioration.'

The United States Veterans' Administration has elaborated the following:-

'Occupational Therapy is that form of treatment, which includes any occupation, mental or physical, definitely prescribed and guided for the distinct purpose of contributing to and hastening recovery from disease or injury and of assisting in the social and institutional adjustment of individuals requiring long and indefinite periods of hospitalisation.'

The following very elaborate and comprehensive definition has been issued by the Boston School of Occupational Therapy, USA:-

'Occupational Therapy aims to furnish a scheme of scientifically arranged activities, which will give, to any set of muscles or related parts of the body in cases of disease or injury, just the degree of movement and exercise that may be directed by a competent physician or surgeon. Stimulating heart action, respiration and blood circulation accurately, as prescribed, and at the same time, it yields some of the joy and satisfaction that wisely selected, wholesome occupation provides in normal life. It thus takes its place with nursing, medicine and surgery as one of the important departments of medical art.'

Various other definitions have appeared from time to time, mostly of a descriptive type, but none sufficiently logical to justify being termed "a definition". The following definition should meet the case:-

Occupational Therapy is the treatment, under expert medical supervision, of mental or physical disease, by means of suitable occupation, whether mental, physical, social or recreational.

This definition shows that Occupational Therapy is a form of therapeusis or treatment differing from all other forms of treatment in its applicability to both mental and physical disease by means of occupation, whether the occupation be mental or physical, social or recreational, provided always that it be suitable and definitely prescribed by competent medical supervisors. The word "suitable" has been introduced into the definition with regard to the occupation prescribed to indicate that every form of occupation, though classed as such, may not be therapeutically desirable. Individual cases require individual attention and what may have curative results in one case or group of cases, may have vastly different results in others. Hence, in the prescription of suitable occupation, many considerations, psychological, physiological, orthopaedic, etc., may enter into the picture.

Psychiatrists, physicians and surgeons associated with Occupational Therapy in their different spheres must have a sound and expert knowledge of the principles of Occupational Therapy. It is not sufficient to have nominal medical supervision. The medical director must be conversant with the theory, and to some extent, the practice of the treatment. It will be noted, too, that the treatment is applicable to both mental and physical disease and this is made clear in all the definitions given. While its use, as an adjunct to the treatment of all forms of mental disease is now fairly universal in most countries, it has also been adapted for bodily ailments and physical disabilities. Medical directors of Tubercular Sanatoria have for long appreciated its advantages as a practical form of treatment in suitable cases. Its recognition in the field of orthopaedics has become widespread and is proving most beneficial in conjunction with physiotherapy and other methods of treatment. It is also building up a reputation for itself in general hospitals in many countries. Here, again, it is co-related with the physiotherapy and other departments and availed of in many cardiac and other suitable cases. As a potent factor in convalescence from all ailments, it has become an important item in the treatment of such cases, especially those of the prolonged type, where the difficulties of planning a satisfactory daily timetable, otherwise, must constitute a tremendous deterrent against recovery.

Also, the definition, in addition to describing the occupation to be prescribed as suitable, qualifies it further as mental or physical. This is inserted to embrace all forms of treatment, from the purely physical occupation, ranging through the recreational to the social type, such as the physical drill, dancing, music, social clubs and libraries, visits, hobbies, games, etc. It must be appreciated that the patient, who looks forward with obvious interest to the perusal of his daily newspaper, is as active a recipient of Occupational Therapy as the patient who passes from the rand to the wale in the completion of a basket. It is this diversity in the application of the treatment that constitutes the novelty, glamour and success of the therapy, which will be amplified in later chapters.

History of Occupational Therapy

In reviewing the history of the use of occupations for curative purposes, it is impossible to say when and where occupations and handicrafts were first utilised as a definite form of treatment. From the very earliest times, it was realised that occupation, whether of necessity or as a hobby, promoted health and well-being and work was suggested as an antidote to worry and depression. Just as rational methods in medicine date from the time of the famous Hippocrates, the Father of Medicine (460-370 B.C.), it is not surprising that the first authentic reference to the utility of occupation as a curative agent should emanate from another famous Greek physician, Galen, who is reputed to have said, sometime about the year 170 A.D., that "employment is nature's best physician and is essential to human happiness". Many similar references were made in succeeding years. Philippe Pinel, about 1790 and his successor, Esquirol who, with William Tuke in England about the same period, sponsored the adoption of more humane methods of treatment for the mentally ill, also advocated the use of occupations as a form of treatment. Esquirol described work as: "A stimulant to all, for by it we distract attention from their illness, we fix their attention on reasonable things; we bring back to them some of the practices of order; we quicken their intelligence and, in this way, we improved the lot of the most unfortunate."

About the same period in Germany, Johann Freiderick Reil wrote a book on insanity, dealing at length with work as a curative agent. In it he described work as "an excellent means to cure insanity. It must be wholesome and, whenever possible, be done in the open air and combined with exercise and change".

About the same period, a little over a century ago in America, Eddy, Arnold and Rush were similarly disposed. The former made special recommendations for treating the insane on occupational lines in New York.

Samuel Tuke, of The Retreat, York, England, is reported to have written to Eddy, as follows:-

"I observe with pleasure that one of the lading features of your new institution is the introduction of employment among the patients, an object which I am persuaded is of the utmost importance in the moral treatment of insanity. It is related of an Institution in Spain, which accommodated all ranks and in which the lower class were generally employed, that a greater proportion of these recovered, while the number of the grandees was exceedingly small."

In 1846, Dr. John M. Galt, Medical Superintendent of the Eastern Lunatic Asylum, Williamsburg, Virginia, U.S.A., wrote:-

"No class of patients is so happy as the labourers; no other convalescents recover so rapidly and favourably; many of these would be completely miserable without labour and their recovery retarded. The patient enters by it into accustomed channels of thought and action, and the mind performs rationally at labour, if insane everywhere else. We think highly of employment to procure rest, give strength, promote appetite and facilitate recovery. When our patients begin to mend, they desire employment. Common amusements of hospitals are useful and far better than nothing, but will not compare with labour as a means of restoration. It is true that 'all work and no play makes Jack a dull boy'. It is no less true, that all play and no work becomes insipid after a while and does not give that healthy impulse to the mind which the idea of utility in labour is sure to impart."

Mention should be made here that, prior to the eighteenth century, sufferers from mental disease were treated as outcasts. Insanity was regarded as a punishment – a visitation from God. Those affected were deemed the victims of demoniacal possession and exorcism was rampant as the sole form of treatment. No special provision was made for proper segregation and, generally, those unmanageable were confined to prisons, chained and manacled, and often cruelly and barbarously treated. This was the degraded position of the insane, which Pinel in France, Reil in Germany, William Tuke in England, devoted most of their time to reform. The chains and manacles were dispensed with and special institutions for the insane were established, until recently, known as 'asylums'. They are now correctly designated as 'mental hospitals'.

Dr. Eamonn O'Sullivan and Dan O'Mahony (Dublin Captain) following a Whit Sunday tournament game in Killarney in the 1950s.

Mick O'Connell – one of the greatest mid-field players the game has ever seen. The Valentia Island man won two of his All-Irelands when trained by Dr. Eamonn in 1959 and 1962.

A magnificent action shot of some of Eamonn's Kerry stars in action against Dublin in the 1959 All-Ireland semi-final. John Dowling, the 1955 Kerry Captain, raises high watched by Seamus Murphy (right), No. 8 Mick O'Connell (Captain) and Tom Long.

St. Finan's Hospital All-Ireland Connolly Cup Winners 1959. Trainer: Dr. E. O'Sullivan Back Row: J. Crowley, J. McCarthy, J. Kelly, M. Brosnan, P. O'Callaghan, J. O'Connell, M. Moynihan (Select.). 2nd Row: T. McCarthy (Select.), J. Scanlon, D. McCarthy, D. Carroll, P. O'Sullivan, P. Roberts, B. O'Connor (Select.).

Front Row: J. Culloty, J. O'Donoghue, M. Moriarty (Capt.), Dr. E. O'Sullivan, T. O'Reilly, J. Cahil, M. Curtin.

Paudie Fitzgerald pictured here with Bishop Denis Moynihan and Dr. Eamonn O'Sullivan. Paudie was one of the great Kerry cyclists. He won the 1956 Rás Táilteann.

Above: *Kerry All-Ireland Medallists 1903-1953. Dr. Eamonn is in the front row, 7th from the right.*

Left: *Ger O'Leary, from Killarney, was a good friend of Dr. Eamonn's. He was a Kerry Selector and one of the men who purchased Jones Road, now Croke Park.*

Above: *Dr. Eamonn with Bishop Denis Moynihan.*

Johnny Culloty leads the Kerry team to their glorious 21st All-Ireland title. The team included: Johnny Culloty, Micheal O'Shea, Din Joe Crowley, Mick O'Dwyer, Eamon O'Donoghue, Brendan Lynch, Mick O'Connell, Pat Griffin, Mick Gleeson, Mick Morris, Seamus Murphy, Seamus Fitzgerald, Tom Prendergast, Liam Higgins and Paud O'Donoghue. This was Kerry's first victory since Dr. Eamonn trained his last winning team of 1962.

Jackie Lyne, Kerry Trainer of the 1969-70 winning teams. He based his methods on what he had learned as a player under Dr. Eamonn.

Monsignor Liam Brosnan (left) with former Kerry star Johnny Culloty. Liam very kindly gave access to his vast collection of historic Kerry photos. Without him this work would be incomplete.

Phil O'Sullivan's final resting place at Calvary Cemetery, New York. Phil captained Kerry to victory in 1924 and he was the man who began Dr. Eamonn on his training career.

The author with Denny Lyne, the man who captained Kerry in the New York Polo Grounds in 1947 where they lost to Cavan. Denny claimed that if Dr. Eamonn had been brought to America as trainer for that final, Kerry would definitely have won.

Above: *One of Kerry's greatest sons, Tom 'Gegga' O'Connor being shouldered off the field having captained Kerry to victory in the 1939 All-Ireland win over Meath. 'Gegga' won five senior All-Ireland medals and six senior county Championships with Dingle. His goal, together with Paddy Burke's in the last five minutes against Roscommon in 1946, secured a dramatic draw for the Dr. Eamonn training side. Kerry won the replay. He got the name 'Gegga' because he was as light as a gig. He was also a Munster Boxing Champion. In front (centre) is Dermot 'Fox' Collins and just visible at the rear is Paddy Looney wearing his famous All-Ireland top hat. 'Gegga' is buried in New York.*

Above: *A rare get-together of All-Ireland winning Kerry Captains. Back Row, left to right: Donie O'Sullivan (1970), Liam Hassett (1997), Denis 'Ogie' Moran (1978), Jas Murphy (1953), Johnny Culloty (1969) and Mickey 'Ned' O'Sullivan (1975). Front Row, left to right: Paudie O'Shea (1985), Mick O'Connell (1959), Sean Kelly (Kerry's first President of the GAA), Jimmy Dennihan (1981) and Tommy Doyle (1986). Also included at the back is Monsignor Liam Brosnan. Johnny Culloty, Mickey 'Ned Ogie' Moran and Paudie O'Shea all managed/trained the Kerry senior team at one time or another from 1969 onwards. Jas Murphy was Dr. Eamonn's winning Captain in 1953 and is the oldest surviving winning Kerry Captain. He resides in Cork.*

**Kerry Team 1924
All-Ireland
Champions**
Back Row: *D.J. Baily,
T. Costelloe,
J. Prendergast,
E. Moriarty, B. Stack,
J. Ryan, D. Fitzgerald,
G. Moriarty, M. J.
Hannafim, P. Foley.*
3rd Row: *Dr. E. O'Sullivan (Trainer), J. Sheehy (Goal), J. Walsh, J. Murphy,
B. Landers, D. O'Connell, P. Russell, J.J. Sheehy, G. McEllistrim (Select.), Dr.
D.J. O'Callaghan.* Front Row: *T. O'Connor, J. McCarthy (Dunboyne House),
C. Brosnan, Miss Farrington, P. O'Sullivan (Capt.), Mrs. J. McCarthy
(Dunboyne House), J. Barrett, J. Collins, J. Hannafin.* On Ground: *J. Baily,
J. Slattery.*

**Kerry Team 1926
All-Ireland
Champions**
Back Row:
*T. Costelloe,
D. O'Connor,
G. Collins, J. Crean,
J. McEllistrim
(Selector), Rev.
D. Kissane,
E. O'Sullivan, P.*

Foley, J. K. Kiely, A. Brosnan, J. Prendergast. 3rd Row: *P. Russell, J. Barrett,
M. Coffey, B. Gorman, P. O'Sullivan, J. Walsh, J. O'Sullivan, D. O'Connell,
J. Riordan, P. Clifford.* Second Row: *Dr. E. O'Sullivan (Trainer),
D.J. Conway, J. Ryan, J. Moriarty, Mrs McCarthy (Dunboyne House), B.
Stack, C. Brosnan, D.J. Bailey.* On Ground: *E. Barrett, J. McElistorin, J.
Slattery, T. Mahony.*

**Kerry Team 1937
All-Ireland
Champions**
Back Row: *Dr.
E. O'Sullivan
(Trainer), J.J. Sheehy,
B. Kennerck,
S. McCarthy, D.
Keeffe, T. 'Gegga'
O'Connor, B. Myers,
B. Dillon, J.J.*
*Landers, B. Casey, T. O'Donnell, J. Keohane, M. O'Rourke, M. Raymond, S.
Brosnan, P. O'Brien.* Middle Row: *C. Geaney, T. O'Leary, J. Flavin, M.
Doyle (Capt.), E. Walsh, B. Reidy, C. O'Sullivan, T. 'Roundy' Landers.* On
Ground: *T. Healy, J. Walsh.*

Kerry Team 1946 All-Ireland Champions
Back Row: G. Teahan, P. Burke, B. Casey, B. Garvey, T. O'Connor. 3rd Row: G. Duggan (*wearing cap*), J. Lyne, F. O'Keeffe, J. Falvey, G. Cremin, T. O'Sullivan,

P. 'Bawn' Brosnan, D Keeffe, J. F. O'Sullivan. 2nd Row: Dr. J. O'Connor, T. 'Gegga' O'Connor, B. O'Donnell, D. Kavanagh, Dr. E. O'Sullivan (*Trainer*), P. Kennedy, E. Walsh, D. Lyne, T. O'Leary. Front Row: E. Dowling, C. O'Connor, M. Moore, B. Kelliher, T. Long, N. O'Donoghue, M. Finucane. Two Insert Pics, back left: *Joe Keohane*, back right: *Joe Merriman*.

Kerry Team in training at Killarney 1953
All-Ireland Football semi-final versus Louth. Kerry 3-6: Louth 10 points.
Back Row: G. Duggan, T. Lyne, J. Cronin, B. O'Shea, N. Kennelly, M. Murphy, N. Roche, P. O'Meara. Middle Row: J. Lyne, T. Ashe,

B. Buckley, S. Murphy, M. Brosnan, N. Fitzgerald, J. Brosnan. Front Row: M. Palmer, C. Kennelly, Dr. E. O'Sullivan (*Trainer*), P. Sheehy, P. Russell (*Assist. Trainer*), G. O'Sullivan, D. M. O'Neill.

Kerry Team 1955 All-Ireland Champions
Back Row: D. McAuliffe, D. O'Shea, S. Murphy, M. Murphy, B. Buckley, M. Palmer, C. Kennelly. 2nd Row: N. Fitzgerald, G. O'Sullivan, N. Roche, J.J. Sheehan, G. O'Shea, T.

Moriarty, J. Cronin. 3rd Row: P. 'Bawn' Brosnan (*Select.*), J. J. Sheehy (*Select.*), J. Dowling (*Capt.*), Dr. E. O'Sullivan (*Trainer*), J. Brosnan, J. Lyne (*Select.*), J. Welsh (*Select.*). Front Row: D. Dillon, P. Sheehy, T. Costelloe, G. O'Mahony, D. M. O'Neill, J. Culloty, T. Lyne.

Kerry Team 1959 All-Ireland Champions
Back Row: T. 'Tiger' Lyons, T. Long, D. McAuliffe, K. Coffey, M. O'Dwyer,
N. Sheehy, M. O'Connell. 2nd Row: S. Murphy, T. Collins, J. Dowling,
P. Hussey, D. Gayney. 3rd Row: S. Murphy, P. Sheehy, M. O'Connell
(Capt.), Dr. E. O'Sullivan (Trainer), T. Lyne, J. Dowling, G. O'Shea. On
Ground: G. McMahon, J. Culloty.

Kerry Team 1962 All-Ireland Champions Back Row: J. Walsh (Select.),
D. McAuliffe, J. J. Barrett, N. Lucey, M. O'Connell, N. Sheehy, S. Roche,
J. J. Sheehy (Select.). 2nd Row: P. 'Bawn' Brosnan (Select.), G. Riordan,
T. O'Sullivan, J. Lucey, K. Coffey, T. 'Tiger' Lyons, T. Long, Rev. Fr. Curtin
(Select.). 3rd Row: T. Crowley (Co. Sec.), M. O'Dwyer, S. Og Sheehy
(Capt.), Dr. E. O'Sullivan (Trainer), P. Sheehy, S. Murphy, J. Brosnan
(Co. Board Chairman). On Ground: P. Ahern, J. Culloty, G. McMahon,
D. Geaney.

Left: **Kerry Team 1964 All-Ireland Final, defeated by Galway**
This was Dr. Eamonn's only loosing final out of nine appearances.
Back Row: D. O'Sullivan, M. Morris, P. O'Donoghue, M. O'Connell, P. Griffin, F. O'Leary, B. Sheehy, M. Fleming, M. O'Dwyer. Front Row: T. Long, S. Murphy, J.J. Barrett, J. O'Connor, N. Sheehy (Capt.), D. O'Sullivan, J. Culloty, P. Hanley.

Right: *Dr. Eamonn presents silver medals to some St. Finan's nurses in 1934.* Front row, left to right: Mai O'Connor, Holly Murphy (Representative from RMPA) and Dr. Eamonn O'Sullivan. Back row, left to right: Paddy Murphy, Batt Bambury, John Moriarty and Jack Smith.

Above: *Dr. Eamonn making a presentation to retiring nurse Tim Moriarty at the 1960 St. Finan's Staff Retirement Ceremony.*

Weeshie Fogarty Discusses Dr. Eamonn O'Sullivan's *Textbook Of Occupational Therapy*

Dr. Eamonn published his highly acclaimed book *The Art and Science of Gaelic Football* in 1955. It sold out in a matter of months. It is still a highly treasured acquisition in any collector's library.

However, what is practicality unknown today is that Dr. Eamonn wrote another book and this was also published in the year of 1955. This 320 page publication deals entirely with Occupational Therapy in Mental Hospitals (as they were know at the time). Entitled *Textbook of Occupational Therapy* this second book was a massive undertaking for Dr. Eamonn. The vast amount of time and research that went into the book must have been immense. It's astonishing that a man who was literally up to his eyes in other projects could devote the time and energy to complete the work. His son Tony, in his interview with me, remembers his father sitting by the fire on winter's evenings, with a board on his lap, busily writing in a school copybook with a pencil, while correcting the script using a rubber to erase mistakes. The question of why Eamonn dropped in and out of training Kerry teams is often asked and now we can see plainly that this man simply had so much to do that he could not find the time to fit everything in between rearing his family and being Resident Medical Superintendent (R.M.S.) of the Hospital, which were undoubtedly huge responsibilities. There were over 1,000 patients resident at the Killarney Mental Hospital at the time. In addition to all these pressures, Dr. Eamonn was writing and publishing two books, planning and overseeing the building of Fitzgerald Stadium and of course training the Kerry football team … and much more.

In retrospect, it is not surprising that Dr. Eamonn wrote this book on Occupational Therapy. He was always a great believer in the benefits of patients being occupied and the results arising from an active mind and body. In March 1933 at Dr. Eamonn's request permission was granted at a meeting of the Killarney Mental Hospital Committee allowing the patients to work on the development of the new Fitzgerald Stadium adjacent to the Hospital. There was some condemnation in the local papers that patients were being used on the project. Dr. Eamonn, however, had no doubt that it was of great therapeutic value to them. As he said himself, it was "the first major undertaking of the subsequently developed Occupational Therapy Department of the Hospital and could be described as its 'Opus Magnum'".

Later, in a letter to the Hospital Committee, the Minister for Local Government said he was pleased to learn that the work had a beneficial effect on the health of the patients and that a number of cures had resulted wherefrom. It was only fitting then that the Pavilion and Stand built in the 1970s should have been named in honour of Dr. Eamonn O'Sullivan. Those who helped in the development of the Stadium said in later years that Eamonn's contribution was immense. He himself said that great help came from members of the Hospital staff, three in particular; Denso Hurley, Myo Murphy, and Tim O'Donoghue. Of course he was also lavish in his praise for the 50 or so patients from his Hospital who helped complete this massive undertaking. Members and sympathisers from his own club Dr. Croke's did not spare themselves, he added, particularly on Thursday and also worked in the late evenings, during the summer months.

In 1933, following visits to European hospitals where he studied the latest occupational treatments, Dr. Eamonn established an Occupational Therapy Department in his own Killarney Hospital. Other mental hospitals throughout Ireland quickly followed suit. The treatment in the Killarney Hospital was based on the 'Simon System' – an American-Canadian practice. The services of occupational therapists were now sought after. The work was undertaken by the more skilled members of the nursing staff and special efforts were made to extend the treatment to the more restless and excited patients. In addition to wards, special occupational centres were established for more advanced work.

Dr. Eamonn must have been very pleased with the daily percentages of the total number of patients availing of the new treatment (including those acutely ill), which ranged from 85% to 90%. The development of many special craft centres throughout the male and female sides of the Hospital, plus the implementation of re-education therapy classes, not to mention the establishment of recreational treatment centres, all proved to be great resources for following up treatment in cases of Insulin Therapy and Electro-Convulsive Treatment. As soon as a patient exhibited a positive response to the more intensive physical methods of treatment (like the ones listed above) the patient was immediately submitted, under prescription card, for appropriate occupational treatment. Occupational Therapy thus proved to have an additional reinforcing value in the physical treatments. It often aided in speeding up, in a very appreciable manner, the period of recovery in favourable cases. Dr. Eamonn hoped that the recognition of this reinforcement factor in Occupational Therapy would help to convince the responsible administrators in all hospitals, including the general hospitals, of the advantages of establishing Occupational Therapy centres as a standard form of treatment.

The amount of planning required to implement this vast change in the daily running of the Killarney Hospital was immense. To change the focus of the Hospital from a position where patients spent their days sitting and pacing around the locked wards to organising full days of monitored Occupational Therapy must have taken an enormous amount of the Doctor's time. It was an amazing achievement.

The actual occupational sections were divided into separate areas for male and female patients of the Hospital, incorporating the various occupations in each section. The Special Needs' section offered such activities as weaving, wire-craft, mat making, embroidery, seamstress and soft toy work. The utility section offered work in the laundry, kitchen and dining hall. Ward handicap therapy included; weaving, basketry, leather-craft, floor polishing and various other work around the ward. Printing and bookmaking, carpentry, shoemaking, engineering, painting, farming, gardening, tailoring and masonry were other very useful occupations that the patients were able to participate in.

Dr. Eamonn drew up a recreational therapy plan so that the patients could have some relaxing occupations as well. Patients were encouraged to play cards, chess, draughts, billiards, table tennis and dominoes. Weekly dances and films were introduced and radios were installed in all wards. Outside groups were invited to the Hospital to perform on stage. Debates and question time competitions were encouraged.

Outdoor recreational therapy was begun, including; football, hurling, walking, handball, athletics, golf putting, bowls and tennis. Football matches between patients of other Munster hospitals were organised. Outings to the sea sides were introduced and patients were also taken to the visiting circuses and to the annual local regatta on the Lakes of Killarney.

It is very evident that Dr. Eamonn was greatly attracted to the immense value of occupational projects as a very definite treatment for psychiatric illness and he made a deep study and research of this from his early years as a psychiatrist. It was in the early 1930s that he began to write this superb book, *Textbook of Occupational Therapy'*. He eventually finished and published it some twenty years later. The first 1,000 copies were sold out immediately.

Dr. Eamonn's *Textbook of Occupational Therapy'* has proven to be a very valuable resource to hospitals, in particular mental hospitals, of that period and even today. There was no other book on the subject available. The foreword to the book included in the following chapter was written by Dr. W. R. Dunton., Maryland, USA. Dr. Eamonn's introduction and his chapter on 'Definition and History of Occupational Therapy' will give a flavour of the contents of this wonderful publication. Until now this book was one of the greatest, yet forgotten, achievements of Dr. Eamonn's career and gives yet another fascinating insight into the life of this most talented man.

Killarney Mental Hospital

REPORT ON OCCUPATIONAL THERAPY

As promised I have pleasure in presenting the first report on the Occupational Scheme inaugurated in November 1934, covering the 16 month period to the March 31, 1936. I am happy to be in a position to state that the scheme has been an unqualified success viewed from any and every point.

The essential factor in Occupational Therapy is that it is a form of treatment or therapeusis, and the qualifying adjective merely describes that the treatment is occupational or utilises occupations or handicrafts towards that end. Being essentially a treatment or curative agent it should be regarded solely in the light of all other forms of therapy as a definite expenditure securing very definite practical results; and if it would still be completely measured by its therapeutic results, its financial returns should be subordinated thereto. Dr. Howland in his presidential address to the Canadian Association of Occupational Therapy stated that "it is now beginning to be recognised that Occupational Therapy is a definite factor of treatment in all up-to-date hospitals. It is no longer a luxury, it is a necessity". Its objects are to create interest, confidence and courage; to exercise mind and body in healthy activity; to overcome disability, and to re-establish capacity for industrial and social usefulness. It has special application to Mental Hospital life by its tendency to establish a normal atmosphere where the mentally sick may indulge in normal pursuits. It has a socialising influence and breaks up the monotonous routines so prevalent in most institutions. It becomes an antidote to boredom and depression, and is a very useful substitute for the useless excitement and destructive tendencies exhibited in all forms of mania. The daily teasing of pieces of rags into its component threads, thereby providing useful flock for cushions or suitable cotton waste for the engineer or stoker, has undoubtedly replaced the destruction of clothes and bedding, which are a usual feature of most mental hospitals. It simply transfers the dissipation of useless energy into more utilitarian channels, thus improving the general tone and morale of the hospital life. It is accordingly for these reasons that we should not be influenced in judging the innovation purely from financial viewpoints. Still, I am glad to be able to state that the financial results have completely exceeded our most sanguine expectations, as the figures hereunder will show.

The aim has been as far as possible to manufacture from raw materials the commodities required for the Hospital, which were formerly purchased outside the county, as well as to maintain interest by the introduction of special handicrafts. To date, the following crafts have been introduced and successfully carried on under the guidance of Nurse Mary Murphy on the female side and attendant John O'Connor on the male side. It is to their great credit that without any skilled instruction they have mastered practically all the crafts associated with Occupational Therapy, ably assisted by several nurses and attendants from time to time: Basketry (willow and cane-work); Weaving (tweeds etc.); Carpet Manufacture to special Celtic designs (submitted by Mr. Micheal Reidy, Principal Killarney Technical School); Cocoa Matting (coir yarn dyed in hospital); Mat-making (in wool, cocoa fibre, rubber, jute, rags, leather, wire etc.); Wire Netting; Leathercraft (bags, wallets, etc.); Seagrass chairs and stools (from ash cut in hospital grounds, oak, etc.); Wooden Toys; Painting; Gloves (all kinds); Envelope, Notepaper and Labels; Stitchcraft (knitting, crochet, embroidery, drawn-thread work, etc.); Artificial flowers and paper hats. Mention must also be made of the excellent work performed in the fitting out of the Fitzgerald Memorial Stadium which is a great tribute to the work of the attendants and patients who have spent four industrious years in completing the project.

The total expenditure was as following:
Machinery and equipment	£355-11-11:
Materials:	£890-16-1 (€1,200)
Unused materials in stock on March 31, 1936	£623-19-1 (€800)
Cost of materials used during period	£266-17-0 (€350)

The latter expenditure realised as follows:
Cash sales to the public	£422-4-4 (€550)
Sales to Hospital (L.G.D. prices)	£403-0-11 (€500)
Total receipts	£825-5-3 (€1,000)
Leaving profit for period under review	£558-8-3 (€700)

These figures do not take into account the profit on work performed by the patients in the Tailor's Shop (3 patients); the Shoemaker's Shop (3 patients); the Seamstress' Shop (8 patients); the Kitchen, Laundry, Farm, Garden, Stores, with the Painter, Stoker, Engineer, etc. The percentage of patients occupied in yesterday's date April 22, 1936, taking into account those confined to bed, was 89% on the female side and 87% on the male side.

Signed:
E. M. O'Sulleabhain
Res. Med. Supt.

Adjourned
Consideration
Next meeting.
E. E.W.
April 23, 1936

An Interview with Donal Hickey

JOURNALIST AND AUTHOR

Dr. Eamonn O'Sullivan was a member of the old Killarney Golf Club in Deerpark. In 1936 that club, which was a 9-hole course, a small course, had very few members playing golf in those days. It was a bit of a jolt, to say the least when the land agent for Lord Kenmare increased the rent on the land from a shilling a year to £75 a year, a substantial sum as we can understand at that time. So they began to look around for land for a new golf course.

The club appointed a sub-committee at the time which included Dr. Eamonn. Of course he had just come through the magnificent task of completing the Fitzgerald Stadium at that stage, so he was quite experienced when it came to these developments. The committee met with Lord Castlerosse who was the owner of the Western Demesne in Killarney where O'Mahoney's Point, in Killeen is now situated. Lord Castlerosse was an avid golfer and had tremendous enthusiasm; he simply loved the game. He decided to go ahead and build what would be regarded as a world class golf course back in the Western Demesne.

Dr. Eamonn was very much involved in the establishment of the company, which would become known as Killarney Golf Club Ltd. That was the company which, in effect, owned the course, although Lord Castlerosse himself was the main shareholder. People in Killarney could buy shares from this company. Dr. Eamonn became a local director of the Club when it first became a company. The work started in early 1938 and Dr. Eamonn was on the committee that appointed a Scotsman – Hamilton White, who would be the foreman for the building of the course. He was a very experienced golf course builder who had built courses in Scotland and England and he knew his trade very well. The committee also recruited a big local workforce to get things moving.

It was a major task, when you consider that the land in those days was very much a wilderness, very wooded land, indeed, some a bit boggy. And they had no machinery, of course; it was a pick and shovel job. The late Jim O'Meara, from Knockeenduve, was appointed assistant to Hamilton White, and Jim as we all know, became Green Keeper for Killarney at that time, and was in that position for nearly 40 years. The late Jim O'Meara was a wonderful character. Dr. Eamonn was the first Captain when they moved back from Deerpark to O'Mahoney's Point in 1939; a very distinguished landmark at that time. He also acted as Honorary Secretary for the Club for a number of years in the early 1940s. He again became Captain in 1944.

Golf in those days was not the golf we know today, in the sense that very few people played the game. It was mainly a game for professional people, business people, in other words, the more well-to-do in Ireland. For that reason they needed a lot of revenue. Unfortunately the Club opening in 1939 almost coincided with the start of the Second World War. From the very early stages, Castlerosse envisaged the golf course in Killarney as a major tourist attraction. This meant that people would have to travel here to play golf, but in the war years, travel was greatly restricted – no petrol, cars off the road and all that. So the club found itself in fairly severe financial straits, as they had no visitors coming worth talking about.

Where was the money going to come from? Dr. Eamonn came up with a number of money-making plans such as; whist drives, sweepstakes, raffles. They look very simple today but I'm sure they were very forward-thinking at that time. In the course of my research on the golf book in Killarney, I came across a very interesting letter, which was written by Dr. Eamonn as Club Captain in 1944, showing his dedication to fund raising. In the letter, he was appealing to members to support the raffle because things were so bad in the Club that they needed money from somewhere. One of the most interesting things about the raffle was the prizes – Dunlop 65 golf balls, cigarettes and whiskey. Now golf balls, drink and fags were all supposed to be scarce during the war, but Dr. Eamonn, for some reason, could come up with these fabulous prizes which were attractive in themselves.

So he really was in there at the start of the Golf Club. He made a major contribution. He was there in the bad times, the worst possible times during the war, trying to get the Club going. And he certainly brought them through those years in style.

I don't know about his abilities as a golfer but I understand he got down to a 9 handicap. His wife, Marjorie was one of the top lady golfers in Killarney. They would have been playing in the 1920s and 1930s.

If he was around today, I have no doubt there would be at least one book written about him because of his magnificent achievements, especially in bad times. You must remember that we had no 'Celtic Tiger' back then.

He was a man before his time. I didn't know him personally but his achievements were certainly magnificent. His training of the eight winning All-Ireland football teams spanning six decades and his work for Fitzgerald Stadium are examples of this magnificence. He was regarded as a pioneer as well in psychiatry in terms of rehabilitation and helping the patients to recover through work in the Fitzgerald Stadium. What a fascinating character!

An Interview with Paddy O'Callaghan

"A fine gentleman, a great Kerryman, a great Irishman and a true friend" – these were Paddy O'Callaghan's feelings on Dr. Eamonn O'Sullivan.

When I first met Dr. Eamonn O'Sullivan, I had just been appointed to a number of bodies; a delegate from my club, the Killarney Athletic and Cycling Club, to the Kerry County Board of the National Athletic and Cycling Association of Ireland (N.A.C.A.I.), which at that time was a 32-County organisation, set up by the GAA approximately 50 years previously.

Dr. Eamonn was Chairman of the County Board and had been Chairman of the Provincial Council as well as being appointed Chairman of the National Organisation.

We became very friendly and often travelled to meetings together. We had great discussions on the topics of the day – especially athletics and cycling. We had great discussions about the split that had taken place in athletics which led to the N.A.C.A.I. being banned from 1973 and banned from participating in the London Olympics of 1948. Dr. Eamonn held very strong views on these matters. He believed that there was no place in cycling or athletics for politics. Dr. Eamonn's beliefs and guiding principals stayed with me all my life.

I learned a lot from the discussions which took place between us, and they were of enormous benefit to me as I tackled the many problems that were killing cycling in those years. I joined the executive of the National Cycling Association (N.C.A.), and became International Secretary and went on to become National President. In my capacity as International Secretary, I was responsible for getting N.C.A. teams invited to participate in multi-stage cycling events in France, after an absence of approximately 15 years.

It was at one of those events that I invited a team of cyclists from Russia to come to Ireland to compete in the Rás Tailteann. The invitation was accepted and during that event in 1978 I was invited to go to Moscow to discuss the problems which were causing a stagnation in cycling in Ireland, with Mr. Susyev, who at that time was President of F.I.A.C/F.I.C.P. – the international governing body for cycling, both amateur and professional, in the world. Needless to say, this invitation was accepted and the meetings led to the resolution of the problem. From then on there was one body established to represent the 32 counties of Ireland, a body which every cyclist in Ireland could join. What Dr. Eamonn had taught me during those meetings on all those journeys helped me enormously during these negotiations. I think he would have been proud of me.

I became Vice-President of the new body, The Federation of Irish Cyclists (F.I.C.), which was set up to administer cycling in all of Ireland. I continued my role of International Secretary and I became Treasurer of the new organisation, a position I held for eight years. The F.I.C. is now known as 'Cycling Ireland' and I am no longer involved. I am, at the time of writing, President of Cycling Munster – the Provincial body.

Dr. Eamonn's primary interest of course, was in Gaelic games and in the GAA. In the biographical account of his life, contained within the pages of this book, Dr. Eamonn spells out in great detail his involvement with what is our national sport. On reading this biographical account I found it difficult to understand how he managed to successfully train so many Kerry football teams over 41 years. It must be noted that, for various reasons, he dropped out during that period for short periods of time. However it is still a remarkable overall achievement – especially when you take into account that during that period, he was R.M.S. of a hospital that housed over 1000 patients. While doing this he was writing books on psychiatry, playing Bridge, and for good measure, building Fitzgerald Stadium! He actually worked with all the people who were involved in the construction of the Stadium as well as raising the finances necessary for the job. When all is considered he is truly a remarkable man.

I do not agree with the notion that Dr. Eamonn is forgotten or that his contribution to the social and sporting life of Kerry is no longer relevant. In my list of the ten most influential Kerrymen ever, he, to my mind, would always rate very high indeed. He was a fine gentleman, a great Kerryman, a great Irishman and a true friend.

Maybe sometime in the near future a trophy can be presented to some category at the Provincial Championships to commentate and honour Dr. Eamonn O'Sullivan and help a new generation to understand and appreciate this remarkable man. Also, perhaps the GAA might consider a bust of Dr. Eamonn within the grounds of Fitzgerald Stadium – surely a long overdue tribute.

An Interview with Fr. Tom Looney

Fr. Tom Looney's family is steeped in the Dr. Croke's tradition, the club of Dr. Eamonn. Tom's family tradition; stretches back to Tom 'Crosstown' Looney, 1896 (Captain and grandfather of Fr. Tom) and Paddy Dillon, 1898 (Captain and granduncle of Fr. Tom); both Kerry stars. Tom played football with Dr. Croke's and worked in London during his priesthood, where he set up the Killarney-London Re-Union. His knowledge of Kerry football is immense and his memories of Dr. Eamonn are warm and vivid.

Here Fr. Tom talks openly about his memories of Dr. Eamonn:

Of course, Weeshie, Dr. Eamonn will be remembered for his work above all in the whole area of the Gaelic Athletic Association, and, like Mick O'Dwyer, for the great number of successful All-Ireland Kerry teams he trained. He also trained club teams and trained his hospital team to win the All-Ireland Connelly Cup. As a young fella I spent many a night in the Fitzgerald Stadium watching Dr. Eamonn training the Kerry teams for the big matches. He never seemed to get excited, never shouted at the players and concentrated a lot on skill. You trained with him yourself, in your own work as a psychiatric nurse and also, I know, for the county.

Dr. Eamonn concentrated a lot on improving each individual player. In football terms he concentrated on both sides of a player's body and making it strong – left and right. I remember well how players could punch as well with their left hand as their right, never mind kick with their left foot, or their weaker side, as they say. This all-round skill is gone now however.

Of course the marvellous contribution he made in the whole area of mental care, mental health and therapy must be put on record. The labour that went into building the Fitzgerald Stadium must not go unnoticed. It was a dream for the people of Killarney really and one that's still alive. Jack O'Keeffe is the last of those men who came together for a meeting and decided, along with Dr. Eamonn, to build the Stadium. My late father and my uncle Paddy were at that meeting. They set up a monument to Dick Fitzgerald who died in 1930 and the monument six years later became a marvellous stadium. But I think if it wasn't for Dr. Eamonn's vision, his skill as a doctor and the work of his patients, nothing would have been achieved. It must never be forgotten.

This is something that was not generally known but it was infact Dr. Eamonn's dream that the teams visiting would tog out in St. Finan's Hospital and that, one day, there would be an underground passage down under the terrace. He envisioned those teams coming out to the centre of the field from this underground passage in a marvellous scene of pageantry and of glamour. You don't see it in the European Cup finals, you don't even see it in Croke Park,. but that was his dream for the Fitzgerald Stadium. Sadly, it never happened. Nevertheless the Stadium is there and, in his honour, a stand is called after him.

I remember too I was at athletic championships meetings in the Stadium and I saw the great Olympian Dr. Pat O'Callaghan there, who also worked as a doctor in St. Finan's. Dr. O'Callaghan won two gold medals for the hammer in the Olympics. He would have won another one, only there was a dispute and he couldn't travel. So he worked in Killarney alongside Dr. Eamonn in St. Finan's. They were great friends. He set up the East Kerry Board in the mid-1920s with a few others.

Dr. Eamonn's work overall in medical therapy and care and Occupational Therapy, was very far-seeing. I think it is fair to say that this man, born in Firies village, was really a visionary. The GAA grounds, a lovely set up, in Firies is called after Dr. Eamonn. So he's duly remembered and rightly so. This follows in the tradition his late father J.P. set, as his life is beautifully commemorated in Killorglin in their superb grounds dedicated to his name. Both men had a great love for their culture and for the traditions of their people. But sport was at their core; be it Gaelic football, hurling or athletics. They were an exceptional family in that sense. And his wife – I don't remember her. I think she was Griffin herself; a lovely lady. I remember her brother Paddy in Ballyheigue and afterwards in Tralee, and her sister-in-law Maura; they were all great people.

Dr. Eamonn was always so calm. I was always impressed by his words before a big game. He was quietly confident. Tadghie Lyne was very anxious before the 1955 Final and Tadghie didn't feel like playing and said to Dr. Eamonn, "I think I shouldn't be playing." And

Eamonn said to him, "Okay, Tadghie, we'll put you on. The first ball you get, you close your eyes and kick and we'll see what happens after that." And sure of course, he was man of the match after that. The great confidence he gave Tadghie that day and the courage he gave him to believe in himself are proof of his true talents as a trainer. I think he had that great gift really.

Dr. Eamonn was without doubt one of the all-time unsung great Kerrymen, Weeshie. I was always baffled that no historian had taken time to write something of his life and times. He packed so much into his years, not alone in football but in many unheard of aspects of his work. This book will at least recognize and honour him and future generations, not only here in Kerry, will be able to appreciate just what he achieved.

The End of An Era

Dr. Eamonn O'Sullivan died in the Bons Secours Hospital, Cork on Friday, October 28, 1966. His death marked the passing of one of the great Kerrymen of the twentieth century. His funeral to Rath Cemetery, the following Sunday was one of the largest seen in Tralee for many years.

Members of past and present Kerry teams led by Dr. Jim Brosnan (Chairman of the Kerry County Board GAA), Tadgh Crowley (County Secretary), Micheál O'Ruairc (Kerry delegate to Central Council) and Mr. Jim Barry (Trainer of the Cork hurling team) formed a guard of honour when the funeral arrived in Tralee on the Saturday night.

The funeral on Sunday was a fitting tribute to a great son of The Kingdom. It was attended by officers of the GAA and N.A.C.A., the Gaelic League and Comhaltas Ceoltóirí Eireann, from many counties. In attendance also were representatives of the professional and business life of the county. On the day of the funeral the guard of honour was composed of members of the Dr. Croke's Club, Killarney, Kerry N.A.C.A.I., past and present members of Kerry teams and the Laune Rangers Club, Killorglin. The Tralee Boys Pipe Band played the funeral music.

The funeral cortège halted outside the Austin Stack Park where a three minute silence was observed. His Lordship, Most Rev. Dr. Ds. Moynihan, Bishop of Kerry assisted by Monsignor John Sone, Dean of Kerry, read the prayers at the graveside.

The graveside tribute was paid by Mr. Sean O'Siocháin, General Secretary of the GAA, who began:

> "It was my privilege to make Eamonn's acquaintance first in 1932 when I had been selected to play for the Munster Colleges and on that occasion my feelings for him were respect and admiration and in the years since then, during which time I was proud to regard him as my friend, those feelings of respect and admiration grew with the passage of time and with the increase in my knowledge of this

truly great man. And I confidently state that those very same feelings are what his thousands of friends and acquaintances felt for him and this would be particularly true of the successive generations of Kerry footballers who came under his expert care."

It is correct to say that many great Kerry footballers reigned supreme during Dr. Eamonn's time as trainer but it would be equally correct to say that he took many mediocre and ordinary players and inspired them to greatness. Because Dr. Eamonn's way was not merely that of achieving physical perfection – it was more of the mind, more of instilling into his players those finer qualities of manliness of sportsmanship and of that legitimate pride which the artist is entitled to have in the art in which he excels.

Dr. Eamonn was an eminent doctor and psychiatrist who contributed to his profession and it was our privilege in the GAA that he brought his personal and professional qualifications to bear on the promotion of Gaelic football. He was a whole man, a man of culture, a man of dignity and one who had a true sense of value. He was a man of uncompromising principles and high ideals; there was no place for the second rate in the scheme of things for Eamonn. He was a great Irishman who recognized the potential of the language, the national games and athletics as vital factors in working towards a full life of national endeavour.

In conveying our sympathy to his wife and family, I would like to qualify that expression by emphasizing the privilege which has been theirs in having such a distinguished man as head of their household and I have no doubt but the standards which he set or the example which he gave will sustain them in the days ahead.

We of the GAA have in like-manner been privileged in that he shared so much of his life with us and inspired us with his principles, his courtesy and his dignity. If we are to respect his memory we should respect the things he respected, strive for the things for which he strove and live the fullness of a national life as he lived. Ar dheis Dé go raibh d'anam uasal, a Eamonn. Guímid slán agus beannacht leat go dtí go geasfar ar a chéile arís sinn, fé ghrásta Dé, ar phirceanna na bhFaitheas."

There was a massive turn out of the GAA representatives for the funeral including; Vincent O'Donoghue (Waterford, former President of the GAA), Jim Ryan (Munster Council Chairman), Jack Russell (Tipperary County Board), Rev. D. McCarthy (Chairman of the Limerick County Board), Jim Moloney (Chairman of the Waterford County Board), Jack Barrett, Con Murphy, Derry Gowan, Denis Conroy, Eamon Young, Jim Barry (all representing Cork GAA), Rev. Bro. J. Clancy (Chairman of the Munster Colleges) and members of the Kerry teams from 1903 to 1966. Also Johnny Walsh, Paddy 'Bawn' Brosnan, Murt Kelly, Mick O'Dwyer, Johnny Culloty, Joe Joe Barrett, Niall Sheehy who were just a few of the vast number of Kerry players in attendance of Rath Cemetery bidding their final farewell to their former trainer.

The N.A.C.A.I. came to pay their respect to their Kerry President and among their representatives included; David Browne (Munster Council President and Vice President General Council), Tadgh Crowley (Chairman of the Kerry County Board), Mr. W. Nestor (Secretary of the Cork County Board), Mr. N. Higgins (General Council), Mr. Noel McMahon (Clare) and from Kerry; Pat Finnegan, Pat O'Callaghan and Mr. M. Barrett. All-Kerry Athletic Clubs and many other clubs in the county were represented. Mr. Seamus Conway Cappawhite (Chairman Munster Council, Comhaltas Ceoltóirí Eireann) was present.

Also at the graveside were 90-year-old Denis Curran of Garryruth, Tralee and 84-year-old Denny Breen of Castleisland, both members of the Kerry team which brought the first Senior All-Ireland football title to Kerry and Pat 'Aeroplane' O'Shea of Castlegregory who played for the county in the Kerry versus Wexford games in the 1914-18 period.

Maurice Lawler (Chairman of the Kerry County Council), Dan Spring (T.D.), Tim O'Connor (T.D.), Bill Dennehy (M.C.C), Michael Scanlon (Chairman of the Tralee U.D.C.), Teddy Clifford (Chairman of the Killarney U.D.C.), Dr. Jack O'Connor (R.M.S., St. Finan's Hospital) also attended the obsequies.

The chief mourners were Eamonn's widow Marjorie, his four sons; Jim, Eddie, Anthony and Robert, his sister Mrs. Paddy Breen from Beaufort and his daughters-in-law; Millie, Mary, Maeve and Maura, his brother-in-law Paddy Breen and his sister-in-law Mrs. P. O'Sullivan of Firies. Requiem Mass for the repose of Dr. O'Sullivan's soul was celebrated at St. John's Parish Church, Tralee, on Monday by Rev. F. L. Kelly, C.C. Tralee.

During the following weeks tributes flowed in for the late Dr. Eamonn. The Kerry Council, the County Committee of Agriculture and Tralee Urban Council all paid glowing tributes to the memory

of Eamonn and as a mark of respect, Killarney Urban Council did
not conduct any business at their weekly meeting. Their chairman,
Teddy Clifford, said of the late Dr. Eamonn, "He had been R.M.S.
at St. Finan's Hospital in our town for 30 years or so and was a very
excellent citizen of Killarney. As long as Fitzgerald Stadium exists and
I am sure that superb stadium would not be there but for the work
and guiding light of Dr. Eamonn. He will forever be remembered,
particularly in this town." Mr. Clifford added that they all knew of his
contribution to the GAA and the training of successive Kerry teams,
his passionate interest in athletics, golf and Bridge. On behalf of the
people of Killarney and himself he proposed a vote of sympathy to
the widow and family.

Another member of the Council, Michael Moynihan added
that, "Dr. Eamonn had set a very high standard in both sporting
and medical life in his long association with the town. His lasting
memorial was certainly the Fitzgerald Memorial Park. That Stadium
in itself was of tremendous material value to Killarney and it would
keep his memory forever fresh. His untimely death had cast a dark
gloom over the area." Mike Moynihan had played on the Killarney
team trained by Dr. Eamonn which had won the 1949 Kerry Senior
Football County Championship.

At a specially convened meeting of the Kerry County Board
N.A.C.A.I., held in Tralee, the Chairman Tadgh Crowley said Dr.
Eamonn's passing had dealt a severe blow to the National Athletic
and Cycling Association in Kerry. He was a most able administrator
and a true Irishman. In having Dr. Eamonn as President of the Kerry
County Board one always felt that nothing could go wrong with the
administration of the county. He was completely unselfish in his
efforts to give the youth attractive athletic competition so that they
would benefit physically and mentally from it. His last public function
was to present the tricolour jersey to the race leader at the 'Round
the Houses' stage of Rás Tailteann, in Killarney. We will never see his
likes again.

Dr. Jim Brosnan, Chairman Kerry County Board said, "We are all
shocked to hear of his death. He will be greatly missed by all who were
associated with him and who experienced his kindness in St. Finan's.
He will of course be missed by the legions of Kerry footballers he
trained to bring honours to the county."

Dr. Jack O'Connor, R.M.S. at St. Finan's Hospital paid his tribute
saying, "I consider that Dr. O'Sullivan was a great man. In the
psychiatric field he was probably over 20 years ahead of his time. He
was the first person to introduce industrial therapy on an organized
basis in Irish hospitals; that was in the mid-30s. I personally feel a

sense of great loss at his passing and I know that the staff at St. Finan's shares my feelings. Irish psychiatry is all the poorer for his death and I would like to express my sympathy to his wife and family." Dr. Eamonn had succeeded his father-in-law the late Dr. Griffin as R.M.S. in Killarney in 1933. He had been on the staff of the hospital since 1925.

Dr. Eamonn's death had brought to an end one of the most remarkable and inspiring stories in the glorious history of Kerry football. Indeed it should be said that he played a major role in establishing that enduring tradition of Kerry football we have inherited today. His record breaking feat of training eight All-Ireland winning Kerry teams over the course of five different decades spanning an incredible 41 years (he lost just one final – that of 1964) will forever remain unequalled.

He organized college football, athletic meetings and was the main driving force in bringing the 9-day South of Ireland Bridge Congress to Killarney, in 1944. Dr. Eamonn also became deeply involved with Lord Castlerosse in the construction of Killarney's new golf course around 1938.

Of course his work in the field of mental illness and his pioneering work in Occupation Therapy are legendary. He wrote a text book on Occupational Therapy, which sold world-wide and received high acclaim from all quarters. He still found time to write yet another book; *'The Art and Science of Gaelic Football'*. Without his vision, leadership and ability to realise great dreams, the magnificent Fitzgerald Stadium would never have been built.

God rest you Dr. Eamonn you made us all feel proud,
While we say a silent Ave or sing your praises loud,
Your name shall be remembered
in the Kingdom's hall of fame
As the one who always taught us
to play a sporting game.

Jimmy Cullinane

An Interview with John O'Donoghue

MINISTER FOR ARTS, SPORT AND TOURISM

Dr. Eamonn should so be remembered that he will serve as a role model for future generations of the Gaelic Athletic Association.

I suppose like many great men as time moves on younger generations are inclined to forget them and it's fair to say that Dr. Eamonn O'Sullivan was one of the greatest Kerry Gaels ever born. His career with Kerry in terms of trainer/coach stretched an amazing five decades and whilst he didn't train them every year his record is second to none. Here is a man who trained eight Kerry teams to All-Ireland victory; I think that the only other Kerryman who can lay claim to that is the great Mick O'Dwyer of Waterville. Obviously Mick did it in a far shorter time frame of course. Therefore it's fair to say that Dr. Eamonn was one of the greatest Kerrymen ever to emerge. His birthplace, Firies, can be very proud of him and of course he then spent his life as Resident Medical Superintendent (R.M.S.) in St. Finan's Hospital Killarney.

His involvement with Fitzgerald Stadium is legendary. It is, I suppose, the cradle, the home, the heart and the soul (if the Austin Stack's people will forgive me) of Kerry football down through the years. And then his service to St. Finan's Hospital, Killarney, is something which will never be forgotten.

Here was a great literary man who wrote two books as well as having a keen interest in sport, a medical professional, being a husband, a father and an all-round Kerryman. He richly deserves to be remembered, deserves to be honoured and deserves every tribute which is paid to him.

Now his name doesn't come up very often any more but it is fair to say that if you go back to the older generation and talk to people who have been immersed in the GAA in Kerry and through the country there are those who will unquestionably remember him. I know for example the present Chairperson of the Fitzgerald Stadium in Killarney, Padraig O'Sullivan, has often mentioned Dr. Eamonn to me in glowing and praiseworthy terms, in his bar in Beaufort.

As an eight-year-old boy I remember his one losing All-Ireland Final in 1964. Sadly that was his last year as Kerry trainer and his only loss in nine finals. Now here was a man whose training stretched from Jack Murphy to Mick O'Connell. It is amazing, quite extraordinary, the endurance that this man displayed over those many decades. That endurance is a testament to his self-reliance and in particular to his abiding interest in the Gaelic Athletic Association. What else would you expect from a man from that great Killarney club – Dr. Croke's?

His professional career as a doctor is quite legendary as well and I know for a fact that he won the respect and admiration of anybody who had the privilege of dealing with him in his capacity as R.M.S. of St. Finan's.

I suppose it is fitting at this stage that Kerry should look to its iconic stadia and decide that the time is ripe to remember Dr. Eamonn O'Sullivan. I know that the stand in the Fitzgerald Stadium is called after him together with the Firies playing field but I do think that the time has come perhaps, for us to honour him in a more high-profile way, so that his memory will not be just cherished but also that he will serve as a role model for future members of the Gaelic Athletic Association. So in that context it might be appropriate to remember him with a trophy or naming the new training centre, which the Kerry County Board plans, after him.

So whether as a professional man or a person who was involved in developments like the Fitzgerald Stadium, or through athletics, or as a person who was involved in Gaelic football, here was a man who gave a tremendous amount of his life and gave complete and absolute dedication and commitment to whichever cause he championed. I believe there are few Kerrymen through the twentieth century who can boast of the achievements which he boasts and there is few, if any, who can say they loved Kerry as much.

An Interview with Senator Maurice Hayes

"Kerry football and football generally owes Dr. Eamonn a great debt," said Senator Maurice Hayes.

My mother was from Listowel, which stamps my visa for me on the first night of the races there every year. I am accepted there without any difficulty. Actually my grandfather Maurice Nugent worked on the building of the Laratigue Railway, as the maintenance carpenter. My grandmother lived in a little cottage there just where the station was and my mother's first job was in the Castle Hotel in Ballybunnion. Then she came to work in Wynn's Hotel here in Dublin about 1913. That Hotel was burned out in 1916. She married my father at that time and he was sent off to the war. My father was from Waterford. Mother could not get home and the only place she could get to was Down Patrick, where she had a sister, so she went and stayed there. As I said my father went to the war and of all places he was posted to Mesopotamia, Tom Barry was also there at the same time. I often think if George Bush had the opportunity to meet my father he would never have gone into Iraq.

Kerry was always in the background and it nurtured a great love of football in me. I had a first cousin Tony McAuliffe who played for Kerry in the 1930s and in the All-Ireland Final of 1938 when Galway became the first team to beat Kerry in a replay.

I played minor football for Down but I enjoyed the hurling greatly. I qualified as a teacher and spend seven years in De La Salle School in Down Patrick and was appointed Town Clerk there in 1965. I later joined the Civil Service. That was the time of Sunningdale, 1973; it was the early days of the Social Democratic and Labour Party (SDLP). I was made Head of the Department of Health and later Ombudsman. So I have always been around that nexus of peacemaking. Ombudsman deals with complaints against government bodies. I did a review of the hospitals in the north – a boundary revision. I was also a member of the Patton Commission which brought about acceptable changes in the very difficult question of policing in Northern Ireland. Today I do the forum on Europe down here. I am also involved with the Ireland fund, which is a charity. I also do some writing for the *Independent*. There are other involvements, so I have a very varied life. It keeps you going all right.

Politics is my life but I like people more than politics. I was brought up in a pub, my mother had a small hotel and all of us worked our way through those young years. So you were dealing with people as customers; some of them lonely. It was, I believe, a great training for life and has served me well.

The peace process has been a long haul. Before, it had been one step forward and two steps back, now it is two steps forward and one step back. None of these things go smoothly, you must have faith at the end of the day, and you have to have an essential confidence and faith in human nature. Great people have sacrificed themselves over the years for peace and I firmly believe we are getting near a closure.

I am delighted to see Croke Park open up. Sean Kelly did a great job and it is something all of us in the GAA should be so proud of. It's a wonderful stadium, built by the GAA – a world class stadium. As Sean Kelly said, "It was being kind to one's neighbour to open it, and I think it has brought a sense of well-being to the whole community."

I became Secretary of the Down County Board in 1956 and served in that position until 1964. We immediately began putting new structures in place in the county. There were too many teams competing in leagues within the county and indeed the entire County Board acted as selectors for the county team. I looked at the organization in Kerry and the system of divisional teams which existed there and we decided to start a Barony League in 1953. This change helped to raise standards. It provided better competition for our players. There was also an East Down/South Down split which was very deep and damaging, so we started an All-County league with ten teams in it and we drew up a fixture list at the beginning of the year, so each team knew how many matches they were going to have. This greatly improved the standard in the county. We gave ourselves five years to win an All-Ireland. Cavan were the big stumbling block, we knew that and also we had to give the players faith in themselves. This was the crucial component in the jigsaw. It was like breaking the four minute mile at the time. People said it could not be done but when Bannister did it everyone was doing it. When we broke down the barrier and won the All-Ireland it gave the rest of the six county team's great faith in themselves.

So it was this mental thing which we broke down. There was this view in the North that every Kerry footballer was a giant, that they were invincible. And this is where I came across Dr. Eamonn. He would become a great friend. I had enormous regard and respect for him. I am not quite sure when we first came into contact. I believe I just started writing to him on the basis of his book: *'The Art and Science of Gaelic Football'* and of course his great reputation.

Now there was another Kerryman from Listowel, Michael Morgan Sheehy, who was corresponding with me regularly at that time. He had played a bit for Kerry in the mid-1920s. He was living with his daughter in Surrey. I would get these nice letters from him in lovely sort of prose telling me about football and what we should do, how to prepare the team. He would write his address on the outside of his envelopes and one day my mother saw this address and she said, "When I was growing up there was a man in Listowel called Morgan Sheehy, I wonder is there any relation there." So I wrote to Morgan and I got this most lovely letter back saying that little did he know that when he was writing to the Secretary of the Down County Board he was infact writing to the son of a dear old school-mate. He added how well he remembered my lovely mother and her beautiful sisters embraced in roses in the garden of my grandmother's cottage by the Laratigue. It is a lovely memory for me. So Kerry was the goal standard, it was always there for me, there is no question of that.

I travelled to New York in 1956 with the Kerry and Dublin teams. Kerry, trained by Dr. Eamonn, had won that historic final in 1955. They did not think that a Down team would ever beat Kerry. Having said that, I always found there was a generosity of spirit in Kerry football. They didn't go around worrying, because they knew they were good and they didn't have to prove it every day of the week. So if you beat them you must be good too. They respected people.

Dr. Eamonn was not the trainer in 1960 when we won that first All-Ireland. The way I look on it is that they had dropped the pilot. I don't know why he was not the trainer then, it was an internal Kerry thing. However I still believe that even if Dr. Eamonn was in charge in 1960; Down would still have won, we were good enough to win at the time.

Now one of the things that we played on for that game was the fact that Dr. Eamonn had a theory of zones. People kept to their places and you did not move out of that zone and what we introduced into Gaelic football was mobility. So your full back or half back could move up with the ball and even make or get a score. I think it took Kerry a bit of time to come to grips with this change. In the late 1950s and early 1960s there was a certain static quality about Kerry football. Now one of the things we attempted to do was play Mick

O'Connell out of the game because Leo Murphy's kick-outs were so long. The one player we were most afraid of in that 1960 All-Ireland was Tom Long. We reckoned that Tom Long was the guy who would win that match for Kerry if he wasn't held. Dan McCartan did a great job in marking him. He probably held him in more ways that one, I must add.

I have spent my life in human relations, negotiations, personnel work and all the rest, but the one thing I learned from Dr. Eamonn was that you have got to treat people as individuals. Each one was different, he would say. One guy could take hard training and that same training could kill another one. He told me that people had different moods and there was different ways of stimulating them and getting a big game out of them. I think that was his great contribution – dealing with each individual.

Dr. Eamonn was the man who put the training of teams on a thoughtful, rational, scientific basis. He was not a mercenary; he did it for the love of the game. He harnessed the skills that he had and the professional knowledge he had.

He was certainly a role model for me. Different people affect your life and he was one of those people that touched my life. He was a great man. Paddy O'Keeffe was another amazing man at that particular time, and also helped greatly in building up the GAA. He is mentioned very little in today's world, not unlike Dr. Eamonn. I am not surprised at this because people are inclined to forget events and such after about five years. Anything more than a generation now and people forget. The mind moves on very quickly and I think there is very little interest in the history of the games now.

The first book written on Gaelic football was that by Dick Fitzgerald, the next one was Dr. Eamonn's and then Joe Lennon wrote his. When you look at the set up today, you have trainers, managers, dieticians, physiotherapists and an army of people around the teams. Dr. Eamonn, in contrast was doing all this himself.

While he was involved in Kerry football from 1924 to 1964, Dr. Eamonn did at times take breaks. However when Kerry were in trouble he always came back with great generosity of spirit. Actually we would have liked to have faced Kerry in the 1962 All-Ireland. This was Dr. Eamonn's last winning final. We had gone to America, we trained when we came home and we should have taken a rest. We won our first match against Fermanagh fairly handy. The next game against Armagh was a bit more difficult. The third match was against Cavan in the Ulster Final, which we lost. Kerry beat Roscommon in the Final, I think we would have beaten Kerry in the Final. That Down team was, I believe, worth three All-Irelands.

Dr. Eamonn had a wonderful way of building up a rapport with all his players. They were, in many ways, all his children. He was a gentleman in every sense of the word; quietly-spoken, very thoughtful and well-read. We had a common interest in Bridge and he loved that game. Actually I got to know one of his sons who was working in the North; Tony was a lovely man. He would visit our home, but sadly he died some years ago.

Of course the building of Fitzgerald Stadium was a great thing. It is a jewel there in the heart of Kerry and it is one of the great life experiences to sit in that place and watch a match admire the mountains and look at the sun go down in the evenings.

Another common interest we had was our involvement in the development of Occupational Therapy in our own hospitals. He had begun Occupational Therapy in the 1930s before anywhere else. His idea of using the patients in work as 'Occupational Therapy' was something that I was very interested in. There was a big Mental Hospital in Down Patrick, they were all built about the same time. In fact the first Resident Medical Superintendent (R.M.S.) in Down Patrick was a Dr. Nolan from Lisselton, in Kerry. Then in the mid-1950s they started taking down the walls and started Occupational Therapy. I was responsible for local housing and we were one of the first councils to let out houses to patients from the hospital as half-way houses. I must say that the people in Down Patrick were extremely tolerant and helpful in that respect. These positive changes for psychiatric patients in Ireland were all thanks to the influence of Dr. Eamonn. He was a many-sided man.

He was a visionary in so many ways and the building of the Stadium was vital for the county. You need your own place, your own shrine, so to speak, and it has been vital for the success of Kerry football. There are a lot of visionary's who don't have the capacity to put their dreams into effect but Dr. Eamonn did this. I believe that not only Kerry football but football generally owes him a great debt. In addition, I think the whole discipline of mental health in Ireland owes him a debt for his success in opening those hospitals up.

I will remember him as a decent, kindly man who put up with a young fellow who was cheekily writing him letters seeking advice on how to beat his team. Yes he certainly was a man well before his time.

Self-Outline of Biographical Details

BY DR. EAMONN O'SULLIVAN

Self-Outline of Biographical Details

BY DR EAMONN O'SULLIVAN

Born May 8, 1897, in Firies village, situated approximately midway between Tralee and Killarney and made famous towards the end of the last century in the land league campaign by the "Firies Moonlighters". I attended Firies National School from 1900 to 1909. Nothing eventful during the latter period, except for the great family shock caused by my father's (ar dheis Dé go raibh a anam) early and sudden death on January 13, 1909, at a coursing meeting near Midleton, Co. Cork. Incidentally, he was accompanied to all sporting events by a close relative – Thomas O'Sullivan of the Wireless Station, Waterville; father of Paddy O'Sullivan of the Gresham Hotel. Father was known popularly in Kerry as "the Champion" and "J.P." to his intimates. He was a great figurehead in The Kingdom as he won the All-Round Athletic Championship of Ireland in Ballsbridge in 1891 and was also captain of the then famous Killorglin Laune Rangers Football Team, which was only narrowly defeated by the Dublin Young Islanders in the 1892 All-Ireland Football Final. I have a full recollection of the huge funeral cortege, which left Firies for Churchtown, Killorglin about three miles long, in the days when motor cars were scarcely known. I also vividly remember the coffin being borne through the town of Killorglin by his football comrades, each wearing the blue jerseys of the Ranger's Club.

In September 1909, I was sent to St. Vincent's College, Castleknock, Dublin, where I was resident for just two academic years. Nothing much of note during those two years excluding my bitter disappointment, when I was to have my late brother and sister (only other members of the family) visit me in September 1910 on the occasion of the All-Ireland Football Final between Kerry (holders) and Louth. The visit never materialised as the match was not played.

Kerry officials refused to travel unless given satisfactory travelling facilities to and from Dublin and though securing the assistance of the then Central Council of the GAA, the then Great Southern and Western Railway Co. refused point blank. The railway powers in office then were completely unsympathetic to every form of Gaelic ideal. It is to the eternal discredit of the Louth team and officials that they accepted the medals, by taking a walk-over.

Needless to add, Kerry has never forgotten this unsportsmanlike act, but we had our revenge in full in the Croke Cup Final of 1913, when Kerry readily defeated Louth in a replay on June 29, 1913. This match demonstrated though in a somewhat relative manner, Kerry's illegal deprivation of the 1910 All-Ireland medals. This latter game was made historic in a number of ways. It was the first record attendance of over 30,000 in the GAA and the proceeds from the two games (drawn game and replay) provided the necessary monies, which subsequently enabled the association to purchase the Jones' Road Grounds, (now and since renamed Croke Park) to commemorate the name of the GAA's first and most illustrious patron, the late Archbishop Croke of Cashel; a fearless and powerfully expressed champion of Gaelic Culture.

While in Castleknock College I enjoyed my stay under the sympathetic and understanding supervision of the Vincentian fathers. Although happy in my studies, I had the keen disappointment of being deprived of the opportunity of playing my beloved Gaelic football. I cannot, even to this day, comprehend the attitude of Irish educationalists who consider that foreign football games can be a satisfactory substitute for the Gaelic code. I had preference to play soccer during my first year in Castleknock, and rugby, which was substituted in my second year 1910-1911. It was, therefore, with great delight and satisfaction that I received news from the family that I was to leave Castleknock and suffer that famous and distinguished academy of learning and Gaelic football, St. Brendan's Seminary, Killarney, in September of 1911.

St. Brendan's was, as stated, noted for the brilliance of its classical teachers, all of whom, of my time there, have passed to their eternal reward (ar dheis de go raibh na'hanamacha). It was, as it still is, a great motivation for the preparation of its students for the priesthood, both for the home and foreign missions. It has produced many brilliant classical scholars and outstanding theologians, as well as filing the various other professions with distinction and many of them pre-eminent in their respective fields. The sound theory of 'meno sans in corpore sano' found much favour in the St. Brendan curriculum. Its recognition of the value of sport and physical development was always a feature of the college's activities. It produced many famous footballers among its 61 All-Ireland Senior medallists, the most notable being that wizard of Gaelic forwards – the late 'Dickeen' Fitzgerald of Killarney, who was on Kerry winning teams from 1905 to 1914. I have a vivid recollection of a single coaching lesson he gave the footballers in my last year in St. Brendan's in 1914. I recall distinctly that, equipped with only ordinary street boots, he said to me "I will show you how to curve a ball from near the end line". With consummate ease he screwed a free kick about five yards from the end line, it curved over the bar. I have yet to see a Gaelic footballer repeat this performance.

My ambition in St. Brendan's was centred on the priesthood, and accordingly I entered the world's greatest and outstanding noviciate in 1914 – St. Patrick's College, Maynooth. There I joined such famous Kerry contemporaries as Canon Michael Costelloe, Canon Con Moriarty and Canon Christopher O'Neill – all three hale and hearty and spiritual pillars of strength in their respective parishes of Millstreet, Castletownbere and Rathmore. There were many other subsequently famous dignitaries as contemporaries from the other dioceses, notably the present Bishops of Dromore and Galway, their Lordships most Rev. Eugene Doherty, and most Rev. Dr. Michael Browne. Incidentally, Canon Christy O'Neill is probably one of the most outstanding of the classical scholars produced by St. Brendans. He was a Greek and Latin Medallist of outstanding merit. We all envied him his ease of interpretation of Greek verse and his all-round knowledge of classics.

Maynooth College was awe-inspiring. The enormity and extent of its building, with its imposing entrance, standing out in sharp contrast to the ancient castle reminding us like the Colosseum in Rome of the sharp contrast of antiquity and modernity as they lay side by side. The majestic spire of the senior chapel stood out as a monastic reminder in the quiet, flat and indeed inspiring countryside. When entering its portals for the first time one became lost without direction and felt as confronted by a great 'Taj Mahal'.

Having located the junior house with its two main structures of logic and rhetoric, one gradually became domiciled and adjusted to the routine life of the College. There was quite a nice balance between its spiritual, the natural and the physical. It did not take long to get adjusted to the early rising at 6 a.m. and this was readily acquired by the assistance of the early retiral.

Football, hurling and athletics organised a very reasonable position in the general curriculum arrangement, and all daily recreational periods allowed, "booting", a football around even in close proximity to both the rhetoric and logic buildings. This led to a rather memorable experience for me when I had only been only one to two weeks in residence. I let fly my left leg, 'being a one leg footballer' to a rather rapidly approaching ground ball and drove it back with some force. Unfortunately, it curved rapidly towards the centre of the building and crashed through one of the first floor buildings. I was immediately informed that the window in question was that of the sitting room of the Junior Dean – the late Rev. Malachy Eaton (ar dheis Dé go raibh a anam). I immediately and indeed nervously visited the Dean's room, and proffered my apologies. The impact of the ball apparently had resulted in a shower of glass fragments all over the room. Although Fr. Eaton did receive me kindly, I did get the impression that he was by no means a football enthusiast. Speaking of football, it may be of interest to record that in those days Gaelic, soccer and rugby, were played in both the senior houses and Junior, though Gaelic had a much more dominant time allowance than soccer and rugby combined. It may not be realised that the majority of the diocesan colleges in the west and north in the pre-1916 period exclusively played soccer only. It was, I think the re-kindling of the national spirit after the 1916 Rising to create a new outlook which surprisingly was not followed by some of the other well-known colleges.

My stay in St. Patrick's was unfortunately limited to the pro-years in the junior house, and consequently, I never experienced life with the senior house. An outstanding highlight of the period was the Easter Rising of 1916 when Pearse and his comrades made the supreme sacrifice to re-awaken the national spirit, at that time at such a low ebb. The flood of propaganda let loose in the country following the declaration of the Great War in the summer of 1914 tended gradually to submerge the already limited national outlook of the people as a whole. Many well-intentioned Irishmen fell pray to the spurious promises, so freely delivered at the spate of the British recruiting meetings, spread throughout the entire country. In Maynooth we saw the late Donal O'Brachalla, first Governor Guard of the Irish Free State, who was well-known to all the students as one of the shopkeepers in the College Mart, lead in to the college his band of volunteers. They received a special blessing from the president, the late Monsignor Hogan, before marching to Dublin to join their compatriots. The failure of the uprising only in the physical sense could be detected in the continuous red glare in the night's sky in the direction of Dublin so clearly visible from the College.

1916 and 1917 saw my enforced absence at home because of indisposition, and in October 1917, I entered University College Cork (U.C.C.) to complete the 3rd Arts Degree course. Among our distinguished professors now gone to their respective eternal rewards were Rev. Father Edwin Fitzgibbon O.F.M. Cap., Professor of Philosophy and Tonna O'Donoghue, Professor of Irish. Doctor Edwin that great lover of Gaelic games, had engraved his name in perpetuity, when following the example of Professor George Sigerson, who gave the Sigerson Cup for the Annual Inter-Varsity Gaelic Football Championships in 1911, similarly presented the Fitzgibbon Cup for hurling.

Both of these cups have been annually competed for, for over 50 years, and a recent satisfactory development has been the participation of all the Irish Universities in both cup competitions. During my solitary year in U.C.C., I must say that I have very many happy memories, not least the numerous friends that I met in the College, and in the Mardyke University Grounds. I had the privilege of playing unsuccessfully in the Sigerson Cup Championship in Galway with the outgoing President of U.C.C., Harry Atkins and many others too numerous to mention who now occupy leading positions in the various professions and also some of whom, have since passed untimely away. In retrospect, I must say that I enjoyed my short nine months stay in Cork and found the general tempo of life 'on the campus' as you might say, most friendly and intimate, where one made contact with almost every student in the college. This was in sharp contrast to the position of University College Dublin (U.C.D.), which I will refer to later. Among my classmates was a Capuchin student, who subsequently became the distinguished College Professor of Philosophy, the late Rev. DV.

Leaving U.C.C. in the summer of 1918 arrangements were made for me to avail of the Fr. Fitzgerald bursary to resume studies for the Kerry Diocese in the Irish Pontifical College, Rome. My journey from Firies to Rome in November 1918 was undertaken shortly after the conclusion of the 1914-1918 war and obviously involved many hazards and difficulties arising from the war disruption of travelling facilities. It took exactly seven days over land, in striking contrast to my journey by air in Holy Year 1950 from Shannon taking only seven hours. The English Channel crossing could only be made then by overnight journey from Southampton to Le Havre. The Dover-Calais and Hewhaven-Dieppe Routes were not then in operation. The journey included a stay of three nights in London, one night on the sea journey to Dieppe (to secure the necessary visa) as well as a recommendation from that great lover of Ireland, Most Rev. DV. Omigo, Bishop of Southwark), one night in Paris, and a night journey from Paris to the Frontier Italian tour of Madame, on the French side of the Alps and a final journey under the Alps with a three hour stay in the evening at the city of Torino (Turin). When I discovered that my supply of monies had become exhausted in per force I had to visit the British Consul, a kindly man, who gave me sufficient hire to complete my overland journey to Rome, which I reached next day at 12 noon. I recall the Consul's letter of acknowledgement of my letter reimbursing him for his loan. I distinctly recall him stating, "If everybody having dealings with this office were as prompt as you were in making refunds, then life in this world would be much more pleasant."

The Irish College then was situated in the Via Massarimo in a large building, the property of a Rome Banking Co. The Public Church attached to the College had the special distinction of housing the famous Dan O'Connell's heart; he willed that his body (he died in Palermo) be taken to Ireland and his heart to Rome.

On the expiration of the lease some few years ago, the Irish College transferred to a new building, adjacent to the Basilica of St. John Lateran. I was in the somewhat unfortunate position of arriving in the then Irish College almost immediately following the end of the war when conditions, particularly in the field of food availability, were deteriorating from day to day. Butter was no longer provided, and its only substitute was fat rashers and these rather limited in quantity. Italian table wines were always provided instead of water at the main meal of the day, and this had just gone off the menu shortly after my arrival. The quality of the post-war bread beggared description. It was almost black in colour and correspondingly derrid in flavour. The college could in no sense be held responsible for this situation. It was the general post-war effect over the whole country.

I had another setback when I was informed shortly after my arrival by the then President, the late Monsignor O'Riordan, that I would have to take the entire philosophy course again, I accordingly took the necessary lectures in the Propaganda University, doing one half of the course with the 1st year students and the final half with the 2nd years. All lectures were given in the University in Latin and this took some adjustment, not to mind the well-recognised difficulty all Italians have in pronouncing their ancient language because of the absence of the vowel endings in the modern language, in the vast majority of the words. Disappointed at the time, I was later to appreciate the value of the Roman outlook on the study of psychology and how it measured up to the Irish traditional version as explained so forcefully by our Maynooth Professor at that time, the late Rev. Professor Dr. O'Neill.

Undergoing studies in Propaganda University was a new exciting experience, because of the medley of nationalities represented by clerical students of all colours and from various climes, all dressed in soutanes each country displaying a distinctively coloured waistband. The students of the Irish College, strangely enough, wore a deep red band, while the Polish students had our emerald green. The story has it that many years ago the Irish students, through their Rector, petitioned the then Holy Father requesting a change over to the green band. It was stated that the Pope, after deep and prolonged prayer and meditation explained that Ireland, with its great tradition of worldwide martyrdom for the faith was more truly represented and characterised by the red colour. Incidentally, there was a great and ready affinity between Irish and Polish students ... their inspiration of our national colour, as we thought.

A lengthy visit to Rome is a very special experience, not alone because it houses the headquarters of Catholic Christianity, but because of the mixture of modernity and antiquity lying side by side. One can travel by bus or motor car on a modern tarmacadamed road from Rome and shortly arrived at Hadrians'– the famous palace built in the second century A.D. This building is in a fairly reasonable state of preservation, and one wonders at the brilliantly coloured tiling of the large and many small baths as well as the enduring state of the first floor housing the dining room with its, unusual for us, vomitarium closely adjacent. Rome's wonderful basilicas including St. Peter's is one of the world's largest and most beautiful churches. It would take many months to examine and make satisfactory study of every part and section of the Church, not to mention the Vatican buildings and the numerous and marvellous art galleries, which house such famous masterpieces. One of the great marvels is Michelangelo's famous painting of the last judgement on the ceiling of the Sistine Chapel, the chapel that houses the selection of the popes. It is recorded that Michelangelo had to spend many years lying flat on his back on a specially erected scaffolding, in carrying out the major portion of his masterpiece.

The physical side of our education was well catered for. Hurling and Gaelic football were played weekly, a half-day being devoted to both activities. Dr. Alec Spain, the well-known Dublin gynaecologist, was a classmate of mine, both in Rome and subsequently as medical students during the following years, as we both commenced our medical studies in U.C.D. in October, in 1919. Alec was initiated into the intricacies of Gaelic football in the Pomphili Estate, where we had our weekly matches. Alec subsequently became captain of U.C.D. Rugby Club and that same year was selected on the Irish Rugby Team. We both were close friends and both completed our chemical studies in the Mater Hospital. Another learned classmate, who had a distinguished course in Rome, was the present Monsignor

Arthur Ryan of Belfast who was for a time Professor of Philosophy in Queen's University, Belfast, and now a parish priest in the city.

My stay in Rome was an all too short nine months and it enabled me to make a final decision as to my vocation, when leaving during the summer of 1919. On the advice of my old friend, the late Dr. P.T. O'Sullivan Professor of Medicine in U.C.C., I decided to commence studies for the medical profession in U.C.D. in October of 1919. On arriving at Salsford Terrace, I received a mild shock when I met my classmate from St. Brendan's, Gerald O'Connor, and found that he was just qualified and about to have his medical degree conferred. It caused me to reflect seriously on the fact that I had been leading the spiritual path for five years, and was now only at the commencement of my medical career. By the way Gerald at our last year at St. Brendan's was Captain of the Senior football team, and he and I were honoured by playing in the Munster College team versus the winners Leinster in the U.C.C. Athletic Grounds in the Mardyke, in June 1914. It should be noted that the then Inter-Provincial College Competition was confined to the one annual game between Munster and Leinster. Also, the persons of the team included players from some of the more advanced colleges such as St. Patrick's Training College, Drumcondra. Teenagers like Gerald and I were very definitely over-awed, when we found ourselves opposed by such famous Kerry footballers as Jerry Beckett, who won the All-Ireland medal with Cork, Humphrey Murphy and Maurice Donovan, both All-Ireland medallists on Kerry teams all now deceased. Quite obviously, our stage-fright in the face of such opposition was reflected in our nervous and mediocre performances. Little then did I think that one day, later, I would re-organise the college football and hurling competitions in the four provinces in accordance with the rule laid out in the constitution of the GAA.

During my over five years sojourn in U.C.D., my abiding interests were centred in Gaelic games and athletics, and I took an active part in the organisation and progress of both clubs. It was a source of great inspiration for all of us students to find the active support we received from such college stalwarts as the well-known Dublin All-Ireland medallist, the late Dr. John Ryan; the big-hearted Limerick man. He was joined as an official of the Athletics Club by the late Professor of Anatomy, Dr. E.P. McLaughlin. Both ruled and directed the Athletic Club with an iron if sympathetic hand and the many Inter-Varsity Athletic Championship victories were in no small way due to these two dedicated enthusiasts. My love for athletics perhaps with a strange heredity traditional, which induced me to get the family and relatives at home to present a suitable trophy for this Irish Inter-Varsity Athletic Championship and perpetuate the memory of my father in winning the All-Round Athletic Championship of Ireland in 1891, already referred to.

The J.P. O'Sullivan trophy was won in 1964 by U.C.D. and is at present being held by Iggy Moriarty, a Kerry student, whose father Padraig Moriarty, a chief official in the Dept. of Education, hails from the Dingle Gaeltacht.

My association with college athletics was more administrative than physical. I only competed for the College in the hammer and javelin and both of these events were only included on a trial basis. My minor success was in winning the javelin event in Cork from the big South African Trinity College student, J. Van Druten, with the rather juvenile performance of about 110ft. Incidentally, the javelin was included as a national event in the last All-Ireland Athletic Championships held in Croke Park in 1922. Under GAA rules the N.A.C.A. I was established subsequently by the Administers of the GAA Athletic Council, and the Irish Amateur Athletic Federation. To my surprise I won the javelin championship with a measly throw of 119 ft. odd. I realised then that I had a big advantage over my D.N.P. burly opponents, including the massive discus champion, the late P.J. Bermingham. I had some if very non-technical experience in the event as against my opponents, who were competing in this event for the first time.

During my student days there were many distinguished athletes competing then in 'Varsity Athletics', Dr. Denis Cussen, the Trinity Student from Newcastlewest who dominated the 100 yds. Championships both in the University and as Irish champion, creating a record of 9.8 secs – which still stands. Then also there was one of our Irish champion sprinters; the late Frank O'Dea, who had a brilliant course in dentistry, practising in Merrion Square up to the date of his early and untimely death. He also was U.C.D. Professor in some branch of dentistry. Another Irish 100 yds and Inter-Varsity competitor was my old friend Dr. Harry Conway, who is still with us as a medical officer in Meath, close to the Metropolis. I will recall his short stay with me in Firies about 1903, and his very hazardous journey on the pillion seat of my motorbike to Killarney and Moll's Gap, descending into the picturesque valley at the southern side behind the famous Gap of Dunloe and through the Gap to emerge at Kate Kearney's Cottage. The rough journey through the humpbacked road of the pass through the gap caused a break in the very sturdy spring of the 4 HP Douglas machine. Harry was posted as the star athlete in Tralee at the time in such sports. On the following Sunday he captured a number of prizes including those for the 100 yds. and long jump.

In those days, the College Sports Centre was in Terenure, and I

can say that the vast majority of my weekends, especially on Saturdays,
was spent there, athletics during the summer months with hurling
and Gaelic football taking up most of our time. Our main objectives
were centred in the Fitzgibbon and Sigerson Cup Championships, as
well as the Co. Dublin League and Co. Championship competitions.
I have a vivid recollection of the 1923 and 1924 Sigerson Cup games
in U.C.C. I was then honoured as Captain of what was regarded as
a star-studded team of inter-county footballers, which included Dr.
Tom Pierce of Wexford. We were so conscious of our superiority that
we regarded the opposition as of little consequence, and we were well
and truly rumbled by a good U.C.C. team, which led us a merry dance
in the Final and sent us back to Dublin without the Cup, in a very
chastened mood. I had a difficult task of marking the well-known
Cork County hurler and footballer, the late Dr. Joe Kearney. He gave
me the 'run-round' as chief scorer with a tally of two goals, in the
very heavy and sodden state of the Mardyke pitch. Still our morale
was quickly restored, when we all got lost in the enjoyable revels of
the Sigerson Cup social that night.

I do not know how many times we reached the final of the Dublin
County Football Championships and on each occasion to be foiled
by that great club team of the 1920s, St. Lawrence – the O'Tooles
captained by that great midfielder, Paddy McDonnell, who at present
is spearheading a special social centre in Dublin for the Seana-Gaedhal.
He had a great team of club and inter-county footballers – Joe Norris,
the Synott brothers, Mick O'Reilly, not forgetting Paddy's brother,
Tommy; the goalie. This team's record has only recently been equalled
by the well-known St. Vincent's County Champions.

I well remember that I had some compensation in 1924 in the
Tailteann Games Inter-Provincial Football Final between Leinster
and Munster. Leinster had a tremendous selection from all over the
province, with seven or eight of the O'Tooles players including those
mentioned above. They were regarded as unbeatable and particularly
when faced by a Munster team, depleted very substantially by the loss
of five or six famous Kerry republican players, chief of whom were;
Joe Barrett, John Joe Sheehy and Jackie Ryan.

The Munster team consisted of 14 Kerry players and one from
Clare. As one would have expected Munster were most of the time on
the defensive, but doggedly refused to surrender. Consequently, the
Leinster full backs and opposing forwards were perched almost on
the centre of the pitch and as happens in such situations our famous
right half-back Paul Russell sent a long and high ball well beyond
the centre line. Two of the inside forwards, the brothers Graham
from Dingle, dashed away inside their fullbacks secured possession,

and scored a great goal which converted a one point defeat at that stage to a two point lead, with only some minutes to go. This was ultimately the final result creating a first-class sensation at the time, and we received the Tailteann Games Championship medals of 1924. Among those on the Munster Team were Kerry's famous midfielders, Con Brosnan and Bob Stack, who dominated this section of the game as they did in the subsequent six or seven years, each winning four or five All-Ireland medals. Also, including Paul Russell mentioned above, we had another Killarney player, goalie 'Denso' Hurley. As well on our team was clerical student Mundy Prendeville of Castleisland, who after his ordination won an All-Ireland medal with Kerry. He was subsequently consecrated Archbishop of Perth, Australia, and was then the youngest Archbishop in the Church. I was playing as left-half back being a last minute selection to fill in for one of the Kerrymen who as stated refused to play. I fear that my play fell short of my other colleagues. My sole contribution for my side was scoring two points from 50 yard frees in the second half, which reduced our defeat to that of a single point.

One of the remaining important events during my stay in U.C.D. was the successful fight which the hurling and football club members, with the help of our sympathisers in the athletic club, put under way in securing a place in the sun for Gaelic culture. During my first and second years as student I was forcibly made very much aware of the necessity for this change in securing majority (student) control in the Athletic Council (this consisted of representatives from all the college sports clubs; Gaelic football, hurling, soccer, rugby, hockey, tennis, etc.), the Academic Council representing the various college societies; the Commerce Society, the L&H, the Law Society, the Medical Society, etc. Representation on the students' representative council consisted of those selected from each faculty class – thus each of the five years medical classes, selected one or two from each class.

In addition, each of the various councils had two representatives. In the absence of members with a Gaelic outlook, we decided to end this extraordinary anomaly. We were successful beyond our expectations with the active support of such Gaels as the late Dr. Tommy Daly from Clare, Dublin's diminutive All-Ireland hurling goalie, sprinter and hurler Dr. Harry Conway, who incidentally were both subsequently appointed joint Honorary Treasurer of the Student Council. We also captured the Hon. Secretarial posts, with a huge majority of the entire body. I was pushed into the Presidency and incidentally established a record by holding office for two years in succession – this was mentioned recently in a report in one of the Dublin daily papers, though I doubt that anybody was able to identify me, I was referred to simply as 'Edward O'Sullivan'. We had agreed to give the Vice-Presidency to one of the opposition, an old friend and colleague the late Dr. 'Spot' O'Doherty. He was one of the three brothers from Derry, whose father was the late Catholic Lord Mayor of Derry over 40 years ago. All three brothers carried the nickname 'Spot' and qualified as medicals. The 'Spot' Vice-President was gifted with a real command of typical Irish humour.

He and I were appointed by the College President and Kerryman, the late Dr. Denis Coffey to represent Ireland at two international student congresses. The first was the National Union of the Students Congresses in Oxford, to which practically every country in the world sent delegates, excluding Germany and Russia, who were still suffering from the shock and effects of the Great War. The second conference was organised by the English Union of Students in London and Cambridge in 1924. Following on these conferences, Frank 'Spot' Doherty and I decided to summon student council representatives from all the Irish Universities including Queens, Belfast to a special congress in Dublin. This, the first Irish National Union of Students was established in 1924 and finalised only on my last year in office in U.C.D., though it was revived recently. I was appointed as its first President, the Vice-President from Trinity College selected was a law student the present High Court; Justice Budd.

Qualifying in my final medical examination in March, 1925, I had arranged to take out a three month's post-graduate course in the world-famous Coombe Gynaecological Hospital. It was immediately prior to this that my old friend the late 'Phileen' O'Sullivan announced to the Kerry team, who had arranged to play a trial match against Wexford towards the end of March, that I would train them for their 1924 All-Ireland Final versus the holders, Dublin, which was not played till April 1925. Needless to emphasise, I thought at the time that Phil was joking, but he soon set me right, when I took up my residence, with both the Senior and Junior Teams, in O'Grady's Hotel, Ashe St., Tralee. One can imagine my feelings of trepidation in undertaking something I had no previous experience of. I had to devise a 24-hour schedule of training, which differs little from that one published in 1958 in my book *'The Art And Science of Gaelic Football'*. However, it worked out successfully, as on all eight subsequent final occasions; 1924, 1926, 1937, 1946, 1953, 1955, 1959 and 1962.

These successes were not due to any personal "magical touch" as has often been stated. Given a bunch of first class footballers, and pitting them under a few weeks regimented and satisfactory schedule of training, any understanding coach could not fail with material such as Kerry has regularly produced, provided and that all important element of luck in the course of the game is not markfully against your team.

True, this success story did not apply to last September's 1964 All-Ireland Football Final, when Galway deservedly defeated Kerry by 15 points to 10. It is no reflection on Galway's victory, to say that Kerry on that date never reproduced their magnificent football, when substantially defeating Cavan in the semi-final. It was not Kerry's lucky day; beset by injuries of a most dislocating nature, and other factors, they had to bow to Galway and did so sportingly. Naturally, I had some disappointment as it was a break in previous successes, but I have no hesitation in stating that the current Kerry team is young enough and capable enough of winning an All-Ireland Championship. Remember that Kerry has won 20 All-Ireland titles in the last 60 years and four in the last 11 years. On the law of averages they are due another title in the next year or so.

After our satisfactory victory against Dublin, I entered the Coombe Hospital and after three months of interesting work, I did a medical Locum Tenens in the Rush & Lusk Dispensary Districts. Lusk recalled memories of Tommy Ashe, who was a primary teacher in Lusk up to the time of his tragic sacrifice after a lengthy hunger strike in Mountjoy. With a goodly band of Kerrymen we had the honour of attending his funeral from the Dublin City Hall, where his remains lay in state, to Glasnevin Cemetery, having made the long and tedious journey to Dublin on the night mail train from Tralee, arriving at Kingsbridge about 6 a.m. on the day of the funeral. The imposing funeral cortege was one of the largest of the big Sinn Fein demonstrations which followed during the 1917 Sinn Fein General Election activities throughout this country, when this existing Irish (British) Parliamentary representatives were practically ousted as a result of the swinging national spirit which developed after the 1916 Uprising.

It was during my sojourn in the Coombe that Dr. Charley Carey, the then medical student, wrote to me from Killarney informing me of a forthcoming vacancy in the medical staff of the Co. Mental Hospital at Killarney, in case I might have been interested. Curiously enough, I had definite leanings towards a psychology career and had actually in June applied unsuccessfully for a vacancy on the medical staff of a Liverpool Mental Hospital. After a short holiday in July in the Isle of Man with an old and dear friend, the late Dr. George Duggan, then Assistant Master in the Coombe Hospital, I returned home to Kerry to take an active part in my campaign for the Killarney vacancy. Luckily enough, I was appointed to the vacancy in September, 1925, and took up duty on the first of the next month.

It was a very new and strange experience for me to enter a life of responsibility, in an atmosphere, which was rather unusual and new to me. I was most fortunate to work under the late Dr. Edward G. Griffin (R.M.S.) of the Hospital. If anybody ever was nature's gentleman, it was Dr. Griffin. Here I met a gentle, humble man, with over 30 years of active psychiatric experience, who never once up to the time I succeeded him as R.M.S., when he retired eight years later, uttered a harsh word to anybody. He had one absorbing hobby, the raising of thoroughbred greyhounds. He acquired a tremendous reputation in the coursing world, producing some wonderful puppies. He won many of the coursing cups throughout the country and from his famous Killarney stud he raised that champion of champions, which won the Waterloo Cup in 1921, for Lord Tweedmonth, shortly after he had purchased the dog from Dr. Griffin – Guard's Brigade.

My genuinely high opinion of the doctor had no relation to the fact that I became deeply interested in his third daughter Marjorie Gertrude, immediately following our first meeting. She was a lovely, attractive, tall, slim, gentle-mannered and unspoilt girl, just gone 17 years of age. She was about 11 years younger than me and consequently we agreed on a relatively long engagement, allowing our marriage over till the June 17, 1930. We were subsequently blessed with four manly sons, all of 6 ft or over and three of them now married, giving us to date five lovely grand children, God bless them.

Incidentally, none of the three were married in Ireland, the eldest James P, and the youngest Robert M.T., in England, and the third son Anthony in New York, U.S.A. Jim bore out the influence of hereditary genes by adopting a maritime career, following on the footsteps of a number of Griffin granduncles. Even his grandfather, Dr. Griffin, after qualifying in the then Queen's College, Cork, commenced his career as a naval surgeon before joining the staff of Wakefield Mental Hospital, England, and was subsequently appointed the first occupant of the newly-created post of Asst. Medical Officer, in 1895, becoming Superintendent in 1906 on the death of his predecessor, Dr. Lawrence Griffin, a successful General Practitioner in Killarney. After a period as visiting physician to the Mental Hospital, he was appointed R.M.S. on the transfer of the then R.M.S., Dr. R. Woods, to the post of Supt. of Cork Mental Hospital.

My unmarried son, Eddie and third son Anthony have entered the field of dairy science, each taking out the necessary respective diploma and degree in U.C.C. Anthony, after qualifying and securing his M.Sc. degree with first class honours, was given a scholarship in food science to Cornell University, New York. After five years intensive study he was awarded the doctorate degree in food technology, and was subsequently appointed Lecturer of Dairy Technology in U.C.C. He was recently appointed Principal Research Officer in the Agricultural Institute. Meantime, he has been invited back to Cornell University to do a year's special research work jointly with Professor Frank Kosikowski, who is regarded as one of the world authorities on cheese and cheese production.

Following my arrival in Killarney on October 1, 1925, I immediately resumed my football activities, joining the Dr. Croke's Club. This club enjoyed the special tradition of being one of the few distinguished club's in Ireland, whose date of origin almost coincided with the very inauguration of the Gaelic Athletic Association in 1884. I was soon appointed Captain, then Hon. Sec. of the Club and shortly afterwards on retiring from active play about 1928, I was appointed as Vice-President. On the death of the Club President, Eugene O'Sullivan, Chairman of the then Killarney Urban District Council, about 1942, I was appointed President and still have the honour of holding this office.

It was Eugene O'Sullivan and another Vice-President of the Club, the old footballer John Clifford, who were appointed with me about 1932 to select a suitable playing pitch to commemorate the Dr. Croke's famous All-Ireland footballer already referred to, Dick Fitzgerald, who passed away in 1929. We selected the existing pitch now known as the 'Fitzgerald Stadium'. It involved purchasing, in addition, two adjoining fields. The original field consisted of a large hillock running down from the level of the Mental Hospital well into the centre of the present playing pitch 25 to 30 ft. below, though not to the same extent at each end of the field. The stepping and removal of this hillock and its removal to other parts of the pitch, created a natural stand occupying one half of the pitch and curved at each end to the rear of each goal line.

The work involved the construction of the mass concrete pillars and walls surrounding the Stadium, with the special curved entrance on the main road. All the concrete work was designed by the then Principal of the Killarney Technical School, the late Mr. Michael Reidy, a native of Tralee. The pitch was specially levelled with the centre approximately 12" – 14" higher than the sidelines or end lines. We were indebted to the late town surveyor, Mr. John Galvin, for giving us the necessary levels through the theodolite. Apart from the expert advice, of both these technologists, there was no skilled or other technical advice in connection with the work. Helped by members of the Mental Hospital staff, three in particular, Denis Hurley, the 1924 Tailteann Games, Munster goalie (already referred to) the late Myo Murphy and Tim O'Donoghue, and about 40 to 50 patients from the Mental Hospital daily for a bout four years. Members and sympathisers form the A.F. Croke's Club, and other Mental Hospital staff did not spare themselves particularly on Thursdays and also working in the late evenings during the summer months.

It was the first major undertaking of the subsequently developed Occupational Therapy Dept. of the Hospital and could be described as its 'Opus Magnum'. The estimated commercial cost of the undertaking at the time, was given as about £4,000, while the actual sum available and spent was only about £3,000. It is still not completed, but at its present unfinished state it is capable, with proper stewarding, of housing about 60,000 spectators. Standing on the terrace, mentioned above, holds about 30,000 and the side-line seating, when completed will hold close on 20,000 (at present about 12,000), while the popular side, to the south has accommodation for about 18,000 people.

The Fitzgerald Stadium, apart from Croke Park, has at present the largest crowd accommodation in Ireland. The playing pitch is of the maximum length (160 yds) laid down in the official rules and is ahead of Croke Park in this respect. In fact the playing pitch, at the commencement of construction work, was laid out to a length of 170 yds., which at the time was the maximum mentioned in the rules. There was so much publicity given to the latter fact, that some feel that the Association at its next Congress altered the 170 distance to its current dimension of 160. It is rather tragic that the Fitzgerald Stadium has to a large extent become in the nature of a 'White Elephant' not withstanding the fact that 52,000 people enjoyed in comfort the All-Ireland Hurling Final between the winners Tipperary and Kilkenny in 1937, and some years later, a slightly smaller crowd witnessed the one and only Munster Hurling Final played in the Stadium. It could be a source of great advantage and encouragement to the footballing southwest of the country, not to mention Kerry, to bring the Provincial hurling final to Killarney, even if only every five or six years. It is extremely difficult to reconcile the present policy of centralising the Munster Hurling Final to practically two venues, Limerick and Thurles over the years, and the anxiety and ambition of all of us to see the development of hurling extended to such hurling centres as; Abbeyfeale, Listowel, Dingle, Caherciveen, Macroom, etc.

The Stadium was opened in 1936 with much pageantry, and a double programme of hurling and football – Kerry versus Mayo in football and Cork versus Tipperary, drew a crowd of about 20,000. His Lordship the late Bishop O'Brien of Kerry blessed the grounds and the pitch was officially opened by the then Patron of the GAA, his Grace Most Dr. Harty, Archbishop of Cashel. There was an inspiring parade before the game led by the surviving members of Kerry's All-

Ireland Hurling champions of 1891, immediately followed by those of the Kerry's first All-Ireland champions and then the various All-Ireland medal holders of subsequent years and rear-guarded by the 1936 Kerry Team, with the Mayo and Tipperary and Cork Hurling teams also in the procession.

A detailed sound film of the entire proceedings was taken by the film unit of the well-known Killarney talkie play *'The Dawn'*. Unfortunately, for some inexplicable reason, the finished product never came to light – more's the pity.

Finally, on the question of the Stadium, which stands silently, 'crying out loud' for the full development it deserves. It remains as a permanent memorial to the great footballer it commemorates, but even more so to the gigantic work put into it by the scores of patients, who spent four industrious years in its development. The whole story of its construction has the makings of a modern fairy tale. It has been necessary to put all this on record, because it is remarkable with what brevity can memory be clothed in this mundane world of ours.

As stated previously, my love for athletics and Gaelic games which remained practically a life's passion, steered me straight away to do something for the development of both. I take up first the story of the games, which consumed the greater part of my free time and otherwise. The GAA constitution and rules provided for the establishment of Inter-Provincial Secondary Colleges Championships by the formation of four provincial councils. I secured the prior blessing of the Association meet with the then President of St. Brendan's College, Killarney, the late very Rev. Canon John Breen, President and never-ending lover of Gaelic games and athletics. When first I met the much admired Canon, he remarked on Kerry's great football tradition and achievements. He said, among many other things that, as a very young man, he first met my father 'The Champion' (as he called him), he had admired him so much, that he set him on an athletic pedestal. To use his own words, "when your father shook hands with me, I was so thrilled that I didn't wash my hands for a week."

When I visited the Canon in 1926, and explained my mission, I could readily detect from the light of his eyes that I was preaching unnecessarily to the fully converted. His enthusiasm for my proposal to summon all the secondary schools' principals in the country to a preliminary meeting in Tralee was most heartening. The meeting proved to be a 100% success; all the eligible colleges sent representatives. Canon Breen was to be selected Hon. President, and I as Hon. Secretary of the first 'Kerry Colleges GAA Committee'. I also was appointed the Committee's Representative on the Kerry

County Board. We immediately organised a Senior and Junior County Football Championships. I approached the then Bishop of Kerry, the late Most Rev. Charles Dr. O'Sullivan, who readily gave us a cup for the senior competition, the Dr. O'Sullivan Cup. I was also successful in getting the late Mr. Howard Harrington, of Dunloe Castle, to give us a trophy for the Junior (Under-16) Championship. Mr. Harrington asked that the trophy be named 'The Dunloe Cup' instead of 'The Harrington Cup' as I suggested. It is a most gratifying result of my seven years official connection with the committee of the County Board, that both these competitions have been running uninterruptedly and most successfully since.

Immediately following the inauguration of the Kerry Committee, Canon Breen and I arranged for a meeting in Mallow of all the secondary schools in Munster and immediately the first Provincial College Council was established in 1927. I should mention that Cork County had been carrying out college competitions in Cork City and county for several years previously, a number of trophies having been presented by distinguished churchmen in the area. We were fortunate that a Leinster College's Committee had been functioning for some time under the very active Hon. Secretaryship of the great I.R.A. veteran, the late Eamon Fleming (ar dheis De go raibh a anam). This enabled us to organise in 1927 the first Inter-Provincial Hurling and Football Championship between Munster and Leinster. We held trial matches between north and south Munster, both matches being played at the Mardyke U.C.C. Grounds, Cork, and I am glad to say that the teams selected proved successful against Leinster in Croke Park in May 1927. I still have a photograph of the Munster Football Teams, which included Canon Breen and myself. It is of interest to note that included in this snap is a number of Kerry College boys who became very prominent subsequently as senior footballers – Tim "Roundy" Landers, Michael O'Rourke, Mike Doyle, among others. The Captain of the team was the St. Brendan's Captain, Tadgh McGillicuddy, of Killorglin. Included also was 'Bob' Murphy, now very Rev. John Murphy, P.P. Ballybunion, a brother of the present Chairman of the Cork County Board. 'Weeshie' Murphy, himself an ex-St. Brendan's pupil, and Cork All-Ireland Football medallist.

The next step was the organisation of Prior College Councils in Connaught and Ulster, the Leinster Colleges Committees, having meantime been raised to the status of Provincial Council. With the approval of the Central Council, I spent three days in Connaught, interviewing the principals of the various schools concerned. I spent one day in Galway accompanied by very Rev. Father James O'Dea, the current County Galway Representative of the Central Council.

The second day was spent in Mayo accompanied by Mr. Sean T. Ruane, N.T. of Kiltimagh, the President of the Connaught Council of the GAA. On the third day I covered Sligo and Roscommon. I can record with satisfaction, that I was courteously and hospitably received everywhere and our enthusiastic and representative meeting at Claremorris established the Connaught College's Council and selected officers of 1927-28.

It was a single matter to summon the Ulster College's to a meeting in Armagh and the Ulster Provincial College's Council came into being. The Diocesan Colleges in the North had already been playing a Senior College Competition for some years, when they transferred from soccer to Gaelic football. These colleges and other schools have since become important nurseries and the production of many brilliant Inter-County footballers. I should have mentioned that the Harty Cup Hurling Competition in Munster had been played regularly for a number of years before coming under the auspices of the newly created Munster Colleges Council. In April and May of 1928, therefore, the Inter-Provincial College Football Championships was played in semi-finals and a final. The Hurling Championship was as yet confined to Munster and Leinster.

It was a great privilege to be associated with the establishment of these Provincial Councils and the subsequently developed Central Colleges' Council, where as in Kerry and Munster, Canon Breen and I were selected as Hon., President and Hon. Secretary respectively, and I was also appointed college representative on the Central Council. I had to retire in 1933 from active association with the College committees on my promotion as R.M.S. of Killarney's Mental Hospital, as well as for the various GAA councils. I must admit that during all these activities I met many new friends, many of them distinguished and all so numerous that it has now become impossible for me to remember all the names. I took a deep interest in the administrative work involved, both in the various college councils, as well as those of the GAA itself. It was a nostalgic break in my activities, but my training associations with Kerry football teams in subsequent years, as well as attending many of the big games throughout the country, a very satisfying if minor compensation.

My interest in Gaelic athletics was only equalled by that in athletics proper. Athletics was over the years administered by a special Athletic Council of the GAA and through the Irish Amateur Athletic Association (I.A.A.A.), was much the older body, these bodies clashed when the latter placed a ban on any athletes, following the establishment of the GAA and its taking over control of Athletics. It was this ban by the I.A.A.A. that the illustrious GAA's first Patron

Most Rev. Dr. Croke of Cashel referred to in his second letter to the GAA and not as erroneously stated to what is now called the GAA 'Ban on Foreign Games'. Curiously enough, the showdown between the two controlling bodies came to a sharp and decisive head in Tralee about 1888. The I.A.A.A. organised a sports meeting in the present Austin Stack Park, then the property of the Tralee Cricket Club, while the GAA organised in opposition in a field adjacent to the town. Only a mere handful of people attended the I.A.A.A. meeting, while close on 10,000 enjoyed the GAA sports at which many of Ireland's subsequently famous athletes participated. It was easy to anticipate the immediate result of this clash of regimes. The I.A.A.A. capitulated and immediately removed their ban and athletes were permitted to compete under both rules. Subsequent developments toward the end of the century caused a resumption of disagreement between the two athletic bodies, the GAA introduced a permanent ban against the I.A.A.A. as well as against specified foreign games, now known as 'Rule 27-29' and which still stands.

My love for athletics is second only as with Gaelic games to the work involved in my psychiatric career, which I detail further on. Accordingly, shortly after setting down in the Mental Hospital, I decided that one of my first assignments was to put athletics on a sound organisational footing in Kerry. I got in touch with all the prominent GAA personalities, who had connections with the development of athletics under the auspices of the GAA, including the late Jack Collins who succeeded my father as official handicapper and starter for Co. Kerry before the latter, following a congress decision in 1922, allowed the Athletic Council and the Irish Student Athletic Association to be fused into one controlling body of athletics and cycling, the National Athletic and Cycling Association of Ireland.

The Irish Cycling Association as a separate body dealing with cycling matters also became absorbed in the new body, which then became the sole controlling organisation for cycling and athletics in the 32 counties. This was a very happy transition, which meant that Ireland could be fully represented internationally in both athletics and cycling as a national unit. The general approval of everybody practically in the country for this desirable and satisfactory position should stimulate all of us to reach a suitable repprochement in the current farcical and indeed fantastic situation where we have five controlling bodies concerned in these sports, in this relatively tiny country of ours.

I summoned a meeting on May 19, 1926, in Tralee of all those interested in athletics and cycling and there followed a good attendance. We had among others such sporting stalwarts as Kerry's famous footballer, the late "Dickeen" Fitzgerald, Jerry McEllistrim, a well-known racing cyclist in his younger days and Jack Collins, and the younger members of our prominent athletic family of Currow (already referred to above) – both now deceased. Following a general discussion it was unanimously decided to establish a county board of the N.A.C.A.I. The following officers were elected; Presidents, Dick Fitzgerald, Killarney, the Hon. Sec. Dr. EN.M. O'Sullivan, Killarney and Vincent Neville, Tralee, Hon. Treasurers, Jeremiah O'Sullivan, Tralee and J.J. Foley, Listowel. The Board has been in regular operation, without a break to date. I continued as Hon. Secretary to the end of 1931, when I was appointed Hon. President, the Hon. Secretaryship being taken over by Willie McSweeney, N.T. ex-President of the I.N.T.O., until his untimely death in the early 1940s.

I have remained on as Hon. President and Chairman of the County Board since 1931, and now have had almost 40 years of active association in the control of development of athletics and cycling in The Kingdom. It has been a period of vacillating and changing vicissitudes, where the only common denominator was the lack of adequate finance. Most of the years we have been on the debit side at the end of each year, but we have always been undaunted and never lacked in enthusiasm. In the earlier years the County Board consisted of less than a half-dozen active supporters, but gradually interest mounted and the number of active clubs quadrupled. During the last ten years or so there has been a sudden intensive and most successful upsurge of cycling in the country, particularly in road racing. This timely development coincided with the inauguration of the famous eight-day Rás Tailteann, in which Kerry cyclists to date have played a very prominent role. We recall how Gene Mangan, Dan Aherne, and others hit the headlines for beating Ireland's best and for their great reception when returning to the county victorious.

My association with athletics extended outside the county, to the Munster Provincial Council, and Central Council. Early on I became a member of both Councils and attended for many years regularly at the Munster Conventions and the Annual Congresses of the Association. I was appointed first Hon. President of the Munster Council in the late 1920s and so acted for a number of years. I was rather shocked though deeply appreciative of the honour in my appointment in 1929 to the Presidency of the N.H.C.A.I. unsolicited. I was reluctant at the time to oppose the outgoing President, the late J.J. Keane, of Dublin, who had for many years previously been Chairman of the old Athletic Council of the GAA 'J.J.', as he was known personally to us all, was a well-known figurehead in control of G.A.A., athletics and cycling since he retired from an active athletic career in the early part of the century. It was, however, apparent at the time, even to me, that the general organisation of the Association, particularly in the country, was losing ground. In addition, because of the somewhat tactless and injudicious manner in which he handled the developing difficulties with some of the Belfast members of the Association, which as early as 1926 resulted in the loss of our control of cycling for the 32 counties, we were in 1929 faced with the similar loss of athletic control, as eventually occurred in 1937. It was accordingly put to me, that I should allow my name to go forward for the Presidency, if I wished the national athletic movement to survive.

I was by a reasonable majority elected President, and although I appreciated the honour and the necessity for change, I did feel more than sorry for J.J. Keane, as he was a friend and an admirer of mine. The athletic situation, when I took over, left us still in 32-county control of athletics, but clouds were looming up as Belfast formed an athletic body of their own for the six counties. They were agitating for recognition by the British A.A.A. and made formal application by personal representatives to a meeting of the Triangular Athletic Board, held in Crewe (England, Ireland and Scotland). They put their case in the absence of our delegates, Dr. R.J. Rowlette, Eamon Fleming (both now deceased) and myself.

At the triangular board meeting held immediately after the retiral of the Belfast delegates, we agreed to the request of the English and Scottish members to meet the Belfast delegates at a meeting in Dundalk under the chairmanship of the then Scottish A.A.A. Hon. Secretary, Mr. George Hume. This meeting duly took place a fortnight later in Dundalk and strangely enough, accompanying our delegation was the Hon. Secretary of the Ulster Council of the N.A.C.A.I; Tommy Ferguson. Ferguson is now and has been for some years subsequently, the most active member of the present opposition partitions Belfast body, the N.I.A.A.A. At the meeting, when George Hume, Chairman, had explained its objects I immediately stood up and stated that there was an easy and ready solution for the problem of control. I stated that we were quite prepared to give full regional control for athletics to a Northern Council for the nine counties, (indistinct from the six counties) of Ulster, with the single promise that this united body should appoint two or three representatives to a central executive body in Dublin, with a view to arranging for the National Athletic Championships and the selection of All-Ireland teams for international competitions. This was instantly and unanimously agreed to and it was further decided that there should be, a fortnight later, a joint meeting in Belfast of the N.T.A.A. clubs, and all the Ulster N.A.C.A.I. clubs to form an All-Ulster controlling body.

It came as a great surprise that this proposed meeting never took place, it was not even summoned. One can readily infer that the Belfast and cross channel politicians saw to it that there was to be no unity in athletic control, and this was before the Belfast body was recognised by England. Such interference has bedevilled a number of conferences held later in Dundalk, even as recently as three or four years ago. With this knowledge it is easy to appreciate that all efforts towards unity will fail, until those interested in athletics in Belfast as well as their partitionist friends in the Dublin A.A.U. (this Dublin was not in existence in 1929) decided that to achieve unity, they must join the N.A.C.A.I. so as to re-assume 32-county control and thus join all the other sporting bodies with one exception; who sponsor fully representative Irish teams in International competition. We could add, in this respect, that we trust that the English A.A.A. will give the same support for this, as they have done recently to secure an all-German team for partitioned Germany, as well as in partitioned Korea. Hitherto, the English A.A.A. have been the 'enfant terrible' in this whole problem, and Mr. Jack Lynch, the Minister for Industry and Commerce, who kindly offered his services of mediation in the matter recently, must by now be well aware of this apparently inseparable barrier.

Gaelic games and athletics, though among my chief hobbies and taking a big slice of my life's activities, had minor rivals in some other recreations, namely golf and Bridge. Although my association with competitive Contract Bridge goes back to the early t1930s, I had been playing Auction Bridge since my early medical student days, but with nothing approaching the intensity of my Contract Bridge operations. The transition from auction to contract took place about 1930, and spread rapidly from New York to this side of the Atlantic, and within 12 months had developed a large following in Ireland. It was a matter of gradual but progressive organisation that following the establishment of the Contract Bridge Association of Ireland, branches and then clubs followed rapidly. A branch was established in Tralee and almost immediately afterwards a club was established in Killarney, about 1932. My wife and I joined the Club as comparative beginners at the game. The late Sir Maurice O'Connell and Mr. Anthony McGillycuddy were the chief founders and play took place weekly at the Lake View Hotel, Fossa, as it was subsequently known and continued successfully there till a year or two before the last war.

The Club was well supported from its very inception, members from Tralee and Killorglin attending fairly regularly. When Sir. Maurice O'Connell decided about 1937 to convert his residence into a hotel (The Lakeview); the Club had to transfer to the town. It had short-lived successive venues at the Great Southern Hotel, the Lake Hotel and the International Hotel, where it remained for quite a number of years without a break. On its transfer to Killarney I took over control of the Club, first as Hon. Secretary and directed the tournaments almost twice weekly and two or three weeks later, I was elected President and Chairman of the Club and have been uninterruptedly in charge since, even though I am living in Tralee for over two years, the members of the Club have refused to relieve me of this honour.

The running of the Bridge Club was not only an easy matter but it was a pleasant responsibility and even though I generally directed the weekly tournaments, it was a labour of love, due to the general cooperation and loyalty of the members. Early on when Sir Maurice O'Connell and Anthony McGillycuddy retired from the club, I prevailed on each of them to present trophies for the Club Championships Competitions.

Hence, the Lakeview Cup for the team-of-four Championship and the McGillycuddy Cup for the pairs Championship have been competed for each winter since 1937 and my wife and I have an unbroken record of taking part each year since, in both competitions with indeed mixed success. Although we have won the Kerry Pairs Championship on one occasion for the Kingdom Cup, we have never succeeded in winning the McGillycuddy Cup, though we have been runners up on a number of occasions. We have however appeared on winning teams of four for the Lakeview Cup three or four times. We have also a trophy for the Individual Championship since just after the last war, and my wife has the record of having won this trophy on at least four occasions. I have been lucky to win it only once, and can recall that on one occasion I occupied the last place of the 28 contestants. Bridge has a sporty resemblance to golf, in the manner in which one can become so absorbed in both games. Some degree of skill is necessary in both but the element of luck forms a prominent part in both such games. Many people have referred to it as 'the golf bug' and the 'Bridge Mania'. Quite a high percentage of enthusiastics in both games take a deep interest in both activities, and age is no determining factor in this anomaly.

Our Bridge activities have not been confined solely to those of the Club; the Killarney South of Ireland Bridge Congress constitutes a success story in itself since 1944. It is of interest to record its history. The late Dr. Thomas Magnier of Fermoy, who was a popular and well-known figure in Bridge circles from the very inception of the C.B.A.I., was selected President of the Association for the year 1943-44. To commemorate the honour paid to him, he secured the approval of the executive of the C.B.A.I. for the inauguration of a South of

Ireland Bridge Congress. The Annual West of Ireland Congress at Galway and the East of Ireland Congress at Dundalk each whit weekend had been running successfully for some years previously. Successful congresses at Dún Laoghaire were held for a few years before the last war, but lapsed and were revived about the 1950s and now are a regular annual feature of Dublin Bridge activities.

Dr. Magnier of Fermoy had the problem of selecting a suitable southern venue for his venture. Quite wisely he selected Killarney not withstanding strong opposition from some of friends in the Cork Branch, who felt that Cork City was a natural choice. Tommy Magnier, however, was very conscious of the tourist potential of Killarney and particularly of the unequalled facilities available in the first class hotels in 'Beauty's Home'. The subsequent history of the Killarney Congress has proved the wisdom of his keen judgement.

The receipt of Tommy's letter to me in the early summer of 1944, with the war still hanging actively in both Europe and the East, came in the nature of a mild shock. I had never as yet been at a Bridge Congress and consequently lacked the detailed knowledge of organisation. However, my main worry was the fact that we could not undertake any financial responsibility, as our club funds were negligible in amount. I was instantly reassured by Dr. Magnier that they only required that we should take responsibility for organising the playing conditions in a suitable hotel. It meant soliciting all the extra tables available in town and district and we used the Great Southern and International Hotels for the different Congress Championship competitions.

The first congress in 1944 was an outstanding success from every point of view. Owing to the fact that the war was not yet over, the Congress membership was entirely all-Irish. This first nine day convention of Irish Bridge players created something new in congresses – a special atmosphere, where playing the game was only a part of the week's activities, and in any case play was confined to four hours, 8 to 12 midnight only. Visitors, therefore, had the opportunity to spend Sunday fishing on the lakes, playing golf on one of the world's finest golf courses or sightseeing generally. In addition, close of play each night was followed by impromptu concerts, in which there was no dearth of artists or variety. This social and friendly atmosphere continued to be a unique feature of the Killarney Congress and was responsible for the fact that one visit has meant a series of visits for most.

In 1945 the 25th Congress was equally successful and notable for the fact that there were eight cross-channel visitors, including; R. Niaman, an English International player and two Welsh Internationals.

Apparently, those eight visitors became unsolicited ambassadors and as a result 30 visitors from Scotland, Wales and England attended in 1946.

This quota included many, still famous international players, the well-known player and broadcaster from Leeds; Harold Franklin, as well in the Scottish International; Clement Ellis from Glasgow. Incidentally, Ellis has the unique distinction of attending every annual Congress to date since 1946 and after his 15th successive visit; we elected him as Honorary Vice-President of the Congress Committee. Harold Franklin among many others has been a prominent congress visitor, on very many occasions. Other prominent visiting international players from time to time included; Capt. Edward Keyson, Newcastle-On-Tyne who is now editor of one of the two English monthly Bridge magazines. The two Tarlo brothers from London, the well-known English International and Bridge Correspondent of the London *Sunday Times* and Capt. Ricardo of Cardiff (one of the largest golf hitters in the game – reported to have held the record distance in driving).

The Congress too is probably one of the largest (9 days) in the world and its popularity grows annually. The late Kevin O'Farrell, who died recently, acted as joint Hon. Secretary with me, until he became Treasurer of the Committee's funds a few years later and I was appointed to my present position as Chairman of the Congress Committee. The Congress celebrated its coming of age last year (1964) and has now decided to procure a valuable trophy to commemorate Dr. Magnier's name as founder of the Congress. The Congress has from its commencement been held namely in the International Hotel, until about 1950 when it was transferred to the Lake Hotel. In The Lake the nine days are taken over exclusively by Bridge visitors and 75% of these are from Scotland, England and Wales. It is a great tribute to the popularity of the event that the majority of the visitors at the end of each Congress book their accommodation for the following year. None of the other Irish Congresses even the Dun Laoghaire Congress has anything like the cross-channel support as Killarney. But not withstanding this unique position of the fact that it can fill the hotels with close on 300 visitors for nine days in the early part of the season, it is an extraordinary thing that the Congress now in mid-May wends its way without the slightest publicity, more particularly in our own local newspaper. With the exception of one Tostal year, Bord Fáilte has given no support for this very valuable tourism potential. In fact, the local coordinator of the tourism committee is hardly aware of the Congress's aid towards increasing substantially the number of visitors.

It is in fact making a very special contribution in bringing these visitors to Killarney in the early part of the season; an off-period in fact and also guarantees an individual stay of nine days. It is very surprising that the local weekly newspaper, for the past few years has made no reference of any kind to the existence of the Congress. This is in sharp contrast to the fact that the Dublin dailies have Special Resident Correspondents in attendance who send special reports nightly to Dublin. As one who has been present at every congress, excluding 1956, when I was in the U.S.A. with the Kerry football team on tour, I had at the concluding dinner and presentation of prizes listened to some wonderful eulogies of Killarney and its scenery. Some of these were quoted in poetry and their publication whether locally or elsewhere, would provide powerful propaganda for the world's most beautiful 'Eden of the West'.

Next I turn to golf, which has provided very many joyful moments in my recreational periods, though it did also for a number of years involve very much administrative work. I had always been attracted to the game, but owing to my multifarious activities I was unable to take up the game seriously before 1937. I remember well the period, 1937, immediately following Kerry's victory in that year's All-Ireland Final, after a replay v Cavan in October (I had trained the team only for the replay). My wife and I on the day, following this replay, bought each a set of golf clubs in Dublin and decided to give serious application, in trying to master this most baffling game, indeed a game most humbling to one's ego.

Both of us had been active members, for three or four years previously, of the tennis section of the Killarney Golf Club, which kept two excellent grass courts in the old Deer Park links. One can appreciate that with the vagaries of our summer weather, active Tennis playing was reduced to a very short season, though we enjoyed many very pleasant challenge games with; Listowel, Tralee, Macroom, Mitchelstown and some of the many Cork clubs for a few years each summer. We both, however, found that there was an obvious strain, in trying at the beginning of each tennis season to revive the physical fitness we had lost during the autumn, winter and early spring.

This fact influenced me in making the change over from tennis to golf. Accordingly, we both joined the Killarney Golf Club, situated then in the well-known Deer Park. I fear however that my wife did not persevere with the game to the same extent as I did. I had always done some putting from time to time, even as a medical student and consequently was able to make reasonable progress with all forms of iron plays. I developed most annoying difficulties in handling the woods, particularly with the driver and was often reduced to abandoning both the driver and the brassie and relying exclusively on the lighter and shorter spoon. I had of course to put in the usual penitential period of two or three years before I felt that I was approaching average standards.

It was not till I got some lessons from John Doran, the Ballybunion Golf Professional about 1940, that I really improved. I had a rather full swing with the driver, but the ball seemed to wander in every possible direction and in Ballybunion, with its defiant and meandering sandhills and very heavy course rough, this inaccuracy of direction proved costly in keeping up an ample supply of balls, apart from unsatisfactory scoring. Doran advised shortening of my swing, to a smaller arc and put me practising this for a week. I carried out instructions rigidly and noticed that on my return to the professional that I had developed a fairly straight line drive, but distance was correspondingly reduced. This, however, paid dividends and resulted in an almost instantaneous improvement. Doran confessed to me when I was returning to Killarney that he felt I would never persevere with this shortening of my swing. Well I did adjust myself to it and to conclude this golfing episode my limit handicap of 24 came down fairly rapidly to the single figure of 9. I was never able to play to this and towards the latter half of my golfing career my handicap gradually also returned to 18 and that became a fixture of my retiral from the game about five years ago. It is said that the main ambition of the average golfer is to play to a single figure and achieve a 'hole-in-one'. Perhaps I can have some degree of satisfaction that I did reach an unplayable single figure, but I did also hole out from my iron tee shot at the fourth hole in that attractive and intriguing seaside golf links at Dooks. I also had some satisfaction in that, though I never won a captain's prize, I was successful in winning many Open Cup competitions, including the County Kerry Medical Trophy and the Fielding Cup (which incidentally, I succeeded in getting Mr. Fielding, of Fielding's Pharmacy, Cork to present to the Kerry Medical Society, which I founded about 1942 and is still operating).

So much for my interest in playing the game, but as in most things, I could not resist the challenge of devoting a good deal of my time to the administrative side. As I said above I commenced play in the Old Deer Park 9-hole links in 1937, and shortly after this, the then late Lord Castlerosse commenced construction of the new 18-hole Championship course about 1938. The Deer Park course is one of the oldest links in Ireland and one of the founders of the club was my wife's father and my predecessor as R.M.S. of Killarney Mental Hospital, Dr. Edward G. Griffin, the great personality which I have already referred to.

Lord Castlerosse, later Earl of Kenmare, secured the services of the well-known golf course architect, the late Sir Gray Campbell, who was fortunate to get the Scottish golf course construction foreman. Between all three (Castlerosse was a Cambridge University scratch golfer himself) they produced one of the world's outstanding golf courses in the western district along the northern shore of the large and beautiful lower lake.

Overseas visitors, since the opening of the course on October 1, 1939, when the last global war was getting into full swing, have paid glowing tributes to the magnificence of the links, whether viewed from the golfing or scenic point of view. I recall writing into the Green Tee Book about 15 years ago the unsolicited remarks made to me one afternoon by a New Zealand golfing enthusiast, who was touring Killarney and many other countries, as follows. "I have played in the leading golf courses of more than 18 countries throughout the world, and nowhere have I seen such tremendous golfing conditions to this by no means inferior to the lovely setting, surrounded by mountain and lake with unrivalled colouring and magnificence." Many prominent golfers, including Henry Cotton, have paid similar verbal and written tributes to the excellence and unrivalled nature of the Killarney course. Its golfing challenge can be gauged from the fact that with scratch score conditions of 75; nobody has returned a score below 70 in official competitions. In the International Professional Tostal Tournament, about 1954 which was supported by all the leading professional players from England, Scotland, Wales and Ireland. Among the many there were Dia Rees from Wales, Eric Brown from Scotland Garry Player and four others from South Africa, with the three leading Irish professionals; Harry Bradshaw, Christy O'Connor, and Fred Daly from Belfast. In the Tostal Stroke Competition proper, the winner; Eric Brown was the only player to return a score of 70 in dry, calm and practically ideal play conditions.

A unique feature of the course, apart from its championship calibre and beautiful unrivalled setting is that the 18 holes are spread over a very wide area of ground, and none of the holes is similar to the other 17. There are many testing holes such as the 13th, which was mainly designed by Castlerosse, in replacing another hole. The 18th is a 3-par hole and is probably one of the most intriguing golf holes in the world. It could be accurately described as a real 'target hole'. With very little approach ground, it is situated with the lake on its right and the banked roadway on the left, with a fairly massive rhododendron growth further on the left. When the lake is in a flooded state and surrounds the green on the west and north side, it can be readily appreciated that one's drive, from the terrace must of the 'Bull's Eye' variety. Further for very many days, particularly in winter, gale-like winds blow in across the green from the south-western side. This adds another serious hazard in play and if records in stroke play for the 18th were kept it would probably cause surprise how often winning scores, on even securing a 5 at this hole, have been well and truly wrecked by bad tee-shots.

I recall about 1945, when among the competitors in the O'Callaghan Cup on St. Patrick's Day, were our two well-known plus – two Irish International golfers; Jimmy O'Brien of Cork and local Dr. Billy O'Sullivan (both Irish champions in their time), both reached the 18th tee with cards shaping for the low 70s and had to face a semi-gale blowing across from right to left. Apparently Brien hit two shots into the unplayable rhododendrons on the left not allowing enough for the wind conditions. On the other hand Billy O'Sullivan allowed too much for the gale and put two well-hit shots into the lake on the right of the green. The conditions caused two sensational scores – Brien's 9 and O'Sullivan's 10. This true to life story, as would be expected gave much encouragement and inspiration to us 'rabbits'.

Special qualities of the links, not the least of which is its most unusual seaside qualities, have been universally acknowledged. A low-handicap Portmarnock player informed me in 1939, shortly after the course was officially opened on October 1, 1939, that he had never played or even seen a course anywhere inland so closely approaching Portmarnock, in its texture and dry underfoot conditions. I remember during 1942, when a friend and I played over the course immediately following three and a half days of non-stop rain and every hole except the 18th was not alone playable but completely dry underfoot. The swell in the lower lake meant that the entire green and approach were under water, reaching up to the top of the bank, leading to the edge of the avenue on the left, approaching the clubhouse. To complete our round, however, we were able to play from the 17th green to the first hole as a 3 par, instead of the 18th.

The importance and indeed testing qualities of the course have been recognised, as a venue for all the important championships and other events. These included the Irish Open Amateur Championship (twice). The quadrangular Amateur Internationals, Ireland, Scotland, Wales, England and the Irish Ladies Championship, etc. Very many golfing societies, some more than once, have arranged their meetings on the course, and these are facilitated with exceptionally reasonable terms. The Irish Professional Golfers Championship has not, as yet, selected Killarney as a venue, but this cannot be postponed for very long. It has been said that the 'tiger-nature' of the course, where in some holes only the very long hitters could carry to the fairway, has not been to the liking of a few of these professionals. Certainly, I believe the big sponsored tournament (now under Messrs. Carroll's auspices), should be fixed for Killarney at some stage. It certainly would obviate the exceedingly low score returns of such a top-course as Woodbrook.

I should place on record here that Killarney would never have achieved the huge advantages, now being derived from the course were it not for the interest of Lord Castlerosse both in Killarney and golf. He succeeded in getting his father the 5th Earl of Kenmare, to give almost the entire land of the Western demesne free by forming a controlling company in which locals from the town and hotels took preference shares to the amount of £2,500. The Kenmare family produced the balance in ordinary shares, to the value of about £25,000 which included the value of the land.

I hold one ordinary share and 25 preference shares and was appointed Chairman of the Directors for the first few years of the war. The complete running of the club was left in my hands and that of preference shareholder directors, Dr. J. M. O'Sullivan and Mr. Henry Dowling, Solicitor. I acted as Hon. Secretary of the Club for the first 5 years, or so and had the unique honour of being the first Captain of the Club. I was Captain of the old Deer Park Club in the last nine months of its existence, and hence Captain of the new course for its first four or five months. Lord Castlerosse was Captain for the following year, as can be seen on the gilt-painted list to date in the bar of the clubhouse. I was given a special honour of being selected captain for the second time in 1944. This could be described as an 'act of vindication' as a personal approval, when somebody tried to discredit me, probably some months previously.

I remained as Hon. Secretary for a few years and then Castlerosse drafted a constitution for the Club which permitted the administration of the Club by a small committee, of which all the directors were ex-office members and did not require to be selected at the Annual Meeting as is the case of the five members elected to the committee. Complete control of the financial side of the Club was however reserved for the directors exclusively. The committee arrangement, which allows them the complete running of the Club, has worked and is working satisfactorily.

The successful growth of the Club can be gauged from the fact that for the first year or two, the green fees taking of two or three hundred pounds per annum has now reached to close on the £3,000 mark.

Now living in Tralee, I resigned as Chairman of the Directors, though still maintaining my interest as a director. Castlerosse's niece, Mrs. Beatrice Grosvenor, President of the Club, has taken over the Chairmanship. She is keeping up actively the Kenmare interest in the

Club. The Club and property is now the private concern of the local company and the articles of association provides for its permanent continuation as a golf course, as long as it is used for the promotion of the game, otherwise the property reverts back to the Kenmare Estate.

I have now disposed of some of my most active recreations and pass on finally to my psychiatric career. Almost immediately after graduating, I plunged into this speciality and have never since regretted the challenge associated with such an almost unchartered medical field, when I first found that conditional treatment appeared to be the overriding factor of the therapeutic armamentarium of the 1920s. Sedative and restraint procedures then seemed to be the only weapons at our disposal. However, the importance of hospital regimentation with its regular hours for solid, natural food and even regular though lengthy hours of sleep have achieved a deeply therapeutic effect – which appears to have been lost on most of our authorities to date. There were other forms of treatment in vogue in the late 1920s apart from sedative therapy. The 'Continuous Bath' type treatment was producing some encouraging results in the medical and extremely restless and aggressive patient, even though it was consonant with some risk.

The drug treatment of that very old disease, from which Caesar was reputed to have suffered proving satisfactory; other new drugs were undergoing research.

The first direct breakthrough was made by Sakal of Vienna, when he introduced deep 'Insulin Coma' treatment, for one of the most intractable, and recovery-defying diseases – schizophrenia – affecting mainly patients at the adolescent period of life, 16 to 30 years, is still in vogue, but unfortunately has been in recent times fairly generally discarded. Killarney was one of the first hospitals in Ireland to use this treatment with good results. It was still in active operation in St. Finan's up to my retiral in July, 1962. The introduction of 'Insulin Coma Therapy' was followed later by the use of various drugs of the cardiazol type. These drugs, though, producing excellent results, had most alarming side effects, some fatal on its patients, and have been discarded.

It was not till 1942, when the two Italians; Bini and Cerlatti produced convulsent effects by the use of electricity, that one could term this one of our major psychiatric advances. It has almost a specific effect on all types of depressive reactions. We introduced the treatment known in short as E.C.T. in Killarney in 1944 and its use rapidly spread to most parts of the globe. Its dramatic results in all forms of melancholia, suggested to us that it should have similar successes with the various confusional parychoses. We were pleasantly surprised by the magic-like effect it had on one of our first such cases. This was a woman so affected, in which after three months in St. Finan's was still completely confused, with no idea of time or space. She was visited weekly by her husband and though she answered his questions, distressingly for him, she had no idea who he was. Towards the end of her course of treatment the husband on his next visit could scarcely credit the fact that she was practically her usual normal self. When I asked her when she first realised that she was in the hospital, she said, "after the last treatment, when I asked one of the nurses."

It was somewhat later that the type of drugs described as 'tranquillisers' were put on the market by the drug firms under a variety of proprietary names. The exaggerated and eulogistic recommendations of the properties of those drugs by the manufacturers has created a rather fantastic craze in their use throughout the world. On my visit to New York in 1956 with the Kerry and Dublin football teams on tour, I was amazed and even alarmed at the extent which psychiatrists over there more or less abandoned the E.C.T. even in some of the best known hospitals. I referred to this in a special paper on my *'Psychiatric experiences in the U.S.A.'* and which was subsequently published in one of the medical journals.

About this time one of our leading Dublin psychiatrists, who had previously read a paper on the tranquillisers, expressed an over-dedicated enthusiasm for this type of drug therapy. I am afraid too many psychiatrists are over-impressed by the unusual exuberance of the manufacturer's printed recommendations, many of the latter having a somewhat distorted conception of the variations found in depressive disorders resulting from so very many different and wide ranged causative factors. Hence, in quite a wide range of depressive conditions, these recommendations are far removed from clinical accuracy.

Personally, I cannot share this enthusiasm. I feel that drugs as having temporary effects and governed by the recognised effects of immunity, cannot be regarded as a specific form of therapy. The extent of their continuous use in many individual cases can only be alarming and dangerous for a number of cases. As a follow up to E.C.T. in certain types of conditions some of those drugs have a useful therapeutic place. Not withstanding the fluctuations in popularity of all these various treatments, since psychiatry became a speciality and in particular since it became a precise science, one form is as old as psychiatry itself, namely 'Occupational Therapy'. There is recorded confirmation of its use from the very institution of Mental Hospitals in the early part of the last century, or as they were originally termed 'Asylums'. Though without clinical knowledge, Galen (the famous second century physician) among the many voluminous and general treatises which he wrote, published his famous dictum; "Employment is nature's best physician and is essential to human happiness." This could be regarded as Occupational Therapy's charter.

Occupational Therapy (O.T.), however, did not emerge as an active clinical science till after the 1914-18 war during which America and Canadian armies sent to the western European front hastily trained C.T. personnel, then called 'aides'. They provided a very useful rehabilitation service for the wounded soldiers. This created a worldwide impetus towards the general use of O.T. and the treatment gradually developed a more scientific clinical application. Incidentally, special credit must also be given to the Americans for the inauguration, as an essential war tactic of psychological screening of war recruits. The other well-known combatants, including the British were without this screening, with the result that mentally defective recruits were sent to the battle areas, where they instantly broke down under the stress of explosives and other warfares.

I have from the very start of my psychological career been deeply interested in the promotion of O.T. as a definite form of psychiatric treatment. I initiated it in Killarney Mental Hospital, when I became R.M.S. in 1933. I should, however, say that O.T. achievement in Killarney really dated from the commencement of the construction of the Fitzgerald Stadium, with the permission of my predecessor the late Dr. E.W. Griffin, in 1932, which I have already referred to. This construction unit became an important and probably the largest O.T. project ever operated and its therapeutic content was most satisfying. Very many patients, to the disadvantage of the Stadium owe their complete rehabilitation to the therapeutic and satisfying effects of their work there. The therapeutic effects of this satisfying work led to the complete rehabilitation of many patients.

The gradual extension of the treatment from special sections of the various wards of St. Finan's led to a large and regular increase in the number and extent of the crafts used. The O.T. Dept., as a whole reached after a few years the exceptionally and possible unequalled high O.T. percentage rate of 90% of the patients, including those confined to bed. The introduction of the co-managerial system, as far as St. Finan's was concerned, led to such a curtailment in the operation of the O.T. Department, generally and particularly in many of the crafts which from sales, individual and contract, created annual profits of over one thousand pounds per annum. The first crafts to suffer extinction were the dye-craft, machine-knitting and various weaving looms and these were, in fact, the mainstay of the huge annual profit figures. The dyecraft and weaving departments by special arrangements with leading city firms had become for a number of years official contractors for the local authorities of the 26 counties. Managerial approval of the success of the O.T. Department by closing down these sections proved successful from the therapeutic as well as the commercial aspect, revealed the strange and inexplicable psychology of the lay, non-technological mentality.

As stated from the start of my medical career, I was specially attracted by the immense value of occupational projects as a very definite, successful and indeed pleasant form of psychiatric treatment. O.T. as previously mentioned was in use in most Mental Hospitals, almost since their inception, but its therapeutic value, up to the 1930s was regrettably subordinated to the utilitarian and other aspects. From 1925, I made a deep study and research in O.T. and as a result I decided in 1935 to write a textbook of O.T., mainly because I felt that most books on the subject fell very far short in detail and in clinical application, and did not give a suitable description of the psychological disorders requiring treatment. This textbook printed by *The Kerryman* Ltd., Tralee, was published by the well-known English medical publishers, Messrs. H.K. Lewis & Co. Ltd. of London in 1955. The book was favourably received all over the world, and the first edition of one thousand copies was sold fairly rapidly. I received a request from the publishers to issue a second edition. Unfortunately, *The Kerryman* Co. did not preserve the original lead-type setting. There was also a request from a Spanish firm of publishers in Madrid for permission, on a suitable payment basis, to publish an edition in Spanish, but unfortunately Franco's Spanish Government refused permission for the export of the pesetas concerned.

I retired in July, 1962, from the post as R.M.S. at St. Finan's, having reached the statutory retiral age of 65 a few months earlier. The wisdom and justice of this statutory order is highly questionable. It is objectionable too because of its discriminatory nature. When it underwent parliamentary approval it applied only to medical members of local authority hospitals. All the medical members remunerated by the local authorities were excluded with regard to any age limit, until a few years ago, when even then discrimination was again in evidence as the age of 70 years was established for district dispensary medical officers. This latter age limit sounds less urgent, as it does prove retrograde to retired doctors, and particularly psychiatrists, and other specialists, when they have at least five or more years of useful and experienced service. Retired now on a pension amounting to half of my salary prior to retiral has necessitated in my case and am very happily continuing active work, as a private consultant and specialist.

In conclusion, to date February 1965, I continue to enjoy my interest in active psychiatry, though in September last I decided to retire from the active training of Kerry football teams. And so Buidheachas le Dia, live in pleasant relaxation, enjoying my interest in Gaelic games, athletics, Bridge and administrative golf, etc.